KT-443-120

The Anarchical Society

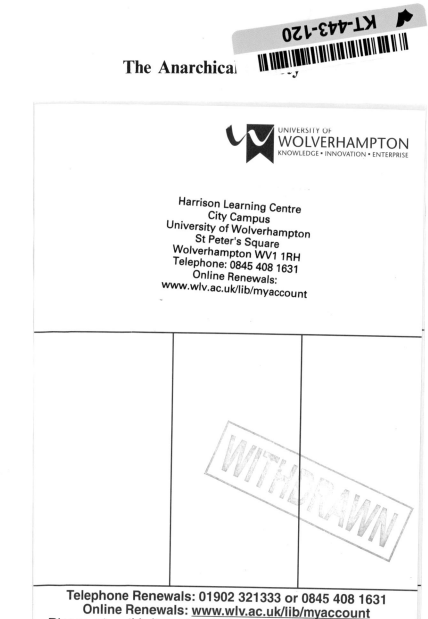

UNIVERSITY OF
WOLVERHAMPTON
KNOWLEDGE • INNOVATION • ENTERPRISE

Harrison Learning Centre
City Campus
University of Wolverhampton
St Peter's Square
Wolverhampton WV1 1RH
Telephone: 0845 408 1631
Online Renewals:
www.wlv.ac.uk/lib/myaccount

WITHDRAWN

Telephone Renewals: 01902 321333 or 0845 408 1631
Online Renewals: www.wlv.ac.uk/lib/myaccount
Please return this item on or before the last date shown above.
Fines will be charged if items are returned late.
See tariff of fines displayed at the Counter.

The Anarchical Society

A Study of Order in World Politics

Third Edition

Hedley Bull

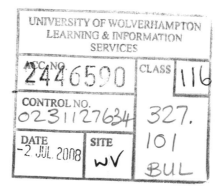

UNIVERSITY OF WOLVERHAMPTON
LEARNING & INFORMATION
SERVICES

ACC NO. 2446590 CLASS 116

CONTROL NO. 0231127634 327.

DATE -2. JUL. 2008 SITE WV 101

BUL

Columbia University Press
New York

Columbia University Press
Publishers Since 1893
New York   Chichester, West Sussex

Copyright © Hedley Bull 1977
Foreword to the 2nd edition © Stanley Hoffmann 1995
Foreword to the 3rd edition © Andrew Hurrell 2002

All rights reserved

ISBN 10: 0-231-12762-6 (cloth)   ISBN 10: 231-12763-4 (paper)
ISBN 13: 978-231-12762-2 (cloth)   ISBN 13: 978-0-231-12763-9 (paper)

A complete Cataloging-in-Publication record is available from the
Library of Congress.

c   10   9   8   7   6   5   4   3   2   1
p   10   9   8   7   6   5   4

Contents

For Emily, Martha and Jeremy

Foreword to the Third Edition:
The Anarchical Society 25 Years On

Andrew Hurrell

The status of *The Anarchical Society* as a classic text is clear. It provides the most elaborate and powerful exposition of the view that states form amongst themselves an international society; and it develops this idea as a powerful vantage point from which to analyse and assess the possibilities of order in world politics. It also remains a fundamental teaching text, not just as the exemplar of a particular position or as the representative of the so-called English School;[1] but also for its capacity to unsettle established and comfortable positions, for the clarity of its exposition, and for the sharpness of Bull's writing and his intellectual rigour. Clearly a very great deal has changed in the twenty-five years since the book was first published. The first part of this Foreword links *The Anarchical Society* to some of the main developments that have taken place within International Relations theory in this intervening period. The second section sets Bull's approach and some of his conclusions against some of the major changes that have occurred in the structures and practices of world politics.[2]

The Anarchical Society and the Study of International Relations

Bull's importance in the academic study of International Relations has long been recognised, but, as Stanley Hoffmann suggests in the foreword to the second edition, precisely where and how his work fits in is more contested.

Realism and Neorealism

Even a cursory reading of *The Anarchical Society* suggests Bull's many affinities with realism, not least his emphasis on the role of power in international relations and the fact that the 'institutions' of international society that he analyses in *The Anarchical Society* include war, the Great Powers, the balance of power and diplomacy. Indeed, in a very important sense, the balance of power remains the most important foundation for Bull's conception of international society. Without a balance of power and without sustained and stable understandings between the major powers on the conduct of their mutual relations, then the 'softer' elements of international order (international law, international organisations, the existence of shared values) would be so many castles in the air. Bull also stressed the critical function of realist analysis – unmasking the pretensions of those who purport to speak on behalf of international or global society and underlining the extent to which, even when shared, universal or solidarist values will tend to further the interests of particular states. Finally, Bull's idea of international society grew out of his very close critical engagement with classical realists such as Carr and Morgenthau and retained many of their concerns, especially the relationship between power, law and morality.

Despite textbook stereotypes, a realist is not simply someone who writes about states and believes in the importance of power. Bull did both of these things but did not see himself as a realist: 'I am not a realist', he said unequivocally in a 1979 lecture.[3] He emphasised the extent to which the classical realism of Carr, Kennan or Niebuhr was rooted in particular historical circumstances. It was part of the intellectual temper of a particular age – a period when conflict and anarchy was 'in fact the main ingredient in I[nternational] R[elations] at the time'. From Bull's perspective, both classical realism and, even more, its neorealist variant (as in the hugely influential work of Kenneth Waltz) pay insufficient attention to the framework of rules, norms and shared understandings on which international society depends. This does not imply that norms somehow control the actions of states, acting upon them from outside. But it does mean that they shape the game of power politics, the nature and identity of the actors, the purposes for which force can be used, and the ways in which actors justify and legitimise their actions. Thus, on Bull's account, even conflict and war take place within a highly institutionalised set of normative structures – legal, moral and political. As he puts it: '. . . war is as a matter of fact an inherently normative phenomenon; it is unimaginable apart from rules by which human beings recognise what behaviour is appropriate to it and define their attitude towards it. War is not simply a clash of forces; it is a clash between the agents of political groupings who are able to recognise one another as such and to direct their force at one another only because of the rules that they understand and apply.'[4]

Similarly, even the quintessentially realist 'institution' of the balance of power appears not as a mechanical arrangement or as a constellation of forces that pushes and shoves states to act in particular ways from outside. It should, rather, be understood as a conscious and continuing shared practice in which the actors constantly debate and contest the meaning of the balance of power, its groundrules, and the role that it should play. Equally Great Powers are to be studied not simply in terms of the degree to which they can impose order on weaker states or within their spheres of influence on the back of crude coercion, but rather in terms of the extent to which their role and their managerial functions are perceived as legitimate by other states. Power remains central to Bull's analysis of international relations, but power is a social attribute. To understand power we must place it side by side with other quintessentially social concepts such as prestige, authority and legitimacy. International society is therefore centrally concerned with norms and institutions. But this does not necessarily lead, notwithstanding the influence of the seventeenth-century international lawyer Hugo Grotius on Bull's work, to a soft, liberal Grotianism concerned solely with the promotion of law and morality as is so often mistakenly assumed.

The distance and differences between Bull and neorealism are particularly clear: the international system simply cannot be viewed solely in material terms as a decentralised, anarchic structure in which functionally undifferentiated units vary only according to the distribution of power. Central to the 'system' is a historically created, and evolving, structure of common understandings, rules, norms, and mutual expectations. Indeed it was the dominance of Waltzian neorealism in the 1980s and early 1990s that explains the relative marginalisation of international society perspectives in that period.

Neo-liberal Institutionalism

On the face of it one would expect a significantly greater degree of overlap and commonality between Bull and liberal or rationalist institutionalists. In the first place the object of explanation is similar. The central problem is to establish that laws and norms exercise a compliance pull of their own, at least partially independent of the power and interests which underpin them and which are often responsible for their creation. There is also some degree of overlap in terms of how rules and institutions function. Institutionalists are concerned with ways in which institutions make it rational for states to cooperate out of self-interest. They view norms and institutions as purposively generated solutions to different kinds of collective-action problems. There is certainly a good deal of this kind of thinking in Bull's work: the notion that states will further their own interests by mutual respect for each others' sovereignty, by recognising certain limits on the use of force, and by accepting the principle that agreements between them should be honoured. Bull recognises that interest-driven cooperation can indeed be built on Hobbesian assumptions and a contractualist and rationalist logic runs through much of his discussion of the institutions of international society.

Yet there are also important differences between Bull and many institutionalists. One relates to Bull's distrust of attempts to understand cooperation purely in terms of abstract ahistorical rationalism. Bull was concerned with the processes by which understanding of common interest evolved and changed through time. Denying that 'Grotian theorists' had any great confidence in abstract human reason, he wrote that:

> Grotius and other exponents of the natural law theory certainly did have 'confidence in human reason', but the Grotian idea of international society later came to rest on the element of consensus in the actual practice of states, and it is on this rather than on 'human reason' that (in common with other contemporary 'Grotians') I rest the case for taking international society seriously.[5]

Standing back, we can see that Bull examined international society from two distinct directions, one analytical, the other historical. On the one side, he arrived at his understanding of international society by thinking through, in purely abstract terms, those essential elements that would have to be present for any society of states to be meaningfully so described. But, on the other, he insisted that, however plausible this abstract reasoning might be, it had to be set against the cultural and historical forces that had helped shape the consciousness of society at any particular time and had moulded perceptions of common values and common purposes.

This emphasis on historically constructed understandings leads to a second area of divergence: the extent to which successful cooperation often depends on a prior sense of community or, at least, on a common set of social, cultural or linguistic conventions. Rationalist models of cooperation may indeed explain how co-operation is possible once the parties have come to believe that they form part of a shared project or community in which there is a common interest that can be furthered by cooperative behaviour. But, from Bull's perspective, rationalist approaches neglect the factors which explain how and why contracting is possible in the first place and the potential barriers that can block the emergence of such a shared project – perhaps because institutionalist analysis has been so dominated by studies of cooperation amongst liberal developed states that enjoy a compatibility of major values and a common conceptualisation of such basic concepts as 'order', 'justice', 'state', 'law', 'contract' and so on. Yet so much of Bull's work was concerned with precisely these kinds of problems – the constant fascination with the boundaries of international society, with the criteria for membership, and with the position of groups that lie on or beyond its margins (infidels, pirates, barbarians).

Constructivism

Almost all constructivists make at least passing reference to Bull and recent writings have sought to compare Bull and the English School explicitly with constructivism.[6] Constructivism is far from a unified position and is becoming ever less so. Yet a number of claims unite much constructivist writing on international relations, including the view that international norms are constitutive as well as regulative; the claim that norms, rules and institutions create meanings and enable, or make possible, different forms of social action; and the idea that many of the most important features of international politics are produced and reproduced in the concrete practices of social actors.

It is evident that Bull was deeply committed to the centrality of norms and institutions in international politics and to the notion that society is constituted through diverse political practices built around shared, inter-subjective understandings – that is, understandings that exist between and amongst actors. Take, for example, his approving characterisation of the objectives of *Diplomatic Investigations* (one of the other classic texts of the English School):[7]

> Above all, perhaps, they saw theory of international politics not as 'models' or 'conceptual frameworks' of their own to be tested against 'data' but as theories or doctrines in which men in international history have actually believed.[8]

Equally Bull's core definition of international society highlights *shared* conceptions of interests and common values and the *shared consciousness* of being bound by legal and moral rules.

And yet there are problems with trying to squeeze Bull into a constructivist mould that is too confining. He differs greatly from the influential constructivist work of Alexander Wendt in the much greater emphasis that he places on the actual historical evolution of different types of international society.[9] Similarly he places more emphasis on international law as a concrete historical practice and set of normative structures which merit far more direct engagement than has been the case in most constructivist scholarship (and indeed within International Relations theory generally). Although ideas and language matter, Bull's philosophical realism distinguishes him from many of the more strongly reflectivist or discursive constructivists (and still more from post-modernism). Bull rejected the notion that international relations could be ever studied *solely* in terms of shared understandings rather than in terms of the interaction between material and social facts. For Bull, ideas mattered to the extent that they are taken up and acted upon by powerful states, and the relevance of particular norms and institutions would always be linked to the underlying distribution of material power. Finally, in contrast to more self-consciously 'critical' constructivists, Bull believed that brute material facts and cold power politics could act as a powerful check on both the aspirations of practitioners and the methods of the analyst.[10]

Other Approaches

The Anarchical Society also needs to be related to two other important bodies of academic work: the history of ideas about international relations and international normative theory.

Commentators routinely stress the importance of history in English School writing – both the historical method and the need to historicise international society itself. But within the English School, and certainly for Bull, the history of thought about international relations occupies a particularly important place. After all, Bull's three competing traditions of thought (Hobbesian, Grotian and Kantian), which he took and developed from Martin Wight and around which the book is constructed, were themselves the product of one reading of how the history of thought on international relations had evolved within Europe from the late fifteenth century.

The continued importance of this approach cannot be underestimated. The neglect of history and the relentless presentism of Political Science are all too evident. Examples abound, as in the common belief that it was only in the 20th century that realists came to stress the importance of systemic forces; that Kant is merely an early democratic peace theorist or, worse still, a believer in pro-democratic interventionism; or that we had to wait until the arrival of constructivism to discover that sovereignty was a constructed and contested concept.

All human societies rely on historical stories about themselves to legitimise notions of where they are and where they might be going. For Bull, a central element in the study of International Relations is about uncovering actors' understandings of international politics and the ways in which these understandings have been gathered into intelligible patterns, traditions, or ideologies. The past matters because of the changing, contested, plural, and completely unstraightforward nature of the concepts with which we map the international political landscape.

At the same time it is clear that contemporary readers of Bull's work will need to engage with the large amount of work that has been produced in this area over the past twenty-five years. Thus the study of classical theories of international relations has grown significantly; there have been important reassessments of the major traditions of thought on the subject; Westphalia has been demythologised; and others have traced the evolution of the constitutional structures of international society and the revolutions in sovereignty that have taken place. And finally, there has been a very important move into the area of 'international relations' on the part of those working on the history of political thought and on the development of historical concepts and ideologies – a move which has expanded immensely the degree of sophistication in the study of the subject. A good deal of this work forces us to reconsider some of Bull's specific claims (for example, his reading of Kant) and even to rework quite radically his central theoretical category of a 'Grotian tradition'. But specific critiques and re-readings should not lead us to neglect the continued importance of the history of thought in the way in which International Relations is both taught and studied.

Finally, it is important to look briefly at the relation between Bull's work and the explosion of writing on moral and ethical issues in world politics. Here the criticisms of Bull are often sharper. For the critics, Bull (and the English School more generally) opened up a fertile realm of classical political thought but conceived of 'classical theory' in narrow and impoverished ways. The result was to separate the subject of International Relations from the far richer traditions of political and social theory to which it is necessarily intimately connected, and to downplay or ignore a range of fundamental questions about state, community and nation that could never be satisfactorily addressed solely from the perspective of the society of states. Much of this criticism is clearly justified, above all, if the aim is to develop a normative theory of international or world order. The range of intellectual resources available has expanded enormously over the past twenty-five years and anyone working in this area would very soon move beyond *The Anarchical Society*.[11]

It is important to remember, however, that Bull's own purpose, while related, was a somewhat different one. The subtitle of his book is not 'A Study of Order' but 'A Study of Order in World Politics'. What makes Bull's approach fascinating, but also sometimes frustrating, was that he was interested in the relationship between order as fact and order as value, and with the bridges that have been, or might be, constructed between theory and practice. He was therefore centrally concerned with the legal and moral understandings of order and justice as they had developed within and around international society; with the political and material prerequisites of a meaningful moral community; and with the complex and often dispiriting ways in which the procedural and substantive rules of international society are connected to concrete institutions, to power-political structures and to the often very rough trade of world politics.

Thus, unlike most political theorists, Bull's particular contribution is his insistence on the inevitably close links between the struggle for moral consensus and questions of political practice: for example, how particular normative issues are related to patterns of unequal power, to the coherence of states and state structures, and to the legitimacy of international norms and institutions. Bull's work suggests that many of the most pressing and intractable ethical dilemmas in the field of world politics are as much about the legitimacy of practice, power and process as they are about philosophical foundations. This is certainly not the only approach to the study of normative issues in world politics, but it remains an important one.

The Anarchical Society and Contemporary World Politics

For many readers *The Anarchical Society* appears outdated because Bull so often emphasised continuities between past and present. As a result he seemed to downplay the dynamic forces at work in global politics and to fail to recognise the extent to which the system was moving decisively 'beyond Westphalia'. Factors such as the impact of economic globalisation and political democratisation, the increased importance of transnational civil society, the increased density, scope and range of international institutions, the multiple problems that result from the break-up of states and ethnic self-assertion have developed to such a point that, for many commentators, Bull's narrow focus on the society of states is now wholly inadequate and outdated.

It is clearly the case that much of Bull's work was heavily shaped by the concerns of the Cold War and of superpower rivalry; that he was openly sceptical about the possibility of radical change in the character of superpower relations; that he gave very little space in his work to economic factors and forces; that, at least in this book, he expressed little interest in formal international institutions, including the United Nations; and that he was generally critical of 'Kantian' optimism about the spread and impact of liberal democracy – the set of claims that would subsequently develop into democratic peace theory. It is also clearly the case that *The Anarchical Society* was intended as a defence of a state-based international society as the best available means for the management of power and the mediation of difference. In response to charges of outdatedness, four points can be highlighted.

Systemic Change and Transformation

One response is simply to see *The Anarchical Society* as providing a model exposition of how to think about claims for change. Bull did not ignore change but he did advocate sobriety in analysing change. He argued consistently that contemporary trends and features which appear novel – from transnational corporations to the privatisation of violence in the form of terrorist groups or warlords – look more familiar when approached from a sufficiently long historical perspective. Equally, he suggested that we can gain much from comparing the present with previous epochs of change – hence his suggestive, if underdeveloped, ideas about 'neo-medievalism' and of a 'neo-Grotian moment'.

A further possibility is simply to view Bull's rather sober and sceptical conclusions as a mark in the sand against which more recent work should be judged. Pedagogically it makes great sense for students to read Bull alongside the many works of the 1990s that have stressed the idea of systemic transformation, especially in the context of globalisation. Which parts of Bull's picture still hold? Which do not? And why?

But a final possibility is to argue that he was often right to be sceptical. Clearly his own arguments cannot simply be replayed and there will be important differences of emphasis and of empirical application. And yet as the claims of the 1990s about globalisation have been subjected to scrutiny and criticism, the pattern of argumentation that we see in Bull's work and some substantive conclusions recur: that the historical novelty of current globalising forces has been exaggerated; that there was never a neat 'Westphalian model' in which understandings of sovereignty and norms of non-intervention were stable and uncontested and that can be easily contrasted with the complexities of the post-Cold War world; and that the decline in state capacity has been overdone. Not only has globalisation been driven by state policies but state retreat is reversible and the power resources available to states are still critical and distinctive – Microsoft matters but so, too, do the marines.

Normative change and transformation

A second point to stress is that Bull's primary concern was not with change in general but with change within the international legal and normative structure of international society. This is arguably the aspect of the debate on globalisation and transformation that has been least well developed. On one side, ideas about 'post-sovereign states' or 'multi-layered geo-governance' do indeed point to potentially very important changes, but they are embedded in a discourse of transformation that is in most cases extremely difficult to pin down. On the other side, those who stress continuity within the Westphalian order often rely on such a one-dimensional view of the role of norms and such a very thin notion of the legal order that it becomes impossible to make sense of the tremendous changes that have indeed taken place, above all in the period since 1945.

There are different ways forward. Thus some have picked up on Bull's distinction between pluralist and solidarist versions of international society and have suggested that, contrary to the scepticism expressed in *The Anarchical Society*, a consensus has in fact developed around such expanded normative goals as humanitarian intervention.[12] In still more strongly progressivist mode, but still owing much to Bull's work, Linklater has explored how the changing conditions of global politics may be opening political and moral spaces for the transformation of political community.[13]

There are still other possibilities: for example, taking on board the degree to which regionalism has become an important characteristic of contemporary world politics but examining and comparing these 'regional international societies' within the framework of Bull's ideas and concepts. Or thinking through the notion of 'world society', whose importance Bull stresses but which is left underdeveloped in his work, and the complex ways in which international and world society relate to each other. Following this line of enquiry might lead the analyst to consider the structure of rules, norms and institutions that lie beyond the state. Thus, if one set of legal and normative developments look to an improved society of states united by a far higher degree of solidarity, another looks beyond the state, or at least comes to view the state within the context of a broader legal and normative order. This image builds on many of the trends already visible in the contemporary international legal system: the pluralism of the norm-creating processes; the role of private market actors and civil society groups in articulating values which are then assimilated in inter-state institutions; and the increased range of informal, yet norm-governed, governance mechanisms often built around complex networks, both transnational and trans-governmental. Moves in this direction would involve a substantial reengagement with the changing practices of international law and with recent work within that field – another somewhat neglected legacy of Bull's approach.

Culture and Context

One of the most important features of Bull's work is his view that international relations could neither be understood nor studied solely from the perspective of the powerful. What is so striking in retrospect is not that he wrote under the shadow of the power-political and ideological conflicts amongst the major powers that dominated so much of the twentieth century, but that he argued so consistently that these conflicts represented only one dimension of world politics. Thus, for Bull, the Cold War had to be set against the transformations produced by decolonisation, the rise of what came to be called the Third World, and the clash between North and South. Typically, too, he insisted that these transformations were part of a broader process of historical evolution that he labelled the revolt against western dominance.[14]

As mentioned above, this perspective involved close attention to the boundaries of international society and the criteria for member-ship. It also led to a recurring line of questioning and argument – that a durable international society must depend on a sense of legitimacy, and that this, in turn, must reflect the interests and values of the weaker members of international society. It is true that there remains a good deal of ambiguity here. Who needs to be accommodated? Only those capable of mounting a revisionist challenge or the truly excluded and powerless? But Bull's central point remains: understanding cooperation will involve understanding not just clashes of power and shifting prudential calculations of interest amongst the strong, but also the policies of weaker states and how their conceptions of international order and justice have varied across time and space.

The methods and approaches reflected in Bull's work retain their value today. They suggest that serious academic research may necessitate less emphasis on the research tools of that mythical being, the universal social scientist; less emphasis on metatheoretical disputation; and rather more stress on the linguistic, cultural and historical knowledge and resources needed to make sense of the variation of understandings of international and world society in different periods and places. Bull's call to look beyond International Relations as an American social science helps explain the continued receptivity to his ideas outside of the United States and Europe – for example, in Latin America and Japan.

This line of enquiry is partly about power: how far and how securely are emerging, revisionist or revolutionary states or groups integrated within the institutions of international society? But it is also, critically, about culture. Cultural diversity has also long been a central problem for all those who ask, 'How broad and how deep is international society?', 'How strong is the consensus on the nature of a desirable world order and the means by which it might be achieved?'. Part of Bull's concern was with a *procedural* and not a *substantive* value consensus – the extent to which states have been able to create a shared framework of rules and by which clashes of interests and conflicting values can be mediated. But he was also deeply concerned with the impact of the expansion of international society beyond its historic, European core; and with the degree to which modernisation and increased interdependence were, or were not, producing a unified and unifying global culture. Here it should be noted that Bull did not believe that international society *necessarily* rested on the existence of a common value system as accounts of Bull's writing often suggest.[15] The role of culture is an empirical question to be investigated, not an analytic assumption.

It is clear that Bull's preoccupation with culture and cultural forces is by no means outdated; there is a link here with recent debates on the degree to which globalisation involves powerful pressures towards homogenisation and convergence, but also towards resistance and backlash. It is also clear that, as the international legal order moves in more solidarist and transnational directions and as the 'waterline of sovereignty' (to use David Kennedy's phrase) is lowered, so the political salience of societal and cultural difference rises. International rules relating to human rights, to the rights of peoples and minorities, to an expanding range of economic and environmental issues impinge very deeply on the domestic organisation of society. Divergent values therefore become more salient as the legal order moves down from high-minded sloganising towards detailed and extremely intrusive operational rules in each of these areas and towards stronger means of implementation (through the proliferation of sanctions and conditionalities). Culture does not necessarily matter but difference and diversity do. Understandings of world order vary enormously from one part of the world to another, reflecting differences in national and regional histories, in social and economic circumstances and conditions, and in political contexts and trajectories.

The State System and International Order

At the core of *The Anarchical Society* is the question, 'To what extent does the inherited political framework provided by the society of states continue to provide an adequate basis for world order?'. Bull's writing can be related directly to the debates on global governance that have been so prominent since the end of the Cold War. Much of this writing has been rationalist in method and technocratic in character. Institutions are analysed in terms of how self-interested egoists overcome the many collective-action problems arising from increased interdependence and interaction. States are seen as competing with international bodies and civil society groups to provide cost-effective and efficient solutions to governance problems. In contrast, Bull's legacy points us in two directions. In the first place, it suggests the need to focus less on theoretical understanding of how particular institutions or regimes emerge and develop, and more on assessing the overall character of institutionalisation in world politics, the normative commitments of different varieties of institutionalism, and the adequacy of existing institutions for meeting practical and normative challenges. Second, whilst it is important to maintain the emphasis on norms, rules and institutions, Bull's concerns highlight the need to shift the focus back to the first-order political questions of power, values and legitimacy.

More importantly, it cannot be overemphasised that Bull's preoccupation in *The Anarchical Society* is not with world politics in general, but with the nature and possibilities of international order. Bull never argued that states were the only legitimate objects of study in world politics, nor that they are, or would necessarily remain, in 'control'. He was in fact rather pessimistic about the prospects for international society. Thus, in response to a reader's comments on *The Anarchical Society*, he wrote in 1975:

> I am not sure that it is correct to say . . . that in the book I see 'an international society emerging'. I think I rather argue that international society exists but is in decline.[16]

The reasons for this decline have partly to do with the degree to which the normative ambition of international society has expanded so dramatically, and partly with the erosion of its political foundations. Equally, he was perfectly aware of the potentially transformative nature of what has come to be called globalisation. But he was less sure that these new elements provided an adequate basis for order (or, for that matter, justice) within international society.

It is certainly the case that, even within its own terms, Bull's conception of inter-state order was too starkly divorced from the social and economic structures within which states and societies are embedded. It is also the case that, as is often noted, his work tended to downplay political economy and his view of the state's capacity to direct the direction and scope of economic developments was strained, even in the mid-1970s. Any contemporary analysis of order and governance needs to place order within the state system against the other two arenas within which all social order needs to be understood and certainly social order within the context of globalisation: civil society on the one hand (including what is now termed transnational civil society), and economic markets on the other.

And yet it remains plausible to argue that these alternative global structures of order are either weak (for example, transnational civil society, especially when it comes to the management of social violence and conflict), or efficient but unstable (as in the case of the global economy). Yes, the past twenty-five years have seen an intensification of economic and social globalisation, but the inequalities and discontents of globalisation have generated increased political strains both internationally and within many states. Yes, there have been significant moves in the direction of solidarist consensus; but it is very hard to argue that globalisation leads easily or unproblematically to shared values, resilient institutions, or to a meaningful global moral community. Yes, the density of the norms, rules and institutions of international society has increased tremendously, often pushing in a liberal direction. Yet Bull's scepticism may still be merited: Whose solidarist or liberal order? What kind of liberal and liberalising order is it that seeks to promote democracy but ignores distributive justice and brushes aside calls for the democratisation of global decision making? How stable and how legitimate can such a liberal order be when it depends so heavily on the hegemony of the single superpower whose history is so exceptionalist and whose attitude to international law and institutions has been so ambivalent?

We are still left with Bull's concern with two fundamental tensions in the constitution of international society: first, between those rules and institutions that seek to mediate amongst different values and conceptions of the good, and those that seek to promote, and perhaps enforce, a single set of universal values; and second, between the vaulting normative ambitions of contemporary international society and its still-precarious power-political, institutional and cultural foundations. Although sometimes seen as optimistic, complacent, or even nostalgic, Bull was constantly worried by what he called *premature global solidarism* – that too many hopes, too many demands, and too many moral claims were being placed on the still thin fabric of international society. Contemporary readers will disagree as to whether Bull's own conclusions remain valid; but his questions and the framework for analysing them provided by *The Anarchical Society* remain one of the most important points of departure for any study of order in world politics.

Nuffield College, Oxford   ANDREW HURRELL

Notes

1   Writing on, and within, the English School of International Relations has increased dramatically. For a full bibliography, *see* www.ukc.ac.uk/ politics/englishschool.buzan

2   A more complete account and assessment can be found in Kai Alderson and Andrew Hurrell (eds), *Hedley Bull on International Society* (Basingstoke: Macmillan, 2000), chapters 1–3. These chapters both draw on Bull's unpublished papers and contain fuller references to the literature referred to in this Foreword.

3   'Power Politics', lecture, Sunningdale, 23 April 1979. Bull Papers, Bodleian Library, Oxford.

4   'Recapturing the Just War for Political Theory', *World Politics* 31, 4 (1979): 595–6.

5   Letter to Shaie Selzer, Macmillan Publishers, 14 November 1975, Bull Papers.

6   *See*, for example, Tim Dunne, 'The social construction of international society', *European Journal of International Relations* 1, 3 (1995): 367–90; and Ole Waever, 'Four meanings of international society: A transatlantic dialogue', in Barbara Allen Roberson (ed.), *International Society and the Development of International Relations Theory* (London: Pinter, 1998), especially 93–8.

7   Herbert Butterfield and Martin Wight (eds), *Diplomatic Investigations* (London: George Allen & Unwin, 1966).

8   Review of Michael Donelan (ed.), *The Reason of States*, *Times Literary Supplement*, 28 March 1978.

9   Contrast Bull's Hobbesian, Grotian and Kantian traditions with Alexander Wendt's three 'cultures of anarchy', *Social Theory of International Relations* (Cambridge: Cambridge University Press, 1999).

10   For distinctions within constructivism, *see* Karin Fierke and Knud Erik Jorgensen (eds), *Constructing International Relations. The Next Generation* (London: M.E. Sharpe, 2001).

11   For a survey and assessment, *see* Andrew Hurrell, 'Norms and Ethics in International Relations', in Walter Carlsnaes, Thomas Risse and Beth Simmons (eds), *Handbook of International Relations* (London: Sage, 2002): 137–54.

12   *See*, for example, Nicholas Wheeler, *Saving Strangers* (Oxford: Oxford University Press, 2000). It is worth noting that Bull examined the possibilities of change in norms concerning intervention well before the subject became fashionable. Hedley Bull (ed.), *Intervention in World Politics* (Oxford: Oxford University Press, 1984).

13   Andrew Linklater, *The Transformation of Political Community. Ethical Foundations of the Post-Westphalian Era* (Cambridge: Polity, 1998).

14   Hedley Bull and Adam Watson (eds), *The Expansion of International Society* (Oxford: Oxford University Press, 1984).

15   Stephen Krasner, *Sovereignty. Organized Hypocrisy* (Princeton, NJ: Princeton University Press, 1999), 47.

16   Letter to Shaie Selzer, Macmillan Publishers, 14 November 1975, Bull Papers.

Foreword to the Second Edition: Revisiting *The Anarchical Society*

Stanley Hoffmann

The Anarchical Society is widely recognised today as a classic of the literature on international relations on account not only of its content but also its lucid and crisp prose. It is also seen as the most masterful work in what is called the British school of international relations, or the British approach to international relations (with his dislike of pomposity, Bull would have shied away from the word 'school'). This approach derives its originality from its view of international relations as a complex set of relations among states that form an international society, and not simply a 'system of states'.

We may ask ourselves why so important a book did not receive the recognition it deserved on initial publication in 1977 particularly in the United States – the country where the attempt to develop a discipline of international relations distinct from diplomatic history and international law has gone farthest. The answer is that its 'Britishness' did not fit with the prevailing American approaches. The emphasis on *society* (however anarchical) seemed strange to realists who, around Hans Morgenthau, studied international relations from the perspective of power-seeking and competing states, or to neo-realists who, following Kenneth Waltz, focused on the effects of the distribution of power in the international system on the inevitable contests of states. For realists and neo-realists, whatever order exists in this endless 'state of war' results from the states' attempts to organise ever-shifting balances of power. Bull devotes a chapter to these, but does not assume that they constitute the alpha and omega of interstate order. However, his book did not satisfy the champions of the other (and older) American approach to international relations – the idealism which, in the spirit of Woodrow Wilson, wishes to reform and to moralise, and sometimes even to transcend, the system of states; looks at war and balances of power with dismay, and at diplomacy with distrust; and invests hope in effective and authoritative international institutions. Bull's work, for all its emphasis on common rules, institutions and interests, is too firmly anti-utopian, too closely tied to the system of sovereign states – to what it is now a cliché to call the Westphalian system – to please those for whom states are the problem, not the solution, in so far as order is concerned. Bull's work was too 'Grotian' for the Machiavellians and the Hobbesians, too statist for the Kantians and the cosmopolitans.

Some two-and-a-half decades after its publication, we can judge more serenely the significance of a book which does not constitute the author's last word, and from which Bull may have departed even more if he had not died so prematurely. I will discuss here its importance in two respects: first, as a general approach to international relations, and second, as a way of understanding the present international system.

As a general approach, *The Anarchical Society* draws our attention to 'the element of co-operation and regulated intercourse among states'. Bull tells us, on the one hand, that *every* international system can be analysed in such terms (even the Cold War's bipolar system, about which his cool reasonableness proved entirely right); but on the other hand he carefully reminds us that in the international system there is also 'the element of war and struggle for power among states', as well as 'the element of transnational solidarity and conflict, cutting across the divisions among states'. How important the 'interstate society' aspect is, he does not prejudge: it is a matter for empirical investigation. A comparison with Waltz is instructive. Both accept the 'anarchy framework': international relations is the politics of autonomous states, without a common superior. It is the domain of self-help. Both therefore stress the importance of the distribution of power, and particularly of the distinction between the great powers and the lesser ones. (Bull goes on to a distinction of the types of great power behaviour in their spheres of influence.) But Bull's approach is richer. Concerned almost exclusively with the 'state of war', Waltz, in discussing the international system, does not go beyond a binary classification – bipolar versus multipolar systems. Bull's approach would lead itself to a typology based on how much 'society' there is in each system: the distinction between bipolar and multipolar ones would thus lose some of the importance that Waltz, or Raymond

Aron, gave to it; and the nature of the relations between the strong and the weak would be seen as largely dependent on how much of a society the system is, on the character of its rules and on the content of the states' common interests.

Indeed, when he examines the interaction among states, Bull is interested in things other than the relations of power: common concerns, rules and institutions. This allows him to examine wars not only as the frequent outcomes of power clashes, but also as possible instruments of order, aimed at curbing the ambitions and excesses of trouble-makers: after all, limited wars were a tool for the balancing of power. It also allows him to examine patterns of order that are neither the balance of power nor war: diplomacy and international law.

This approach has two great merits. It reintroduces into the study of the international system three factors left out by Waltz's own reductionism: transnational ideas, which can generate common norms and interests, international institutions, and interdependence (how states 'perform' self-help: co-operatively, unilaterally, or conflictually, depends to a considerable extent on their degree of interdependence). Also, it draws our attention to the relationship between the interactions among states on the one hand, and their nature and their own institutions on the other. In other words, it looks not merely at the distribution of power among the units, but also at the units themselves. The *scope* of international society (as compared with transnational society) depends on the ratio of free enterprise versus government regulation within the units' political systems. The intensity or *depth* of international society depends on how much the units have in common. The *substance* or content of international society depends on the dominant ideas, ideologies or cultures.

This does not mean that Bull's broad and sweeping outline is without ambiguities or problems. Bull, in his discussion of order, states that it assumes 'a sense of common interests in the elementary goals of social life': order thus seems to belong in, and to emerge from, his 'element of society'. But a pattern such as the balance of power can – when it is a product of mechanical, self-interested moves – be part of the 'state of war', just as it can be part of 'society' when it corresponds to a sense of common concerns, and is deliberately 'contrived'; it can be a Hobbesian *or* a Grotian phenomenon. The two aspects of interstate relations – state of war and international society – are hard to distinguish, both because the 'anarchy problematique' does not mean a constant war of all against all – a convergence on co-operation may result from the calculations of self-help, a point made, also in the 1970s, by the so-called neo-liberal institutionalists – and because, conversely, many features of international society are fragile, and can be undermined when those calculations change.

Bull is not explicit enough in analysing the relations between power and the common rules and institutions of international society (although his rather merciless discussion of order versus justice, and particularly of human rights, contains tentative answers). Nor does he go behind the fuzzy notion of common interests: where do they come from (external imperatives? domestic pressures?) and how do they become binding? Above all, in this book, he did not tell us enough about the formation of international society. We need to know more about its origins. These can be both the patterns of interdependence, and the state of war, which often led to the coercive inclusion into the network of rules and institutions of entities previously left out. We need to know more about the mechanisms of international society: since the diffusion of ideas, technology and goods operates through the units, one must study particularly the effects (and different styles) of hegemonic power. We need to know more about the material underpinnings of international society, or about the respective roles of common values or cultures, and of material factors. Bull puts a strong emphasis on cultural cohesion, but historically it often turned out to be brittle and easily destroyed by the 'state of war'. The variations in the ratio of society to state of war, depending on the period, the region of the world, and the issues, are another element that the book, given its generality, does not cover adequately. Bull's approach leads one to asking such questions, and he himself was beginning to answer some of them at the end of his life.

The Anarchical Society can also be seen as an approach to understanding the contemporary international system – a system in which economic interdependence is compelling, where the network of common rules and institutions is dense, where the utility of force has decreased both because of the nuclear danger and because of the irrelevance of war to many of the conflicts economic interdependence breeds. It is also a world in which the states remain the central actors, and where the diversity of cultures (even if it is not seen as leading to a 'war of civilisations') puts into question the solidity of international society and often challenges its rules. The co-operation of self-interested actors that the theorists of 'international regimes' have explored is a reality for which Bull's work provides a framework.

Nevertheless, here too, question marks abound. First, we find, today, factors Bull did not foresee or integrate into his analysis. There is little in his book about the economic dimensions of international relations (here, he is closer to the realists than to many of the eighteenth-, nineteenth- and twentieth-century liberals); and yet we have witnessed the formation not only of an interstate economic society but also of a transnational world economy, in which private groups and individuals are the actors, and where, thanks to the revolution in communications, decisions are taken – under no central political and few national political controls – which can overwhelm the resources available to states, and constrain their theoretical sovereignty. It is impossible now to separate as rigorously as Bull did the 'transnational' from the 'international' elements of world politics and of order. Moreover, the problem today is not the hypothetical and elusive world state, or even the deliberate reform of the state system; it is the weakness of so many states, racked and wrecked by ethnic or religious conflicts, inadequate institutions and resources, lack of legitimacy, etc. In a sense, all theorists of international relations have taken for granted the notion of a 'system of states' – in conflict or in co-operation. The dichotomy in their minds has been: systems of several states versus imperial systems. But what happens when the number of failed or disintegrating states increases faster, by far, than the capacity of international society to deal with the resulting chaos? Its rules and institutions are inadequate, and the states' common interest tends to be defined as short-term prudence and avoidance of involvement.

The questions to which the study of the present, post-Cold War, system leads one inevitably are questions Bull left unanswered. How much can society actually flourish in an anarchic milieu? Can the factors of sociability prevail over the antagonisms that exist both in the system of states and in the transnational sphere – or under what conditions? Will the importance of economic interdependence in both these realms 'spill over' into, and reduce, the domain of conflict, or will they simply coexist – or else will the conflicts erode society? Can a global international system without a common culture be a genuine and strong society, even if there are dense networks of rules and institutions? What happens to world order when the states challenge it through internal violence and weakness as well as through their customary external violence and aggressiveness, and when transnational society's own rules and institutions create more turbulence than order? Again, these are questions that come straight out of Bull's approach. They could provide students of international relations with a research agenda whose very richness shows the usefulness of the paradigm put forward in this remarkable book – not only for further empirical scrutiny of world politics, but also for normative reflections on the possibility of introducing more ethical concerns into the practices of actors on the world stage, a vast and difficult subject that Bull refused to confront in this 'purely intellectual' inquiry. Next to this agenda, and however sketchy Bull's account of international society may appear, all the competing paradigms look like dead-ends, or like short and narrow paths.

STANLEY HOFFMANN

Preface

In this book I have sought to expound systematically a view of international society and international order that I have stated only in piecemeal fashion elsewhere.

It owes a lot to my former colleagues in the International Relations Department of the London School of Economics, and especially to C. A. W. Manning. It has benefited greatly from the discussions of the British Committee on the Theory of International Politics, in which I have taken part for some years. I owe a profound debt to Martin Wight, who first demonstrated to me that International Relations could be made a subject, and whose work in this field, to use one of his own metaphors, stands out like Roman masonry in a London suburb. His writings, still inadequately published and recognised, are a constant inspiration.

At some points in the argument I draw on the ideas of my Oxford teacher, H. L. A. Hart. In several chapters I dispute the views of my friend Richard A. Falk of Princeton. I believe, however, that his is one of the most significant points of departure in the study of world politics today, and the attention I devote to refuting him should be taken as a compliment. I am particularly grateful to my friend and colleague, Professor J. D. B. Miller, for his criticism and encouragement.

This book is the product neither of refined theoretical techniques nor of any particularly recondite historical research. When still an undergraduate I was very impressed (I now think too impressed) by the dictum of Samuel Alexander, the author of *Space, Time and Deity* (London: Macmillan, 1920) that 'thinking is also research'. My book reflects the limitations of an attempt to deal with a large and complex subject simply by thinking it through.

An earlier version of Chapter 4 appeared as 'Order vs Justice in International Society' in *Political Studies,* vol. xix, no. 3 (September 1971). An earlier version of Chapter 8 appeared as 'War and International Order', in *The Bases of International Order: Essays in Honour of C. A. W. Manning,* ed. Alan James (Oxford University

Press, 1973). I am grateful to the publishers for permission to reproduce passages from these essays.

My greatest intellectual debt is to John Anderson, Professor of Philosophy in the University of Sydney from 1927 to 1958, a greater man than many who are more famous. He had little to say directly about the matters discussed in this book, but the impact of his mind and his example has been the deepest factor in shaping the outlook of many of us whom he taught.

HEDLEY BULL

Introduction

This book is an inquiry into the nature of order in world politics, and in particular into the society of sovereign states, through which such order as exists in world politics is now maintained. I have sought answers to three basic questions:

(i) What is order in world politics?

(ii) How is order maintained within the present system of sovereign states?

(iii) Does the system of sovereign states still provide a viable path to world order?

The three parts of the book explore, in succession, these three questions.

It will be helpful if, at the outset, I indicate the basic elements in my approach to this subject. First, I am concerned in this book not with the whole of world politics but with one element in it: order. Sometimes when we speak of world order (or of *the* world order) what we have in mind is the totality of relationships among states, the international political system as a whole. Here, by contrast, I am thinking of order as a quality that may or may not obtain in international politics at any one time or place, or that may be present to a greater or lesser degree: order as opposed to disorder.

Of course, the element of disorder looms as large or larger in world politics than the element of order. Indeed, it is sometimes held (mistakenly, as I shall argue) that there is no such thing as order in world politics at all, and that we can speak of international order or of world order only as some future, desirable state of affairs which we should strive to bring about but which does not exist at present and has not existed in the past. But while it is important to remember that order is at best only one element in world politics, it is upon this element that I wish to focus attention. Thus when, in Part 2, I consider such institutions of the society of states as the balance of power, international law, diplomacy, war and the great powers, it is their functions in relation to order that I seek to explore, not the place they occupy in the international political system as a whole.

Second, order in this study is defined (in Chapter 1) as an actual or possible situation or state of affairs, not as a value, goal or objective. Thus it is not to be assumed that order, as it is discussed in this study, is a desirable goal, still less that it is an overriding one. To say that such and such an institution or course of action helps to sustain order in world politics is not to recommend that that institution should be preserved or that course of action followed.

Of course, in common with most men I do attach value to order. If I did not think of order in world politics as a desirable objective, I should not have thought it worthwhile to attempt this study of it. Indeed, it is doubtful whether any serious theory of political ends or values fails to attach some value to order in human relationships.

But, as I argue in Chapter 4, order is not the only value in relation to which international conduct may be shaped, and is not necessarily an overriding value. One of the themes of the present time, for example, is the clash between the preoccupation of the rich industrial states with order (or rather with a form of order that embodies their preferred values) and the preoccupation of poor and non-industrial states with just change. Similarly, we often hear that order in international politics should be subordinated to freedom or liberty – the coalition against Napoleon, for example, saw itself as fighting for the liberties of European nations against a system that provided order but extinguished these liberties, and today it is often said that within the American and Soviet spheres of influence order is imposed at the expense of the freedom or independence of small states.

To speak of order as if it were an overriding value, therefore, would be to beg the question of the relationship between order and other goals, and this I do not wish to do. A study of justice in world politics, which may be envisaged as a companion volume to the present one, might yield some very different perspectives from those that are expressed here. I am not unaware of these perspectives or unsympathetic to them. But this is a study of order in world politics, and not of justice. I do, in the course of this work, consider how order in world politics is related to demands for justice, and I discuss the extent to which demands for just change have to be satisfied if order in world politics is to obtain. But these excursions into the theory of justice are undertaken only because they are essential to the treatment of order.

Third, I have sought to confine my inquiry into order in world politics to enduring issues of human political structure or institutions, and to avoid consideration of the substantive issues of world politics at the present time. It is often said, sometimes correctly, that the prospects for international order depend on the outcome of some substantive question of the day – as, at present, the control of strategic nuclear weapons, or the development of *détente* between the United States and the Soviet Union, or the containment of the Arab-Israeli dispute, or the avoidance of a world depression, or the reform of the international monetary system, or the limitation of population growth, or the redistribution of the world's food supply. But whatever the substantive issues of the day may be, they have to be dealt with in the context of the existing political structure of the world, and it is in relation to this political structure, and alternatives to it, that I have sought answers to the three basic questions I have posed about order.

Fourth, the approach to order in world politics that is developed here is one that does not place primary emphasis upon international law or international organisation, and which, indeed, treats order as something that can exist and has existed independently of both. Order, it is contended here, does depend for its maintenance upon rules, and in the modern international system (by contrast with some other international systems) a major role in the maintenance of order has been played by those rules which have the status of international law. But to account for the existence of international order we have to acknowledge the place of rules that do not have the status of law. We have also to recognise that forms of international order might exist in the future, and have existed in the past, without rules of international law. It is, I believe, one of the defects of our present understanding of world politics that it does not bring together into common focus those rules of order or coexistence that can be derived from international law and those rules that cannot, but belong rather to the sphere of international politics.

Similarly, the approach followed here does not place major emphasis upon international organisations such as the United Nations and its specialised agencies, and the various regional international organisations. Of course, the part played by these organisations in the maintenance of order in contemporary world politics is an important one, and this is acknowledged at various points in the argument. But to find the basic causes of such order as exists in world politics, one must look not to the League of Nations, the United Nations and such bodies, but to institutions of international society that arose before these international organisations were established, and that would continue to operate (albeit in a different mode) even if these organisations did not exist.

Even the part that is in fact played by the United Nations and other international organisations is best understood not in terms of the official objectives and aspirations of these organisations themselves, or of the hopes commonly placed in them, but in terms of the contribution they make to the working of more basic institutions. It is for this reason that such references as are made to the United Nations and such bodies appear in the chapters dealing with the balance of power, international law, diplomacy, the role of the great powers, and war. It is these latter that are the effective institutions of international society; the League and the United Nations, as Martin Wight once argued, are best seen as pseudo-institutions. I have also been influenced by the feeling that the United Nations, because of the great mass of documentation it engenders, has been overstudied, and that this tends to deflect scholarly attention away from sources of international order that are more fundamental.

Finally, my purpose in writing this book is not to prescribe solutions or to canvass the merits of any particular vision of world order or any particular path that might lead to it. My purpose, or at least my conscious purpose, is the purely intellectual one of inquiring into the subject and following the argument wherever it might lead.

Of course, I do not wish to imply anything so absurd as that this study is 'value-free'. A study of this kind that did not derive from moral and political premises of some kind would be impossible, and, if it were possible, it would be sterile. What is important in an academic inquiry into politics is not to exclude value-laden premises, but to subject these premises to investigation and criticism, to treat the raising of moral and political issues as part of the inquiry. I am no more capable than anyone else of being detached about a subject such as this. But I believe in the value of attempting to be detached or disinterested, and it is clear to me that some approaches to the study of world politics are more detached or disinterested than others. I also believe that inquiry has its own morality, and is necessarily subversive of political institutions and movements of all kinds, good as well as bad.

Part 1

The Nature of Order in World Politics

1

The Concept of Order in World Politics

A study of order in world politics must begin with the question: what is it? I shall indicate what I mean by order in social life generally, and proceed to consider what it means in the system of states and in world politics in general.

Order in Social Life

To say of a number of things that together they display order is, in the simplest and most general sense of the term, to say that they are related to one another according to some pattern, that their relationship is not purely haphazard but contains some discernible principle. Thus a row of books on the shelf displays order whereas a heap of books on the floor does not.

But when we speak of order as opposed to disorder in social life we have in mind not any pattern or methodical arrangement among social phenomena, but a pattern of a particular sort. For a pattern may be evident in the behaviour of men or groups in violent conflict with one another, yet this is a situation we should characterise as disorderly. Sovereign states in circumstances of war and crisis may behave in regular and methodical ways; individual men living in the conditions of fear and insecurity, described in Hobbes's account of the state of nature, may conduct themselves in conformity with some recurrent pattern, indeed Hobbes himself says that they do; but these are examples not of order in social life but of disorder.

The order which men look for in social life is not any pattern or regularity in the relations of human individuals or groups, but a pattern that leads to a particular result, an arrangement of social

3

life such that it promotes certain goals or values. In this purposive or functional sense, a number of books display order when they are not merely placed in a row, but are arranged according to their author or subject so as to serve the purpose or fulfil the function of selection. It was this purposive conception of order that Augustine had in mind when he defined it as 'a good disposition of discrepant parts, each in its fittest place'.[1] This is a definition which, as we shall see, involves a number of problems, but because it presents order not as any pattern but as a particular kind of pattern, and, because it places the emphasis on ends or values, it provides a helpful starting point.

Augustine's definition at once raises the question: 'good' or 'fittest' for what? Order in this purposive sense is necessarily a relative concept: an arrangement (say, of books) that is orderly in relation to one purpose (finding a book by a particular author) may be disorderly in relation to another purpose (finding a book on a particular subject). It is for this reason that disagreement obtains as to whether or not a particular set of social arrangements embodies order, and that social and political systems that are in conflict with one another may both embody order. The social and political systems of the *ancien régime* and of Revolutionary France, or today of the Western world and the socialist countries, each embodies a 'disposition of discrepant parts' that is 'good' or 'fittest' for some different set of values or ends.

But while order in this Augustinian sense exists only in relation to given goals, certain of these goals stand out as elementary or primary, inasmuch as their fulfilment in some measure is a condition not merely of this or that sort of social life, but of social life as such. Whatever other goals they pursue, all societies recognise these goals and embody arrangements that promote them. Three such goals in particular may be mentioned. First, all societies seek to ensure that life will be in some measure secure against violence resulting in death or bodily harm. Second, all societies seek to ensure that promises, once made, will be kept, or that agreements, once undertaken, will be carried out. Third, all societies pursue the goal of ensuring that the possession of things will remain stable to some degree, and will not be subject to challenges that are constant and without limit.[2] By order in social life I mean a pattern of human activity that sustains elementary, primary or universal goals of social life such as these.

Because this definition is central to all of what follows in the present study, it is worth lingering over it to add some points of clarification. It is not suggested that these three basic values of all social life – sometimes called those of life, truth and property – represent an exhaustive list of the goals common to all societies, or that the term 'order' can be given content only in relation to them. But they are certainly to be included in any list of these basic goals, and they illustrate the idea of a basic goal.

All three goals may be said to be *elementary:* a constellation of persons or groups among whom there existed no expectation of security against violence, of the honouring of agreements or of stability of possession we should hardly call a society at all. The goals are also primary in the sense that any other goals a society may set for itself presuppose the realisation of these goals in some degree. Unless men enjoy some measure of security against the threat of death or injury at the hands of others, they are not able to devote energy or attention enough to other objects to be able to accomplish them. Unless there can be a general presumption that agreements entered into will be carried out, it is not conceivable that agreements can be entered into to facilitate human co-operation in any field. Unless the possession of objects by persons or groups can be to some degree stabilised or settled (it is not material here whether this is through private or communal ownership, or with what kind of mixture of the one and the other) then given that human beings are what they are, and given that the things human beings want to possess have only limited abundance, it is difficult to imagine stable social relations of any sort. Of course, as Hume and others have argued, the need which societies feel to stabilise possession is conditional. If men in their wants of material things were wholly egotistical, the stabilisation of possession by rules of property or ownership would be impossible – just as if men were wholly altruistic in relation to these wants, such stabilisation would he unnecessary. Equally, if there existed total scarcity of the things men wish to possess, rules of property would be impossible to make effective, and if there were total abundance of these things, rules of property would be unnecessary. But given the facts of limited human altruism and limited abundance of the things men want, the attempt to stabilise possession of these things is a primary goal of all social life. The three goals are also *universal* in the sense that all actual societies appear to take account of them.

A further point of clarification is that in defining order in social life as a pattern of human activities, a 'disposition of discrepant parts' that sustains elementary or primary ends such as these, I am not seeking to argue that these goals should have priority over others; nor, indeed, at this point in the argument, am I seeking to endorse them as valuable or desirable at all. I do contend that unless these goals are achieved in some measure, we cannot speak of the existence of a society or of social life; that the achievement of other goals presupposes the achievement of these basic goals in some degree; and that in fact all societies seek to promote them. This does not mean, however, that when a conflict arises between these goals and others, societies either do or should always give priority to them. In fact, as in periods of war or revolution, men frequently and sometimes, it may be argued, rightly, resort to violence, dishonour agreements and violate rights of property in the pursuit of other values. As was argued in the Introduction, order is not the only value in relation to which human conduct can be shaped, nor should we assume that it is prior to other values.

It is not argued here that the elementary or primary ends of social life do or should take priority over others, nor is it being contended that these ends are mandatory at all. In particular, I do not wish to embrace the position of exponents of the doctrine of natural law that these and other elementary, primary or universal goals of social life are mandatory for all men, or that the binding force of rules of conduct upholding them is self-evident to all men. It is true that the position I have adopted here can be said to have been part of the 'empirical equivalent' of the natural-law theory, which sought to deal with the elementary or primary conditions of social existence in the idiom of a different era. Indeed, the natural-law tradition remains one of the richest sources of theoretical insight into the matters dealt with in the present study. But it is not part of my intention to revive the central tenets of natural-law thinking itself.

A point of clarification must be added about the relationship of order in social, life, as I have defined it, to rules, or general imperative principles of conduct. Social order is sometimes defined in terms of obedience to rules of conduct; sometimes it is defined, more specifically, as obedience to rules of law. In fact, order in social life is very closely connected with the conformity of human behaviour to rules of conduct, if not necessarily to rules of law. In most societies, what helps to create patterns of conduct that conform to the elementary goals of security against violence, the honouring of agreements and the stability of possession, is the existence of rules prohibiting murder and assault, rules prohibiting breach of contract, and rules of property. However, I have sought deliberately to find a definition of order in social life that excludes the conception of rules. This is because, for reasons discussed in Chapter 3, I believe order in social life can exist in principle without rules, and that it is best to treat rules as a widespread, and nearly ubiquitous, means of creating order in human society, rather than as part of the definition of order itself.

I must also set out the relationship between order in social life, as it is defined here, and social laws of a different kind: not rules, or general imperative principles of conduct, but scientific laws, or general propositions asserting a causal connection between one class of social events and another. It is sometimes said that order in social life is to do with the conformity of conduct in society to such scientific laws – or, more specifically, that conduct which is orderly is conduct which is predictable, that is, which conforms to laws that can be applied to future cases as well as to past and present ones. Once again, there does in fact exist a close connection between order in the sense in which it is defined here, and the conformity of conduct to scientific laws that afford a basis for predicting future behaviour. One of the consequences of a situation in which elementary or primary goals of social coexistence are consistently upheld is that regular patterns of behaviour become known, are formulated as general laws, and afford a basis for expectations about future behaviour. Moreover, if we ask the question why men attach value to order (and it is my contention that almost universally they do, this being as much part of the perspective of a revolutionary as of a conservative), at least part of the answer is that they value the greater predictability of human behaviour that comes as the consequence of conformity to the elementary or primary goals of coexistence. But to define order in social life in terms of scientific law and predictability is to confuse a possible consequence of social order, and reason for treating it as valuable, with the thing itself. Behaviour which is disorderly, in the sense in which the term is used here, may also conform to scientific law, and afford a basis for expectations about the future: the whole theoretical literature of the recurrent features of wars, civil conflicts and revolutions attests to the possibility of finding conformity to scientific law in social conduct that is disorderly.

International Order

By international order I mean a pattern of activity that sustains the elementary or primary goals of the society of states, or international society. Before spelling out in more detail what is involved in the concept of international order I shall first set the stage by indicating what I mean by states, by a system of states, and by a society of states, or international society.

The starting point of international relations is the existence of *states,* or independent political communities each of which possesses a government and asserts sovereignty in relation to a particular portion of the earth's surface and a particular segment of the human population. On the one hand, states assert, in relation to this territory and population, what may be called internal sovereignty, which means supremacy over all other authorities within that territory and population. On the other hand, they assert what may be called external sovereignty, by which is meant not supremacy but independence of outside authorities. The sovereignty of states, both internal and external, may be said to exist both at a normative level and at a factual level. On the one hand, states assert the right to supremacy over authorities within their territory and population and independence of authorities outside it; but, on the other hand, they also actually exercise, in varying degrees, such supremacy and independence in practice. An independent political community which merely claims a right to sovereignty (or is judged by others to have such a right), but cannot assert this right in practice, is not a state properly so-called.

The independent political communities that are states in this sense include city-states, such as those of ancient Greece or renaissance Italy, as well as modern nation-states. They include states in which government is based on dynastic principles of legitimacy, such as predominated in modern Europe up to the time of the French Revolution, as well as states in which government is based upon popular or national principles of legitimacy, such as have predominated Europe since that time. They include multinational states, such as the European empires of the nineteenth century, as well as states of a single nationality. They include states whose territory is scattered in parts, such as the oceanic imperial states of Western Europe, as well as states whose territory is a single geographical entity.

There are, however, a great variety of independent political communities that have existed in history and yet are not states in this sense. The Germanic peoples of the Dark Ages, for example, were independent political communities, but while their rulers asserted supremacy over a population, they did not assert it over a distinct territory. The kingdoms and principalities of Western Christendom in the Middle Ages were not states: they did not possess internal sovereignty because they were not supreme over authorities within their territory and population; and at the same time they did not possess external sovereignty since they were not independent of the Pope or, in some cases, the Holy Roman Emperor. In parts of Africa, Australia and Oceania, before the European intrusion, there were independent political communities held together by ties of lineage or kinship, in which there was no such institution as government. Entities such as these fall outside the purview of 'international relations', if by this we mean (as we generally do) not the relations of nations but the relations of states in the strict sense. The relations of these independent political communities might be encompassed in a wider theory of the relations of *powers,* in which the relations of states would figure as a special case, but lie outside the domain of 'international relations' in the strict sense.[3]

A *system of states* (or international system) is formed when two or more states have sufficient contact between them, and have sufficient impact on one another's decisions, to cause them to behave – at least in some measure – as parts of a whole. Two or more states can of course exist without forming an international system in this sense: for example, the independent political communities that existed in the Americas before the voyage of Columbus did not form an international system with those that existed in Europe; the independent political communities that existed in China during the Period of Warring States (circa 481– 221 B.C.) did not form an international system with those that existed in Greece and the Mediterranean at the same time.

But where states are in regular contact with one another, and where in addition there is interaction between them sufficient to make the behaviour of each a necessary element in the calculations of the other, then we may speak of their forming a system. The interactions among states may be direct – as when two states are neighbours, or competitors for the same object, or partners in the same enterprise. Or their interactions maybe indirect – the consequence of the dealings each of them has with a third party, or merely of the impact each of them makes on the system as a whole. Nepal and Bolivia are neither neighbours, nor competitors, nor partners in a common enterprise (except, perhaps, as members of the United Nations). But they affect each other through the chain of links among states in which both participate. The interactions among states by which an international system is defined may take the form of co-operation, but also of conflict, or even of neutrality or indifference with regard to one another's objectives. The interactions may be present over a whole range of activities – political, strategic, economic, social – as they are today, or only in one or two; it may be enough, as Raymond Aron's definition of an international system implies, that the independent political communities in question 'maintain regular relations with each other' and 'are all capable of being implicated in a generalised war'.[4]

Martin Wight, in classifying different kinds of states system, has distinguished what he calls an 'international states system' from a suzerain-state system'.[5] The former is a system composed of states that are sovereign, in the sense in which the term has been defined here. The latter is a system in which one state asserts and maintains paramountcy or supremacy over the rest. The relations of the Roman Empire to its barbarian neighbours illustrate the concept of a suzerain-state system; so do the relations of Byzantium to its lesser neighbours, of the Abbasid Caliphate to surrounding lesser powers, or of Imperial China to its tributary states. In some of what Martin Wight would call 'international states systems', it has been assumed that at any one time there is bound to be a dominant or hegemonial power: the classical Greek city-state system, for example, and the later system of Hellenistic kingdoms, witnessed a perpetual contest as to which state was to be *hegemon*. What distinguishes a 'suzerain-state system' such as China-and-its-vassals from an 'international states system', in which one or another state at any one time exerts hegemonial power, is that in the former one power exerts a hegemony that is permanent and for practical purposes unchallengeable, whereas in the latter, hegemony passes from one power to another and is constantly subject to dispute. In terms of the approach being developed here, only what Wight calls an 'international states system' is a states system at all. Among the independent political entities constituting a 'suzerain-state system' such as China-and-its-vassals, only one state – the suzerain state itself – possesses sovereignty, and therefore one of the basic conditions of the existence of a states system, that there should be two or more sovereign states, is absent.

A second distinction made by Martin Wight is between 'primary states systems' and 'secondary states systems'.[6] The former are composed of states, but the latter are composed of systems of states – often of suzerain-state systems. He gives as examples of a 'secondary states system' the relationship between Eastern Christendom, Western Christendom and the Abbasid Caliphate in the Middle Ages and the relationship of Egypt, the Hittites and Babylon in the Armana Age. This is a distinction which may prove a helpful one if a general historical analysis of the political structure of the world as a whole – today almost completely uncharted territory – is ever attempted. The distinction does not help us very much if, as here, we confine our attention to what are strictly systems of states. If the systems of which 'secondary states systems' are composed, each contains a multiplicity of states, then if there is contact and interaction sufficient between these states and other states, the states as a whole form a 'primary states system'. If, on the other hand, the systems concerned do *not* contain states – as Western Christendom did not, for example – then the interactions between such systems are of interest to a theory of world politics, but are not systems of states at all. In terms of our present approach we need take account only of 'primary states systems'.

The term 'international system' has been a fashionable one among recent students of international relations, principally as a consequence of the writings of Morton A. Kaplan.[7] Kaplan's use of the term is not unlike that employed here, but what distinguishes Kaplan's work is the attempt to use the concept of a system to explain and predict international behaviour, especially by treating international systems as a particular kind of 'system of action'.[8] Here nothing of this sort is intended, and the term is employed simply to identify a particular kind of international constellation.

It should be recognised, however, that the term 'system of states' had a long history, and embodied some rather different meanings, before it came to have its present one. It appears to have begun with Pufendorf, whose tract *De systematibus civitatum* was published in 1675.[9] Pufendorf, however, was referring not to the European states system as a whole, but to particular groups of states within that system, which were sovereign yet at the same time connected so as to form one body – like the German states after the peace of Westphalia. While the term 'system' was applied to European states as a whole by eighteenth-century writers such as Rousseau and Nettelbladt, it was writers of the Napoleonic period, such as Gentz, Ancillon and Heeren, who were chiefly responsible for giving the term currency. At a time when the growth of French power threatened to destroy the states system and transform it into a universal empire, these writers sought to draw attention to the existence of the system, and also to show why it was worth preserving; they were not merely the analysts of the states system, but were also its apologists or protagonists. Of their works, the most important was A. H. L. Heeren's *Handbuch der Geschichte des Europaischen Staatensystems und seiner Kolonien,* first published in 1809. The term 'states system' first appeared in English in the translation of this work that was published in 1834, the translator noting that it was 'not strictly English'.[10]

For Heeren the states system was not simply a constellation of states having a certain degree of contact and interaction, as it is defined here. It involved much more than simply the causal connection of certain sets of variables to each other, which Kaplan takes to define a 'system of action'.[11] A states system for Heeren was 'the union of several contiguous states, resembling each other in their manners, religion and degree of social improvement, and cemented together by a reciprocity of interests'.[12] He saw a states system, in other words, as involving common interests and common values and as resting upon a common culture or civilisation. Moreover, Heeren had a sense of the fragility of the states system, the freedom of its members to act so as to maintain the system or allow it to be destroyed, as the Greek city-state system had been destroyed by Macedon, and as later the system of Hellenistic states that succeeded Alexander's empire had in turn been destroyed by Rome. Indeed, Heeren in the 'Preface' to his first and second editions thought that Napoleon had in fact destroyed the European states system, and that he was writing its epitaph. Such a conception of the states system differs basically from what is called an international system in the present study, and is closer to what I call here an international society.

A *society of states* (or international society) exists when a group of states, conscious of certain common interests and common values, form a society in the sense that they conceive themselves to be bound by a common set of rules in their relations with one another, and share in the working of common institutions. If states today form an international society (to what extent they do is the subject of the next chapter), this is because, recognising certain common interests and perhaps some common values, they regard themselves as bound by certain rules in their dealings with one another, such as that they should respect one another's claims to independence, that they should honour agreements into which they enter, and that they should be subject to certain limitations in exercising force against one another. At the same time they co-operate in the working of institutions such as the forms of procedures of international law, the machinery of diplomacy and general international organisation, and the customs and conventions of war.

An international society in this sense presupposes an international system, but an international system may exist that is not an international society. Two or more states, in other words, may be in contact with each other and interact in such a way as to be necessary factors in each other's calculations without their being conscious of common interests or values, conceiving themselves to be bound by a common set of rules, or co-operating in the working of common institutions. Turkey, China, Japan, Korea and Siam, for example, were part of the European-dominated international system before they were part of the European-dominated international society. That is to say, they were in contact with European powers, and interacted significantly with them in war and commerce, before they and the European powers came to recognise common interests or values, to regard each other as subject to the same set of rules and as co-operating in the working of common institutions. Turkey formed part of the European-dominated international system from the time of its emergence in the sixteenth century, taking part in wars and alliances as a member of the system. Yet in the first three centuries of this relationship it was specifically denied on both sides that the European powers and Turkey possessed any common interests or values; it was held on both sides that agreements entered into with each other were not binding, and there were no common institutions, such as united the European powers, in whose working they co-operated. Turkey was not accepted by the European states as a member of international society until the Treaty of Paris of 1856, terminating the Crimean War, and perhaps did not achieve full equality of rights within international society until the Treaty of Lausanne in 1923.

In the same way Persia and Carthage formed part of a single international system with the classical Greek city-states, but were not part of the Greek international society. That is to say, Persia (and to a lesser extent Carthage) interacted with the Greek city-states, and was always an essential factor in the strategic equation, either as an outside threat against which the Greek city-states were ready to combine, or as a power able to intervene in the conflicts among them. But Persia was perceived by the Greeks as a barbarian power; it did not share the common values of the Greeks, expressed in the Greek language, the pan-Hellenic games or consultation of the Delphic oracle; it was not subject to the rules which required Greek city-states to limit their conflicts with one another; and it was not a participant in the *amphictyonae* in which institutional co-operation among the Greek states took place, or in the diplomatic institution of *proxenoi*.

When, as in the case of encounters between European and non-European states from the sixteenth century until the late nineteenth century, states are participants in a single international system, but not members of a single international society, there may be communication, exchanges of envoys or messengers and agreements – not only about trade but also about war, peace and alliances. But these forms of interaction do not in themselves demonstrate that there is an international society. Communication may take place, envoys may be exchanged and agreements entered into without there being a sense of common interests or values that gives such exchange substance and a prospect of permanence, without any sense that there are rules which lay down how the interaction should proceed, and without the attempt of the parties concerned to co-operate in institutions in whose survival they have a stake. When Cortes and Pizarro parleyed with the Aztec and Inca kings, when George III sent Lord Macartney to Peking, or when

Queen Victoria's representatives entered into agreements with the Maori chieftains, the Sultan of Sokoto or the Kabaka of Buganda, this was outside the framework of any shared conception of an international society of which the parties on both sides were members with like rights and duties.

Whether or not these distinguishing features of an international society are present in an international system, it is not always easy to determine: as between an international system that is clearly also an international society, and a system that is clearly not a society, there lie cases where a sense of common interests is tentative and inchoate; where the common rules perceived are vague and ill-formed, and there is doubt as to whether they are worthy of the name of rules; or where common institutions – relating to diplomatic machinery or to limitations in war – are implicit or embryonic. If we ask of modern international society the questions 'when did it begin?' or 'what were its geographical limits?' we are at once involved in difficult problems of the tracing of boundaries.

But certain international systems have quite clearly been international societies also. The chief examples are the classical Greek city-state system; the international system formed by the Hellenistic kingdoms in the period between the disintegration of Alexander's empire and the Roman conquest; the international system of China during the Period of Warring States; the states system of ancient India; and the modern states system, which arose in Europe and is now world-wide.

A common feature of these historical international societies is that they were all founded upon a common culture or civilisation, or at least on some of the elements of such a civilisation: a common language, a common epistemology and understanding of the universe, a common religion, a common ethical code, a common aesthetic or artistic tradition. It is reasonable to suppose that where such elements of a common civilisation underlie an international society, they facilitate its working in two ways. On the one hand, they may make for easier communication and closer awareness and understanding between one state and another, and thus facilitate the definition of common rules and the evolution of common institutions. On the other hand, they may reinforce the sense of common interests that impels states to accept common rules and institutions with a sense of common values. This is a question to which we shall return when, later in this study, we consider the contention that the global international society of the twentieth century, unlike the Christian international society of the sixteenth and seventeenth centuries, or the European international society of the eighteenth and nineteenth centuries, is without any such common culture or civilisation (see Chapter 13).

Having elaborated our conception of states, of a system of states, and of a society of states, we may return to the proposition with which this section began: that by international order is meant a pattern or disposition of international activity that sustains those goals of the society of states that are elementary, primary or universal. What goals, then, are these?

First, there is the goal of preservation of the system and society of states itself. Whatever the divisions among them, modern states have been united in the belief that they are the principal actors in world politics and the chief bearers of rights and duties within it. The society of states has sought to ensure that it will remain the prevailing form of universal political organisation, in fact and in right. Challenges to the continued existence of the society of states have sometimes come from a particular dominant state – the Habsburg Empire, the France of Louis XIV, the France of Napoleon, Hitler's Germany, perhaps post-1945 America – which seemed capable of overthrowing the system and society of states and transforming it into a universal empire. Challenges have also been delivered by actors other than states which threaten to deprive states of their position as the principal actors in world politics, or the principal bearers of rights and duties within it. 'Supra-state' actors such as, in the sixteenth and seventeenth centuries, the Papacy and the Holy Roman Emperor, or, in the twentieth century, the United Nations (one thinks especially of its role as a violent actor in the 1960–1 Congo crisis) present such a threat. 'Sub-state' actors which operate in world politics from within a particular state, or 'trans-state' actors which are groups cutting across the boundaries of states, may also challenge the privileged position of states in world politics, or their right to enjoy it; in the history of modern international society the revolutionary and counter-revolutionary manifestations of human solidarity engendered by the Reformation, the French Revolution and the Russian Revolution are principal examples.

Second, there is the goal of maintaining the independence or external sovereignty of individual states. From the perspective of any particular state what it chiefly hopes to gain from participation in the society of states is recognition of its independence of outside authority, and in particular of its supreme jurisdiction over its subjects and territory. The chief price it has to pay for this is recognition of like rights to independence and sovereignty on the part of other states.

International society has in fact treated preservation of the independence of particular states as a goal that is subordinate to preservation of the society of states itself; this reflects the predominant role played in shaping international society by the great powers, which view themselves as its custodians (see Chapter 9). Thus international society has often allowed the independence of individual states to be extinguished, as in the great process of partition and absorption of small powers by greater ones, in the name of principles such as 'compensation' and the 'balance of power' that produced a steady decline in the number of states in Europe from the Peace of Westphalia in 1648 until the Congress of Vienna in 1815. In the same way, international society, at least in the perspective of the great powers which see themselves as its guardians, treats the independence of particular states as subordinate to the preservation of the system as a whole when it tolerates or encourages limitation of the sovereignty or independence of small states through such devices as spheres-of-influence agreements, or agreements to create buffer or neutralised states.

Third, there is the goal of peace. By this is meant not the goal of establishing universal and permanent peace, such as has been the dream of irenists or theorists of peace, and stands in contrast to actual historical experience: this is not a goal which the society of states can be said to have pursued in any serious way. Rather what is meant is the maintenance of peace in the sense of the absence of war among member states of international society as the normal condition of their relationship, to be breached only in special circumstances and according to principles that are generally accepted.

Peace in this sense has been viewed by international society as a goal subordinate to that of the preservation of the states system itself, for which it has been widely held that it can be right to wage war; and as subordinate also to preservation of the sovereignty or independence of individual states, which have insisted on the right to wage war in self-defence, and to protect other rights also. The subordinate status of peace in relation to these other goals is reflected in the phrase 'peace and security', which occurs in the United Nations Charter. Security in international politics means no more than safety: either objective safety, safety which actually exists, or subjective safety, that which is felt or experienced. What states seek to make secure or safe is not merely peace, but their independence and the continued existence of the society of states itself which that independence requires; and for these objectives, as we have noted, they are ready to resort to war and the threat of war. The coupling of the two terms together in the Charter reflects the judgement that the requirements of security may conflict with those of peace, and that in this event the latter will not necessarily take priority.

Fourth, it should be noted that among the elementary or primary goals of the society of states are those which, at the beginning of this chapter, were said to be the common goals of all social life: limitation of violence resulting in death or bodily harm, the keeping of promises and the stabilisation of possession by rules of property.

The goal of limitation of violence is represented in international society in a number of ways. States co-operate in international society so as to maintain their monopoly of violence, and deny the right to employ it to other groups. States also accept limitations on their own right to use violence; at a minimum they accept that they shall not kill one another's envoys or messengers, since this would make communication impossible. Beyond this, they accept that war should be waged only for a 'just' cause, or a cause the justice of which can be argued in terms of common rules. They have also constantly proclaimed adherence to rules requiring that wars be fought within certain limits, the *temperamenta belli*.

The goal of the keeping of promises is represented in the principle *pacta sunt servanda*. Among states as among individuals, co-operation can take place only on the basis of agreements, and agreements can fulfil their function in social life only on the basis of a presumption that once entered into they will be upheld. International society adjusts itself to the pressures for change that make for the breaking of treaties, and at the same time salvages the principle itself, through the doctrine of *rebus sic stantibus*.

The goal of stability of possession is reflected in international society not only by the recognition by states of one another's property, but more fundamentally in the compact of mutual recognition of sovereignty, in which states accept one another's spheres of jurisdiction: indeed, the idea of the sovereignty of the state derived historically from the idea that certain territories and peoples were the property or patrimony of the ruler.

The above are among the elementary or primary goals of modern international society, and of other international societies. It is not suggested here that this list is exhaustive, nor that it could not be formulated in some other way. Nor is it any part of my thesis that these goals should be accepted as a valid basis for action, as legislating right conduct in international relations. It should also be said that at this stage in the argument we are concerned only with what may be called the 'statics' of international order and not with its 'dynamics'; we are concerned only to spell out what is involved in the idea of international order, not to trace how it is embodied in historical institutions subject to change.

World Order

By world order I mean those patterns or dispositions of human activity that sustain the elementary or primary goals of social life among mankind as a whole. International order is order among states; but states are simply groupings of men, and men may be grouped in such a way that they do not form states at all. Moreover, where they are grouped into states, they are grouped in other ways also. Underlying the questions we raise about order among states there are deeper questions, of more enduring importance, about order in the great society of all mankind.

Throughout human history before the nineteenth century there was no single political system that spanned the world as a whole. The great society of all mankind, to which allusions were made by exponents of canon law or natural law, was a notional society that existed in the sight of God or in the light of the principles of natural law: no actual political system corresponded to it. Before the latter half of the nineteenth century world order was simply the sum of the various political systems that brought order to particular parts of the world.

However, since the late nineteenth century and early twentieth century there has arisen for the first time a single political system that is genuinely global. Order on a global scale has ceased to be simply the sum of the various political systems that produce order on a local scale; it is also the product of what may be called a world political system. Order in the world – say, in 1900 – was still the sum of the order provided within European and American states and their overseas dependencies, within the Ottoman empire, the Chinese and Japanese empires, within the Khanates and Sultanates that preserved an independent existence from the Sahara to Central Asia, within primitive African and Oceanic political systems not yet destroyed by the European impact – but it was also the consequence of a political system, linking them all, that operated all over the world.

The first global political system has taken the form of a global system of states. What is chiefly responsible for the emergence of a degree of interaction among political systems in all the continents of the world, sufficient to make it possible for us to speak of a world political system, has been the expansion of the European states system all over the globe, and its transformation into a states system of global dimension. In the first phase of this process the European states expanded and incorporated or dominated the rest of the world, beginning with the Portuguese voyages of discovery in the fifteenth century and ending with the partition of Africa in the nineteenth. In the second phase, overlapping with the first in point of time, the areas of the world thus incorporated or dominated broke loose from European control, and took their places as member states of international society, beginning with the American Revolution and ending with the African and Asian anti-colonial revolution of our own times. It is true that the intermeshing of the various parts of the world was not simply the work of states; private individuals and groups played their part as explorers, traders, migrants, missionaries and mercenaries, and the expansion of the states system was part of a wider spread of social and economic exchange. However, the political structure to which these developments gave rise was one simply of a global system and society of states.

But while the world political system that exists at present takes the form of a system of states, or takes principally this form (we shall contend later that a world political system is emerging of which the system of states is only part), world order could in principle be achieved by other forms of universal political organisation, and a standing question is whether world order might not better be served by such other forms. Other forms of universal political organisation have existed in the past on a less than global scale; in the broad sweep of human history, indeed, the form of the states system has been the exception rather than the rule. Moreover, it is reasonable to assume that new forms of universal political organisation may be created in the future that do not resemble those that have existed in the past. In Part 3 of this study we shall consider the questions whether the present states system is giving place to some other form of universal political organisation, and whether world order would be best served if it did give place to some such other form.

Here we need only stress that in this study world order entails something different from international order. Order among mankind as a whole is something wider than order among states; something more fundamental and primordial than it; and also, I should argue, something morally prior to it.

World order is wider than international order because to give an account of it we have to deal not only with order among states but also with order on a domestic or municipal scale, provided within particular states, and with order within the wider world political system of which the states system is only part.

World order is more fundamental and primordial than international order because the ultimate units of the great society of all mankind are not states (or nations, tribes, empires, classes or parties) but individual human beings, which are permanent and indestructible in a sense in which groupings of them of this or that sort are not. This is the moment for international relations, but the question of world order arises whatever the political or social structure of the globe.

World order, finally, is morally prior to international order. To take this view is to broach the question of the value of world order and its place in the hierarchy of human values, which I have so far avoided, but which I discuss in Chapter 4. It is necessary to state at this point, however, that if any value attaches to order in world politics, it is order among all mankind which we must treat as being of primary value, not order within the society of states. If international order does have value, this can only be because it is instrumental to the goal of order in human society as a whole.

2

Does Order Exist in World Politics?

We have now made it clear what is meant in this study by order in world politics. The question we must now ask is: does it exist?

Order in world politics may one day take the form of the maintenance of elementary goals of social life in a single world society or great society of all mankind. How far the system of states is giving place to such a society, and whether or not it is desirable that it should, are questions that will be considered later in this study. It could not be seriously argued, however, that the society of all mankind is already a going concern. In the present phase we are still accustomed to thinking of order in world politics as consisting of domestic order, or order within states, and international order, or order among them.

No one would deny that there exists within some states a high degree of domestic or municipal order. It is, however, often argued that international order does not exist, except as an aspiration, and that the history of international relations consists simply of disorder or strife. To many people the idea of international order suggests not anything that has occurred in the past, but simply a possible or desirable future state of international relations, about which we might speculate or which we might work to bring about. To those who take this view a study of international order suggests simply a design for a future world, in the tradition of Sully, Cruce, St Pierre and other irenists or peace theorists.

This present study takes as its starting-point the proposition that, on the contrary, order is part of the historical record of international relations; and in particular, that modern states have formed, and continue to form, not only a system of states but also an international society. To establish this proposition I shall begin by showing first that there has always been present, throughout the history of the modern states system, an idea of international society, proclaimed by philosophers and publicists, and present in the rhetoric of the leaders of states. Second, I shall seek to show that this idea is reflected, at least in part, in international reality; that the idea of international society has important roots in actual international practice. Third, I shall set out the limitations of the idea of international society as a guide to the actual practice of states, the precarious and imperfect nature of the order to which it gives rise.

The Idea of International Society

Throughout the history of the modern states system there have been three competing traditions of thought: the Hobbesian or realist tradition, which views international politics as a state of war; the Kantian or universalist tradition, which sees at work in international politics a potential community of mankind; and the Grotian or internationalist tradition, which views international politics as taking place within an international society.[1] Here I shall state what is essential to the Grotian or internationalist idea of international society, and what divides it from the Hobbesian or realist tradition on the one hand, and from the Kantian or universalist tradition on the other. Each of these traditional patterns of thought embodies a description of the nature of international politics and a set of prescriptions about international conduct.

The Hobbesian tradition describes international relations as a state of war of all against all, an arena of struggle in which each state is pitted against every other. International relations, on the Hobbesian view, represent pure conflict between states and resemble a game that is wholly distributive or zero-sum: the interests of each state exclude the interests of any other. The particular international activity that, on the Hobbesian view, is most typical of international activity as a whole, or best provides the clue to it, is war itself. Thus peace, on the Hobbesian view, is a period of recuperation from the last war and preparation for the next.

The Hobbesian prescription for international conduct is that the state is free to pursue its goals in relation to other states without moral or legal restrictions of any kind. Ideas of morality and law, on this view, are valid only in the context of a society, but international life is beyond the bounds of any society. If any moral or legal goals are to be pursued in international politics, these can only be the moral or legal goals of the state itself. Either it is held (as by Machiavelli) that the state conducts foreign policy in a kind of moral and legal vacuum, or it is held (as by Hegel and his successors) that moral behaviour for the state in foreign policy lies in its own self-assertion. The only rules or principles which, for those in the Hobbesian tradition, may be said to limit or circumscribe the behaviour of states in their relations with one another are rules of prudence or expediency. Thus agreements may be kept if it is expedient to keep them, but may be broken if it is not.

The Kantian or universalist tradition, at the other extreme, takes the essential nature of international politics to lie not in conflict among states, as on the Hobbesian view, but in the trans-national social bonds that link the individual human beings who are the subjects or citizens of states. The dominant theme of international relations, on the Kantian view, is only apparently the relationship among states, and is really the relationship among all men in the community of mankind – which exists potentially, even if it does not exist actually, and which when it comes into being will sweep the system of states into limbo.[2]

Within the community of all mankind, on the universalist view, the interests of all men are one and the same; international politics, considered from this perspective, is not a purely distributive or zero-sum game, as the Hobbesians maintain, but a purely co-operative or non-zero-sum game. Conflicts of interest exist among the ruling cliques of states, but this is only at the superficial or transient level of the existing system of states; properly understood, the interests of all peoples are the same. The particular international activity which, on the Kantian view, most typifies international activity as a whole is the horizontal conflict of ideology that cuts across the boundaries of states and divides human society into two camps – the trustees of the immanent community of mankind and those who stand in its way, those who are of the true faith and the heretics, the liberators and the oppressed.

The Kantian or universalist view of international morality is that, in contrast to the Hobbesian conception, there are moral imperatives in the field of international relations limiting the action of states, but that these imperatives enjoin not coexistence and cooperation among states but rather the overthrow of the system of states and its replacement by a cosmopolitan society. The community of mankind, on the Kantian view, is not only the central reality in international politics, in the sense that the forces able to bring it into being are present; it is also the end or object of the highest moral endeavour. The rules that sustain coexistence and social intercourse among states should be ignored if the imperatives of this higher morality require it. Good faith with heretics has no meaning, except in terms of tactical convenience; between the elect and the damned, the liberators and the oppressed, the question of mutual acceptance of rights to sovereignty or independence does not arise.

What has been called the Grotian or internationalist tradition stands between the realist tradition and the universalist tradition. The Grotian tradition describes international politics in terms of a society of states or international society.[3] As against the Hobbesian tradition, the Grotians contend that states are not engaged in simple struggle, like gladiators in an arena, but are limited in their conflicts with one another by common rules and institutions. But as against the Kantian or universalist perspective the Grotians accept the Hobbesian premise that sovereigns or states are the principal reality in international politics; the immediate members of international society are states rather than individual human beings. International politics, in the Grotian understanding, expresses neither complete conflict of interest between states nor complete identity of interest; it resembles a game that is partly distributive but also partly productive. The particular international activity which, on the Grotian view, best typifies international activity as a whole is neither war between states, nor horizontal conflict cutting across the boundaries of states, but trade – or, more generally, economic and social intercourse between one country and another.

The Grotian prescription for international conduct is that all states, in their dealings with one another, are bound by the rules and institutions of the society they form. As against the view of the Hobbesians, states in the Grotian view are bound not only by rules of prudence or expediency but also by imperatives of morality and law. But, as against the view of the universalists, what these imperatives enjoin is not the overthrow of the system of states and its replacement by a universal community of mankind, but rather acceptance of the requirements of coexistence and co-operation in a society of states.

Each of these traditions embodies a great variety of doctrines about international politics, among which there exists only a loose connection. In different periods each pattern of thought appears in a different idiom and in relation to different issues and preoccupations. This is not the place to explore further the connections and distinctions within each tradition. Here we have only to take account of the fact that the Grotian idea of international society has always been present in thought about the states system, and to indicate in broad terms the metamorphoses which, in the last three to four centuries, it has undergone.

Christian International Society

In the fifteenth, sixteenth and seventeenth centuries, when the universal political organisation of Western Christendom was still in process of disintegration, and modern states in process of articulation, the three patterns of thought purporting to describe the new international politics, and to prescribe conduct within it, first took shape. On the one hand, thinkers like Machiavelli, Bacon and Hobbes saw the emerging states as confronting one another in the social and moral vacuum left by the receding *respublica Christiana*. On the other hand Papal and Imperialist writers fought a rearguard action on behalf of the ideas of the universal authority of Pope and Emperor. As against these alternatives there was asserted by a third group of thinkers, relying upon the tradition of natural law, the possibility that the princes now making themselves supreme over local rivals and independent of outside authorities were nevertheless bound by common interests and rules. As Gierke puts it:

> The mediaeval idea of a world-monarchy was an idea foreign to the thinkers of the School of Natural Law. They left to the publicists of the Holy Roman Empire the task of continually re-invoking, on reams of paper, the unsubstantiated ghost of the old *imperium mundi*, but they made the indestructible germ of that

dying system of thought yield the new and fruitful idea of *international society.* . . . On the one hand, a tendency continually reappeared to harden international society into a world-State, and to arm it with the authority of a Super-State organised on Republican lines: on the other, the stricter advocates of the theory of sovereignty rejected *in toto* any idea of a natural community uniting all States together. But the doctrine which held the field, and determined the future of international law, was a doctrine which steadily clung to the view that there was a natural law connection between all nations, and that this connection, while it did not issue in any authority exercised by the Whole over its parts, at any rate involved a system of mutual social rights and duties.[4]

The international society conceived by the natural-law thinkers of this period (Victoria, Suarez, Gentili, Grotius, Pufendorf) had the following as its most central characteristics. First, the values which they held to underly the society were Christian. It is true that the prominence accorded by all these thinkers to the idea of a natural law, spelling out the rights and duties of all men everywhere, carried the implication that social bonds existed between Christians and others, as Victoria insisted when he adumbrated the universal laws of hospitality by which Spaniards and Indians were bound in the Americas. It is true that Grotius, by insisting that natural law was the principal source of the law of nations, and that this law would remain valid even if God did not exist, implied that international society might ultimately dispense with its Christian foundations. It is true that the search for principles on which Catholic and Protestant states might find a basis for coexistence led necessarily in the direction of secular principles.

But none of these theorists of international society believed that relations among Christian powers were on the same basis as relations between these and others. Even for Grotius, within the wider circle of all mankind, bound by the principles of natural law, there was the narrower circle of Christendom, bound by volitional divine law, by the inherited customs and rules of *ius gentium,* by canon and Roman law. For the Spanish scholastics, Victoria and Suarez, natural law was not separable from divine law. The signing of treaties, in this period, was accompanied by religious oaths. Christian societies at this time had a strong sense of differentiation from outside powers, and especially from the Ottomans, who presented a real and present threat.

Second, theorists of this period provided no clear guidance as to who the members of international society were; no fundamental constitutive principle or criterion of membership was clearly enunciated. When the conception of the state as the common political form of all the kingdoms, duchies, principalities and republics of modern Europe was itself not yet established, the idea of a society made up principally or exclusively of a single kind of political entity called 'states' could not take shape. In the writings of Victoria and Suarez, and even of Grotius, the political units which are bound by the law of nations are referred to not only by the term *civitates* but also by such terms as *principes, regni, gentes, respublicae.* The doctrine of natural law, on which all the internationalists of this period rested their conception of the rules binding princes and the communities over which they ruled, treated individual men, rather than the groupings of them as states, as the ultimate bearers of rights and duties.

Third, in the idea of international society that prevailed in this period, primacy was accorded to natural law over what today would be called positive international law in defining the source of the rules by which Christian princes and communities were bound. For Grotius natural law was supplemented by the inherited rules of the Roman *ius gentium* and by existing treaty law, such as that contained in the body of mercantile and maritime law developed in mediaeval times, just as it was supplemented by divine law. But princes and peoples were bound by rules in their dealings with one another primarily because princes and peoples were men and thus subject to natural law. This primacy accorded to natural law by the early internationalists reflected their perception that the existing body of positive law bequeathed by the universal society of Western Christendom was out of touch with the new political realities. By invoking the natural law they hoped to liberate the law of nations from the constraints of existing practice and develop rules appropriate to the new situation.

A fourth feature of the idea of international society that emerged in this early period was that the rules of coexistence which it enunciated were inchoate and overlaid with the assumptions of a universal society. It was characteristic of the natural law theorists that they in no case wholly liberated themselves from the ambiguities of the Roman term *ius gentium,* as between its modern meaning of 'international law' or law between states and nations, and its original meaning of a law common to all nations.

This emerges in their attempts to formulate the basic rules which limit violence between the members of international society. Thus the early internationalists all insist, in line with Thomist tradition, that war should be fought only by those with proper authority, for a just cause and by just means. But they do not do more than grope towards the modern doctrines that only public authorities are entitled to wage war, and that only states can be regarded as such authorities. Even Grotius does not seek to proscribe private war, and indeed his own doctrine of the freedom of the seas, as formulated in *Mare Liberum* (1609), arose from his defence of a warlike action of the Dutch East India Company. Nor does he state unequivocally the doctrine that rules of just conduct or just means in war protect both parties and not merely the party whose cause is just. In expounding the need to limit the way war is conducted and to contain its geographical spread, he is inhibited by his commitment to the universalist or solidarist idea that such limitations should not be allowed to inhibit the party whose cause is just. All of the early internationalists except Gentili have difficulty in coming to terms with the idea that is the foundation of later attempts to accept war between states as an institution of international society, that war may have a just cause on both sides, not merely 'subjectively' but objectively.

The carrying over of universalist assumptions is also apparent in the treatment accorded by the early internationalists to rules upholding the sanctity of agreements. The principle *pacta sunt servanda* is one which they all uphold, but they conceive of treaties in terms of an analogy with contracts in private law. Thus in this period it was still widely held that treaties were binding only upon the princes that entered into them, and not on their successors; that treaties, like private contracts, were not binding if concluded under duress; and that they remained binding irrespective of any *clausula rebus sic stantibus,* or proviso that conditions remained the same. The far-sighted Gentili sought to dispute these views, and drawing upon him Grotius later developed a general theory of treaties as a distinct species of contract, but even these thinkers remained under the sway of the private-contract analogy to some degree.

Similarly, universalist assumptions prevented these thinkers from developing any clear conception of sovereignty as an attribute of the member states of international society, or of the exchange of recognition of sovereignty as a basic element in the compact of coexistence. The notion of sovereignty developed by Bodin (in his *Six livres de la Republique* in 1576) did not make its impact on international thought until much later. Traces of the idea are to be found in Suarez's use of the conception of a 'perfect community', or in Grotius's use of the term *summum imperium,* or in the tendency to make use of the Roman-law notion of *dominium* or private property, with its implication that a territory and its people are the patrimony of the ruler, to be bartered at his will. But what is lacking is a conception that makes independence of outside authority in the control of territory and population the inherent right of all states.

A fifth feature of the idea of international society entertained by the early internationalists was that it did not define a set of institutions deriving from the co-operation of states. On the one hand, the existing 'international' or 'supranational' institutions were those of the decadent Empire and Papacy, and did not derive from the co-operation or the consent of states; and on the other hand the tradition of co-operation which states were developing was not yet perceived as taking the place of these institutions.

Thus the early theorists of international society were all contributing to the development of what was later called 'international law', one of the central institutions of the society of states, but they did not, as we have seen, seek to found the law of nations primarily on the actual practice of states, and their preoccupation with natural law and with divine law was one which was bound to inhibit the development of international law as a distinct discipline and technique, different from moral philosophy and from theology.

The institution of diplomacy was in fact developing in this period; resident ambassadors, which had originated in Italy in the fifteenth century, became generalised north of the Alps in the sixteenth century and spread to Russia in the time of Peter the Great. Theorists in this period analysed the new institution and the rules surrounding its operation; most notably, Gentili's *De Legationibus* (1584) provided the first systematic examination of the principle of the inviolability of envoys, and Grotius introduced the notion of the 'extraterritoriality' of the ambassador. But they did not seek to treat the co-operation of states in operating the machinery of diplomatic representation, or the development of 'summit conferences' of heads of government, of which there were a number in this period, as part of the evidence that a society of states existed.

Nor did any of these theorists discuss the balance of power or take any account of it in elaborating their conception of international society. The actual institution of the balance of power, in the sense of a conscious attempt to check the preponderance of any one state, began to develop in the coalition against Philip II, and its preservation was an implicit objective of the Peace of Westphalia of 1648, which marked the end of Habsburg pretensions to universal monarchy. But it was not until much later – until the time of the struggle against Louis XIV – that the balance of power was recognised in international theory as an institution of international society, and the various writers of the earlier period who contributed to the development of the theory (Guicciardini, Commynes, Overbury, Rohan) belonged to a separate tradition of historical and political commentary, whose observations were not integrated into the natural law theory of international society.

Nor, again, did exponents of the latter have any conception of a great power, and its role in international society. They did, indeed, think in terms of a hierarchy of rulers, but this was a hierarchy determined by the status and precedent of the receding universal society, and not by considerations of relative power (that were the terms in which leading writers such as Rohan and Bolingbroke were to discuss great powers in the period) or of the special rights and duties accorded to certain powers by the society of states at large.

European International Society

In the eighteenth and nineteenth centuries, when the vestiges of Western Christendom came almost to disappear from the theory and practice of international politics, when the state came to be fully articulated, first in its dynastic or absolutist phase, then in its national or popular phase, and when a body of modern inter-state practice came to be accumulated and studied, the idea of international society assumed a different form. As natural law gave place to positive international law the ideas of political and legal theorists converged with those of historians, who sought to record the practice of the states system, and of statesmen who were operating it. A history of the idea of international society in this period would have to be concerned with the latter as well as the former, and might deal with Bynkershoek, Wolff, Vattel, J. J. Moser, Burke, G. F. von Martens, Gentz, Ancillon, Heeren, Ranke, Castlereagh, Phillimore, Gladstone and Salisbury.

The international society conceived by theorists of this period was identified as European rather than Christian in its values or culture. References to Christendom or to divine law as cementing the society of states declined and disappeared, as did religious oaths in treaties. References to Europe took their place, for example in the titles of their books: in the 1740s the Abbe de Mably published his *Droit public de l'Europe*, in the 1770s J. J. Moser his *Versuch des neuesten Europaischen Volkerrechts*, in the 1790s Burke denounced the regicide Directory of France for having violated 'the public law of Europe'.[5]

As the sense grew of the specifically European character of the society of states, so also did the sense of its cultural differentiation from what lay outside: the sense that European powers in their dealings with one another were bound by a code of conduct that did not apply to them in their dealings with other and lesser societies. The sense of differentiation, as we have noted, was already present in the era of Christian international society, as indeed it had been present in the distinction recognised by the Greek city-states between their relations *inter se* and their relations with barbarian powers such as Persia and Carthage. But the exclusiveness of the idea of Christian international society had been mitigated by the influence of the doctrine of natural law, which proclaimed the common rights and duties of men everywhere. In the era of European international society the decline of natural law thinking withdrew this mitigating influence. By the nineteenth century the orthodox doctrine of the positivist international lawyers was that international society was a European association, to which non-European states could be admitted only if and when they met a standard of civilisation laid down by the Europeans – the test which Turkey was the first to pass when under Article VIII of the Treaty of Paris of 1856 she was admitted to 'the public law and concert of Europe'.

In the idea of international society elaborated by eighteenth- and nineteenth-century theorists, the ambiguity of earlier thinkers as to what kinds of groups or entities are members of the society of states gives way to a clear statement of the principle that international society is a society of states or nations – even though this is sometimes accompanied by a qualification, as in Westlake's doctrine that while states are the immediate members of the society, men are its ultimate members. 'The Law of Nations', Vattel proclaims simply, 'is the science of the rights which exist between Nations or States, and of the obligations corresponding to these rights'.[6] From this recognition that all members of international society are a particular kind of political entity called 'states', and that entities that do not satisfy the criterion cannot be members, there stem other basic features of the idea of international society in this period, which without it could not have been conceivable: the idea that members all have the same basic rights, that the obligations they undertake are reciprocal, that the rules and institutions of international society derive from their consent, and the idea that political entities such as Oriental kingdoms, Islamic emirates or African chieftaincies should be excluded from membership.

Before the American and French Revolutions these states were, for the most part, hereditary monarchies, and what Martin Wight has called the 'principle of international legitimacy' was dynastic: that is to say, the collective judgement of international society was that dynastic principles should determine questions about rightful membership of the family of nations, about how sovereignty over territory or population should be transferred from one government to another, or about how state succession should be regulated. After the American and French Revolutions the prevailing principle of international legitimacy ceased to be dynastic and became national or popular: that is to say, it came to be generally held that questions of this sort should be settled not by reference to the rights of rulers, but by reference to the rights of the nation or the people.[7] The dynastic marriage, as the means whereby acquisition of territory was made internationally respectable, gave place to the plebiscite; the patrimonial principle to the principle of national self-determination. The actual course of events was no more determined by the national or popular doctrine of international legitimacy than in the earlier period it had been determined by the dynastical or monarchical one, but these doctrines did determine the kind of justifications that could be offered for whatever was done.

In identifying the sources of the rules by which states are bound, theorists of international society in the eighteenth and nineteenth centuries turned away from natural law and towards positive international law; more generally, they took as their guide, not abstract theories about what states should do, but the body of custom and treaty law that was accumulating as to what they did do. Modern examples could be cited in place of the ancient and mediaeval ones that abound in the pages of Suarez and Grotius. The histories of the states system and of the rise and fall of great powers, especially those that came to be written in Germany during and after the the Napoleonic wars, provided a new source of political generalisations and maxims.

When they came to formulate the rules of coexistence, theorists of this period were able to free themselves of the universalist or solidarist assumptions inherited from mediaeval times, and to take account of the unique characteristics of the anarchical society. The term 'law of nations', *droit des gens, Volkerrecht,* not only drove out the term 'law of nature', with which it had previously always been coupled; it came quite clearly to mean not law common to all nations, but law between nations. The transition was completed when the term 'law of nations' itself gave way to 'international law', the term coined by Bentham in 1789 in his *Introduction to the Principles of Morals and Legislation.*

Thus the rules restricting violence that were formulated in this period, by contrast with those of the early naturalists, make it clear that resort to legitimate violence in international politics is the monopoly of the state. From their recognition that a war may have a just cause on both sides, it was a short step to the doctrine that war was simply a political conflict and that the question of the justice of the cause should be banished from international law as being incapable of being settled by international society. Rules limiting the conduct of war, as formulated by these theorists, thus gave equal protection to all belligerents. Neutrality – the device for limiting the geographical spread of war – was recognised by Bynkershoek and Vattel to require impartiality towards both sides, as against the doctrine of Grotius that it had to be qualified by discrimination in favour of the party whose cause was just.

Thus, again, the theorists of this period, in their approach to the rule requiring treaties to be kept, were able to dispense entirely with the analogy with private contracts, and to recognise that treaties concluded by a government were binding upon its successors, and that they were valid even if concluded under duress. In the nineteenth century, moreover, the doctrine that Gentili had first sought to apply to the law of nations, that treaties remained valid only while circumstances remained the same, came to be generally accepted, as was also the addendum that it was for each party to determine whether or not circumstances had changed. This is a doctrine which is sometimes said to be an invitation to international lawlessness, but in the view of the nineteenth-century positivists it provided a means of securing some place for international agreements in the historical process, while also coming to terms with the forces of change.

Likewise, also, theorists of this period were able to recognise sovereignty as an attribute of all states, and the exchange of recognition of sovereignty as a basic rule of coexistence within the states system. They were also able to work out such corollary principles as the rule of non-intervention, the rule of the equality of states in respect of their basic rights, and the rights of states to domestic jurisdiction. For some legal theorists in this period, it should be noted, the idea of sovereignty was bound up with a doctrine of the 'natural rights of states' and of rights of self-preservation which were in effect a denial of the idea of 'international society'. But such ideas are in no way inherent in the treatment of sovereignty as a complex of rights conferred by rules of international law.

Finally, in the eighteenth and nineteenth centuries international society was seen to have visible expression in certain institutions that reflected the co-operation of its member states. International law was recognised to be a distinct body of rules, arising from the co-operation of modern states, and calling for a discipline and technique distinct from that of philosophy or theology; it was seen to be distinct also from matters of private law extending across frontiers, as was recognised in the nineteenth century by the term 'public international law'. The diplomatic system, whose role in relation to international society was now set out in the writings of Callières and other diplomatic theorists, was recognised to be the concern of international society as a whole by the Congress of Vienna, whose Final Act regularised it and brought it into conformity with the doctrine of the sovereign equality of states. The preservation of a balance of power was elevated to the status of an objective consciously pursued by international society as a whole; proclaimed to be this by the Treaty of Utrecht of 1713, that ended the War of Spanish Succession, and absorbed into the mainstream of international legal thinking with Vattel's *Droit des Gens* in 1758, it generated a great corpus of historical and political literature during the Napoleonic era, whose maxims were widely taken to state the conditions of international society's survival, and by some to have legal force. Phillimore, for example, in his *Commentaries Upon International Law* (1854–61), maintained that war or intervention to maintain a balance of power was lawful. Likewise the notion of a 'great power', explored by Ranke in his famous essay, and of its special rights and duties, came to express a new doctrine of the hierarchy or grading of states, in place of the old hierarchy of inherited status and precedent, based on the facts of relative power and the consent of international society, and was formally expressed in the Concert of Europe that sprang, by way of the Congress System, from the Vienna settlement.

World International Society

In the twentieth century, as in the sixteenth and seventeenth centuries, the idea of international society has been on the defensive. On the one hand, the Hobbesian or realist interpretation of international politics has been fed by the two World Wars, and by the expansion of international society beyond its originally European confines. On the other hand, Kantian or universalist interpretations have been fed by a striving to transcend the states system so as to escape the conflict and disorder that have accompanied it in this century, and by the Russian and Chinese revolutions, which have given a new currency to doctrines of global transnational solidarity, both communist, and anti-communist. Ideas of international society in the twentieth century may be said to be closer to those that were entertained in the early centuries of the states system than to those that prevailed in the eighteenth and nineteenth centuries.

In the twentieth century international society ceased to be regarded as specifically European and came to be considered as global or world wide. In the 1880s the Scottish natural lawyer James Lorimer expressed the orthodox doctrine of the time when he wrote that mankind was divided into civilised humanity, barbarous humanity and savage humanity. Civilised humanity comprised the nations of Europe and the Americas, which were entitled to full recognition as members of international society. Barbarous humanity comprised the independent states of Asia – Turkey, Persia, Siam, China and Japan – which were entitled to partial recognition. And savage humanity was the rest of mankind, which stood beyond the pale of the society of states, although it was entitled to 'natural or human recognition'.[8] It is worth noting in passing that Lorimer's distinction is in fact the same one which is made by social scientists today when they distinguish between modern societies, traditional societies and primitive societies.

Today, when non-European states represent the great majority in international society and the United Nations is nearly universal in its membership, the doctrine that this society rests upon a specific culture or civilisation is generally rejected and even the echo of it that survives in the Statute of the International Court of Justice – which lists the law common to civilised states among the sources of international law it recognises – has become an embarrassment. It is important to bear in mind, however, that if contemporary international society does have any cultural basis, this is not any genuinely global culture, but is rather the culture of so-called 'modernity'. And if we ask what is modernity in culture, it is not clear how we answer this except by saying that it is the culture of the dominant Western powers. (This point is discussed further in Chapter 13.)

In the twentieth century, also, there has been a retreat from the confident assertions, made in the age of Vattel, that the members of international society were states and nations, towards the ambiguity and imprecision on this point that characterised the era of Grotius. The state as a bearer of rights and duties, legal and moral, in international society today is widely thought to be joined by international organisations, by non-state groups of various kinds operating across frontiers, and – as implied by the Nuremberg and Tokyo War Crimes Tribunals, and by the Universal Declaration of Human Rights – by individuals. There is no agreement as to the relative importance of these different kinds of legal and moral agents, or on any general scheme of rules that would relate them one to another, but Vattel's conception of a society simply of states has been under attack from many different directions.

In this century, also, the theory of international society has moved away from the emphasis of eighteenth- and nineteenth-century legal and historical positivism on existing practice as the source of norms about international conduct, in favour of a return to natural law principles or to some contemporary equivalent of them; in political as in legal analysis of international relations the idea of international society has been rested less on the evidence of co-operation in the actual behaviour of states than on principles purporting to show how they should behave, such as those proclaimed in the League Covenant, the Kellogg-Briand Pact or the Charter of the United Nations.

Going along with this there has been a reappearance of universalist or solidarist assumptions in the way the rules of coexistence are formulated. The idea that the means states use in war should be limited has been qualified by the reappearance of the distinction between objectively just and unjust causes for which war is waged, as in the attempts to prohibit 'aggressive' war. The idea that neutrals should behave impartially towards belligerent states has been qualified in the same way, as in the doctrine of 'collective security' embodied in the League of Nations Covenant and the United Nations Charter.

The twentieth-century emphasis upon ideas of a reformed or improved international society, as distinct from the elements of society in actual practice, has led to a treatment of the League of Nations, the United Nations and other general international organisations as the chief institutions of international society, to the neglect of those institutions whose role in the maintenance of international order is the central one. Thus there has developed the Wilsonian rejection of the balance of power, the denigration of diplomacy and the tendency to seek to replace it by international administration, and a return to the tendency that prevailed in the Grotian era to confuse international law with international morality or international improvement.

The Reality of International Society

But does this idea of international society conform to reality? Do the theories of philosophers, international lawyers and historians in the Grotian tradition reflect the thought of statesmen? If statesmen pay lip-service to international society and its rules, does this mean that the latter affect their decisions? If the idea of international society played some real part during periods of relative international harmony, as in Europe for long stretches of the eighteenth and nineteenth centuries, was it not extinguished during the wars of religion, the wars of the French Revolution and Napoleon, and the World Wars of the present century? What meaning can it have, for example, to say that Hitler's Germany and Stalin's Russia, locked in a struggle to the death during the Second World War, regarded each other as bound by common rules and co-operated in the working of common institutions? If the Christian and, later, European international system that existed from the sixteenth century to the nineteenth was also an international society, were not the bonds of this society stretched and ultimately broken as the system expanded and became world-wide? Is not the international politics of the present time best viewed as an international system that is not an international society?

The Element of Society

My contention is that the element of a society has always been present, and remains present, in the modern international system, although only as one of the elements in it, whose survival is sometimes precarious. The modern international system in fact reflects all three of the elements singled out, respectively, by the Hobbesian, the Kantian and the Grotian traditions: the element of war and struggle for power among states, the element of transnational solidarity and conflict, cutting across the divisions among states, and the element of co-operation and regulated intercourse among states. In different historical phases of the states system, in different geographical theatres of its operation, and in the policies of different states and statesmen, one of these three elements may predominate over the others.

Thus one may say that in the trade and colonial wars fought in the late seventeenth and eighteenth centuries, chiefly by Holland, France and England, where the object was trading monopoly enforced by sea power and the political control of colonies, the element of a state of war was predominant. In the wars of religion that marked the first phase of the states system up till the Peace of Westphalia, in the European convulsion of the wars of the French Revolution and Napoleon, and in the ideological struggle of communist and anti-communist powers in our own times, the element of transnational solidarity and conflict has been uppermost – expressed not only in the revolutionist transnational solidarities of the Protestant parties, the democratic or republican forces favourable to the French Revolution, and the Communist Internationals, but also in the counter-revolutionist solidarities of the Society of Jesus, International Legitimism and Dullesian anti-communism. In nineteenth-century Europe, in the interval between the struggle of revolutionism and Legitimism that remained in the aftermath of the Napoleonic wars, and the re-emergence, late in the century, of the patterns of great power conflict that led to the First World War, one may say that the element of international society was predominant.

The element of international society has always been present in the modern international system because at no stage can it be said that the conception of the common interests of states, of common rules accepted and common institutions worked by them, has ceased to exert an influence. Most states at most times pay some respect to the basic rules of coexistence in international society, such as mutual respect for sovereignty, the rule that agreements should be kept, and rules limiting resort to violence. In the same way most states at most times take part in the working of common institutions: the forms and procedures of international law, the system of diplomatic representation, acceptance of the special position of great powers, and universal international organisations such as the functional organisations that grew up in the nineteenth century, the League of Nations and the United Nations.

The idea of 'international society' has a basis in reality that is sometimes precarious but has at no stage disappeared. Great wars that engulf the states system as a whole strain the credibility of the idea, and cause thinkers and statesmen to turn to Hobbesian interpretations and solutions, but they are followed by periods of peace. Ideological conflicts in which states and factions within them are ranged on opposite sides sometimes lead to a denial of the idea of international society by both sides, and lend confirmation to Kantian interpretations, but they are followed by accommodations in which the idea reappears.

Even at the height of a great war or ideological conflict the idea of international society, while it may be denied by the pronounce-ments of the contending states – each side treating the other as outside the framework of any common society – does not disappear so much as go underground, where it continues to influence the practice of states. The Allied and Axis powers at the height of the Second World War did not accept each other as members of a common international society, and they did not co-operate with each other in the working of common institutions. But one could not say that the idea of international society ceased to affect the practice of international relations in that period. The Allied powers continued to respect the ordinary rules of international society in their relations among themselves and in their dealings with neutral countries; so did Germany, Italy and Japan. Within both groups of belligerent powers there were persons and movements who sought out the basis of a negotiated peace. The Allied and Axis states each insisted that the others were bound as members of international society to observe the Geneva conventions concerning prisoners of war, and in the case of the Western allies and Germany, in respect of one another's prisoners, in large measure actually did observe these conventions.

Similarly, when the Cold War was being prosecuted most vigorously, the United States and the Soviet Union were inclined to speak of each other as heretics or outcasts beyond the pale, rather than as member states of the same international society. However, they did not even then break off diplomatic relations, withdraw recognition of one another's sovereignty, repudiate the idea of a common international law or cause the break-up of the United Nations into rival organisations. In both the Western and communist blocs there were voices raised in favour of compromise, drawing attention to the common interests of the two sides in coexistence and restating, in secular form, the principle *cuijus regio, eijus religio* that had provided a basis for accommodation in the wars of religion. Thus, even in periods when international politics is best described in terms of a Hobbesian state of war or a Kantian condition of transnational solidarity, the idea of international society has survived as an important part of reality, and its survival in these times of stress lays the foundation for the reconstruction of international society when war gives place to peace or ideological conflict to *détente*.

It may help to make clear the persistent reality of the element of international society if we contrast the relations of states within that system with examples of relations between independent political communities in which the element of society is entirely absent. The relations of Chingis Khan's Mongol invaders, and the Asian and

European peoples whom they subjugated, were not moderated by a belief on each side in common rules binding on both in their dealings with one another. Chingis Khan's conquests did have a basis in the moral ideas of the Mongols themselves: Chingis believed that he had the mandate of heaven to rule the world, that whatever peoples lay outside the *de facto* control of the Mongols were nevertheless *de jure* subjects of the Mongol empire, and that peoples who failed to submit to the Mongol court were therefore rebels against the divinely inspired order, against whom the waging of war was a right and a duty.[9] But these ideas formed no part of the thinking of the peoples who were subjugated and in some cases annihilated by the Mongols.

When the Spanish Conquistadors confronted the Aztecs and the Incas, this similarly took place in the absence of any common notion of rules and institutions. The Spaniards debated among themselves what duties they had towards the Indians – whether their right to invade derived from the claim of the Pope to *imperium mundi*, the duty of a Christian prince to spread the faith, the failure of the Indians to extend rights of hospitality, and so on.[10] But the rights which the Indians were acknowledged – by scholars such as Victoria – to have, were rights deriving from a system of rules recognised by the Spaniards; they did not derive from any system of rules acknowledged by the Indians also. The Spaniards and the Indians were able to recognise each other as human beings, to engage in negotiations and to conclude agreements. But these dealings took place in the absence of any common framework of rules and institutions.

The long history of relations between Europe and Islam provides a further illustration of this theme. As long as modern international society thought of itself as Christian or European, Islam in its successive embodiments was viewed as a barbarian power against which it was the duty of Christian princes to maintain a common front, even if they did not always do so in practice. Islamic thought reciprocated by dividing the world into *dar-al-Islam*, the region of submission to the will of God, and *dar-al-Harb*, the region of war which was yet to be converted. Coexistence with infidel states was possible; diplomatic exchanges, treaties and alliances could be and were concluded; and these relations were subject to rules – but only rules binding on Moslems. There was no conception of a common society in which Islamic and infidel states both had their place; the latter were regarded as having only a provisional existence, and coexistence with them as only a temporary phase in a process leading inexorably to their absorption.

It might be argued that while there is indeed a contrast between cases where a common idea of international society is shared by adversary communities, and cases where no such idea exists, this is of no practical consequence; the language of a common international society spoken by states in the modern international system is mere lip-service. Thus, as Grotius notes, for some states which claim that they have a just cause for going to war with one another, this just cause is often simply a pretext, their real motives being quite otherwise. Grotius distinguishes between causes of war that are 'justifiable', that is to say which are undertaken in the belief that there is a just cause, from causes of war that are merely 'persuasive', that is in which allegation of a just cause is simply a pretext.[11]

The question, however, is whether an international system in which it is necessary to have a pretext for beginning a war is not radically different from one in which it is not. The state which at least alleges a just cause, even where belief in the existence of a just cause has played no part in its decision, offers less of a threat to international order than one which does not. The state which alleges a just cause, even one it does not itself believe in, is at least acknowledging that it owes other states an explanation of its conduct, in terms of rules that they accept. There are, of course, differences of opinion as to the interpretation of the rules and their application to concrete situations; but such rules are not infinitely malleable and do circumscribe the range of choice of states which seek to give pretexts in terms of them. The giving of a pretext, moreover, means that the violence which the offending state does to the structure of commonly accepted rules by going to war in disregard of them is less than it would otherwise be; to make war without any explanation, or with an explanation stated only in terms of the recalcitrant state's own beliefs – such as the Mongols' belief in the Mandate of Heaven, or the belief of the Conquistadors in the Pope's *imperium mundi* – is to hold all other states in contempt, and to place in jeopardy all the settled expectations that states have about one another's behaviour.

Grotius recognises that while international society is threatened by states which wage war for merely 'persuasive' causes, and not for 'justifiable' ones, it is even more threatened by states which wage

asive' causes either; wars which lack causes of
:s of as 'the wars of savages'.[12] Vattel speaks of
/ar without pretext of any kind as 'monsters
name of men', whom nations may unite to

The Anarchical Society

It is often maintained that the existence of international society is
disproved by the fact of anarchy, in the sense of the absence of
government or rule. It is obvious that sovereign states, unlike the
individuals within them, are not subject to a common government,
and that in this sense there is, in the phrase made famous by
Goldsworthy Lowes Dickinson, an 'international anarchy'.[14] A
persistent theme in the modern discussion of international relations
has been that, as a consequence of this anarchy, states do not form
together any kind of society; and that if they were to do so it could
only be by subordinating themselves to a common authority.

A chief intellectual support of this doctrine is what I have called
the domestic analogy, the argument from the experience of
individual men in domestic society to the experience of states,
according to which states, like individuals, are capable of orderly
social life only if, as in Hobbes's phrase, they stand in awe of a
common power.[15] In the case of Hobbes himself and his successors,
the domestic analogy takes the form simply of the assertion that
states or sovereign princes, like individual men who live without
government, are in a state of nature which is a state of war. It is not
the view of Hobbes, or other thinkers of his school, that a social
contract of states that would bring international anarchy to an end
either should or can take place. By contrast, in the thinking of those
who look forward – or backward – to a universal or world
government, the domestic analogy is taken further, to embrace
not only the conception of a state of nature but also that of a social
contract among states that will reproduce the conditions of order
within the state on a universal scale.

There are three weaknesses in the argument that states do not
form a society because they are in a condition of international
anarchy. The first is that the modern international system does not
entirely resemble a Hobbesian state of nature. Hobbes's account of

relations between sovereign princes is a subordinate part of his explanation and justification of government among individual men. As evidence for his speculations as to how men would live were they to find themselves in a situation of anarchy, Hobbes mentions the experience of civil war, the life of certain American tribes and the facts of international relations:

> But though there had never been any time wherein particular men were in a condition of warre one against another; yet in all times Kings, and Persons of Soveraigne authority, because of their Independency, are in continual jealousies, and in the state and posture of Gladiators; having their weapons pointing, and their eyes fixed on one another; that is, their Forts, Garrisons and Guns, upon the Frontiers of their Kingdomes; and continual Spyes upon their neighbours; which is a posture of warre.[16]

In Hobbes's account the situation in which men live without a common power to keep them in awe has three principal characteristics. In this situation there can be no industry, agriculture, navigation, trade or other refinements of living because the strength and invention of men is absorbed in providing security against one another. There are no legal or moral rules: 'The notions of Right and Wrong, Justice and Injustice have there no place. . . . It is consequent also to the same condition, that there can be no Propriety, no Dominion, no *Mine and Thine* distinct; but only that to be every mans, that he can get; and for so long as he can keep it.'[17] Finally, the state of nature is a state of war: war understood to consist 'not in actual fighting; but in the known disposition thereto, during all the time there is no assurance to the contrary'; and to be 'such a warre, as is of every man, against every man'.[18]

The first of these characteristics clearly does not obtain in international anarchy. The absence of a world government is no necessary bar to industry, trade and other refinements of living. States do not in fact so exhaust their strength and invention in providing security against one another that the lives of their inhabitants are solitary, poor, nasty, brutish and short; they do not as a rule invest resources in war and military preparations to such an extent that their economic fabric is ruined. On the contrary, the armed forces of states, by providing security against external attack and internal disorder, establish the conditions under which economic improvements may take place within their borders. The absence of a universal government has not been incompatible with international economic interdependence.

It is also clear that the second feature of Hobbes's state of nature, the absence in it of notions of right and wrong, including notions of property, does not apply to modern international relations. Within the system of states that grew up in Europe and spread around the world, notions of right and wrong in international behaviour have always held a central place.

Of the three principal features of Hobbes's state of nature the only one that might be held to apply to modern international relations is the third – the existence in it of a state of war, in the sense of a disposition on the part of every state to war with every other state. Sovereign states, even while they are at peace, nevertheless display a disposition to go to war with one another, inasmuch as they prepare for war and treat war as one of the options open to them.

The second weakness of the argument from international anarchy is that it is based on false premises about the conditions of order among individuals and groups other than the state. It is not, of course, the case that fear of a supreme government is the only source of order within a modern state: no account of the reasons why men are capable of orderly social coexistence within a modern state can be complete which does not give due weight to factors such as reciprocal interest, a sense of community or general will, and habit or inertia.

If, then, we are to compare international relations with an imagined, pre-contractual state of nature among individual men, we may well choose not Hobbes's description of that condition but Locke's. Locke's conception of the state of nature as a society without government does in fact provide us with a close analogy with the society of states. In modern international society, as in Locke's state of nature, there is no central authority able to interpret and enforce the law, and thus individual members of the society must themselves judge and enforce it. Because in such a society each member of it is a judge in his own cause, and because those who seek to enforce the law do not always prevail, justice in such a society is crude and uncertain. But there is nevertheless a great difference between such a rudimentary form of social life and none at all.

The third weakness of the argument from international anarchy is that it overlooks the limitations of the domestic analogy. States, after all, are very unlike human individuals. Even if it could be contended that government is a necessary condition of order among individual men, there are good reasons for holding that anarchy among states is tolerable to a degree to which among individuals it is not.

We have already noted that, unlike the individual in Hobbes's state of nature, the state does not find its energies so absorbed in the pursuit of security that the life of its members is that of mere brutes. Hobbes himself recognises this when, having observed that persons in sovereign authority are in 'a posture of war', he goes on to say that 'because they uphold thereby the industry of their subjects, there does not follow from it that misery which accompanies the liberty of particular men'.[19] The same sovereigns that find themselves in a state of nature in relation to one another have provided, within their territories, the conditions in which refinements of life can flourish.

Moreover, states are not vulnerable to violent attack to the same degree that individuals are. Spinoza, echoing Hobbes in his assertion that 'two states are in the same relation to one another as two men in the condition of nature', goes on to add, 'with this exception, that a commonwealth can guard itself against being subjugated by another, as a man in the state of nature cannot do. For, of course, a man is overcome by sleep every day, is often afflicted by disease of body or mind, and is finally prostrated by old age; in addition, he is subject to troubles against which a commonwealth can make itself secure.'[20] One human being in the state of nature cannot make himself secure against violent attack; and this attack carries with it the prospect of sudden death. Groups of human beings organised as states, however, may provide themselves with a means of defence that exists independently of the frailties of any one of them. And armed attack by one state upon another has not brought with it a prospect comparable to the killing of one individual by another. For one man's death may be brought about suddenly in a single act; and once it has occurred it cannot be undone. But war has only occasionally resulted in the physical extinction of the vanquished people.

In modern history it has been possible to take Clausewitz's view that 'war is never absolute in its results', and that defeat in it may be 'a passing evil which can be remedied'.[21] Moreover, war in the past, even if it could in principle lead to the physical extermination of one or both of the belligerent peoples, could not be thought capable of doing so at once in the course of a single act. Clausewitz, in holding that war does not consist of a single instantaneous blow, but always of a succession of separate actions, was drawing attention to something that in the past has always held true and has rendered violence among independent political communities different from violence between individual persons.[22] It is only in the context of nuclear weapons and other recent military technology that it has become pertinent to ask whether war could not now both be 'absolute in its results' and 'take the form of a single, instantaneous blow', in Clausewitz's understanding of these terms; and whether, therefore, violence does not now confront the state with the same sort of prospect it has always held for the individual.

This difference, that states have been less vulnerable to violent attack by one another than individual men, is reinforced by a further one: that in so far as states have been vulnerable to physical attack, they have not been equally so. Hobbes builds his account of the state of nature on the proposition that 'Nature hath made men so equal, in the faculties of body and mind, [that] the weakest has strength enough to kill the strongest.'[23] It is this equal vulnerability of every man to every other that, in Hobbes's view, renders the condition of anarchy intolerable. But in modern international society there has been a persistent distinction between great powers and small. Great powers have not been vulnerable to violent attack by small powers to the same extent that small powers have been vulnerable to attack by great ones. Once again it is only the spread of nuclear weapons to small states, and the possibility of a world of many nuclear powers, that raises the question whether in international relations, also, a situation may come about in which 'the weakest has strength enough to kill the strongest'.

The argument, then, that because men cannot form a society without government, sovereign princes or states cannot, breaks down not only because some degree of order can in fact be achieved among individuals in the absence of government, but also because states are unlike individuals, and are more capable of forming an anarchical society. The domestic analogy is no more than an analogy; the fact that states form a society without government reflects features of their situation that are unique.

The Limitations of International Society

We have shown that the modern international system is also an international society, at least in the sense that international society has been one of the elements permanently at work in it; and that the existence of this international society is not as such disproved by the fact of international anarchy. It is important, however, to retain a sense of the limitations of the anarchical international society.

Because international society is no more than one of the basic elements at work in modern international politics, and is always in competition with the elements of a state of war and of transnational solidarity or conflict, it is always erroneous to interpret international events as if international society were the sole or the dominant element. This is the error committed by those who speak or write as if the Concert of Europe, the League of Nations or the United Nations were the principal factors in international politics in their respective times; as if international law were to be assessed only in relation to the function it has of binding states together, and not also in relation to its function as an instrument of state interest and as a vehicle of transnational purposes; as if attempts to maintain a balance of power were to be interpreted only as endeavours to preserve the system of states, and not also as manoeuvres on the part of particular powers to gain ascendancy; as if great powers were to be viewed only as 'great responsibles' or 'great indispensables', and not also as great predators; as if wars were to be construed only as attempts to violate the law or to uphold it, and not also simply as attempts to advance the interests of particular states or of transnational groups. The element of international society is real, but the elements of a state of war and of transnational loyalties and divisions are real also, and to reify the first element, or to speak as if it annulled the second and third, is an illusion.

Moreover, the fact that international society provides some element of order in international politics should not be taken as justifying an attitude of complacency about it, or as showing that the arguments of those who are dissatisfied with the order provided by international society are without foundation. The order provided within modern international society is precarious and imperfect. To show that modern international society has provided some degree of order is not to have shown that order in world politics could not be provided more effectively by structures of a quite different kind.

3

How is Order Maintained in World Politics?

We have now explained what is meant by order in world politics, and shown that in some measure it exists in the modern system of states. The question to which we shall now turn is: how is it maintained?

The Maintenance of Order in Social Life

In all societies, it has been argued, order is a pattern of behaviour that sustains the elementary or primary goals of social life. Order in this sense is maintained by a sense of common interests in those elementary or primary goals; by rules which prescribe the pattern of behaviour that sustains them; and by institutions which make these rules effective.

The maintenance of order in any society presupposes that among its members, or at least among those of its members who are politically active, there should be a sense of *common interests* in the elementary goals of social life. Thus the facts of human vulnerability to violence and proneness to resort to it lead men to the sense of common interests in restricting violence. The fact of human interdependence for material needs leads them to perceive a common interest in ensuring respect for agreements. The facts of limited abundance and limited human altruism lead them to recognise common interests in stabilising possession. This sense of common interests may be the consequence of fear. It may derive from a rational calculation that the limitations necessary to sustain elementary goals of social life must be reciprocal. Or in some cases it may express the ability of the individuals or groups concerned to

51

identify with each other to the extent of treating each other's interests as ends in themselves and not merely as means to an end; that is to say, it may express a sense of common values rather than common interests.

This sense of common interests in achieving the elementary goals of social life may be vague and inchoate, and does not in itself provide any precise guidance as to what behaviour is consistent with these goals, and what behaviour is not. The contribution of *rules* is to provide this kind of guidance. Rules are general imperative principles which require or authorise prescribed classes of persons or groups to behave in prescribed ways. Order in any society is maintained not merely by a sense of common interests in creating order or avoiding disorder, but by rules which spell out the kind of behaviour that is orderly. Thus the goal of security against violence is upheld by rules restricting the use of violence; the goal of the stability of agreements by the rule that they should be kept; and the goal of stability of possession by the rule that rights of property, public or private, should be respected. These rules may have the status of law, of morality, of custom or etiquette, or simply of operating procedures or 'rules of the game'.

Order might in principle be provided in social life without the help of rules. It is conceivable, for example, that orderly patterns of behaviour might be inculcated by means of conditioning, in such a way that men would act consistently with elementary social objectives simply by virtue of a reflex action. In this case rules, directed as they are towards guiding men's choices among alternative courses of action, would not be necessary. It is conceivable, also, that in very small societies, such as families or clans, rules might be dispensed with by an authority which relied solely upon the enforcement of singular commands requiring or authorising particular persons to do particular things, and avoiding resort to any general imperative principle. For these reasons we need to distinguish conceptually between order in social life and the rules which help to create and maintain it. As noted above, to define order in social life in terms of obedience to rules prescribing behaviour that is consistent with elementary social goals would be to mistake an apparently universal cause of order with the thing itself (see Chapter 1).

We need also to take account of the Marxist view that rules serve as the instruments, not of the common interests of members of a society, but rather of the special interests of its ruling or dominant members. This is an important insight into the social function of all rules, and is especially valid in relation to the function of rules of law. It is of course the case that all actual systems of social rules are imbued with the special interests and values of those who make them. Since the influence exerted by members of a society in the process of making the rules is likely always to be unequal, any historical system of rules will be found to serve the interests of the ruling or dominant elements of the society more adequately than it serves the interests of the others.

While it is important to take account of this insight in studying the role of rules, in international society as in other societies, it does not invalidate the present analysis. The special interests of the dominant elements in a society are reflected in the way in which the rules are defined. Thus the particular kinds of limitations that are imposed on resort to violence, the kind of agreements whose binding character is upheld, or the kinds of rights of property that are enforced, will bear the stamp of those dominant elements. But that there should be limits of some kind on resort to violence, an expectation in general that agreements will be carried out, and rules of property of some kind, is not a special interest of some members of a society but a general interest of all of them. The objective of those elements in any society which seek to change the existing order is not to have a society in which there are no restrictions on violence, no rules requiring agreements to be kept, and no rights of property, but rather to change the terms of these rules in such a way that they cease to serve the special interests of the presently dominant elements.

But rules by themselves are mere intellectual constructs. They play a part in social life only to the extent that they are effective. The effectiveness of a rule does not consist in its being carried out by all those persons or groups to which it applies in every instance; on the contrary, any effective rule of conduct is normally violated from time to time, and if there were no possibility that actual behaviour would differ from prescribed behaviour, there would be no point in having the rule. But a rule, to be effective in society, must be obeyed to some degree, and must be reckoned as a factor in the calculations of those to whom it applies, even those who elect to violate it.

Where rules are not mere intellectual constructs but are socially effective in this sense, this is in part at least because there are *institutions* which carry out the following functions. The functions listed below may not be exhaustive, and not all of them may be essential for the effectiveness of a rule in any given case. But something like the following must obtain.

(i) The rules must be *made,* that is to say they must be formulated and promulgated as rules for this society.

(ii) The rules must be *communicated* - they must be stated or advertised in such a way that their content is known to those to whom they apply.

(iii) The rules must be *administered* in cases where acts, ancillary to what is prescribed in the rules themselves, must be carried out if the rules are to be observed. The rules prohibiting or restricting violence in the modern state, for example, may require for their efficacy that steps be taken to establish and maintain police forces, prisons, courts, a department of justice, and so on.

(iv) The rules must be *interpreted* – questions arising about the meaning of a rule, the relationship between rules in cases of conflict, and the existence or non-existence of breaches of a rule, have to be settled if rules are to provide guidance for actual behaviour.

(v) The rules need to be, in the broadest possible sense, *enforced -* if rules are to be effective, there needs to be some penalty attached to non-compliance, whether this penalty takes the form of coercion or some other kind of sanction, or merely that of reciprocal non-compliance by other persons or groups bound by the rule.

(vi) The rules need to be *legitimised* in the eyes of the persons or groups to which they apply. Rules are legitimised to the extent that members of the society accept them as valid, or embrace the values implied or presupposed by the rules. To the extent that the rules are legitimised they do not depend for their effectiveness on sanctions or enforcement.

(vii) The rules must be capable of adaptation to changing needs and circumstances – there must be ways of rescinding or modifying old rules and replacing them with new ones.

(viii) The rules must be *'protected'* against developments in the society likely to undermine the effective operation of the rules. In any society the maintenance of effective rules will depend on conditions, not guaranteed by the rules themselves, but for which the system of rules would be bound to break down.[1]

Order in the Modern State

Within the modern state an institution, or set of connected institutions, is available to help make elementary social rules effective: government. A government is distinguished from other institutions within the modern state by its ability to call on physical force. On the one hand, it possesses actual force at its disposal that is overwhelming in relation to that which is commanded by any other group. On the other hand, it possesses a near monopoly of the legitimate use of force: apart from certain residual rights of self-defence that are accorded to the individual, only the government is able to employ force while being regarded by members of the society at large as within its rights in doing so. It is just as important to a government that its use of force should be legitimate as that it should be overwhelming. These two aspects of a government's coercive power are connected inasmuch as the collapse of a government's legitimacy may make possible a combination of force against it such that its force is no longer overwhelming. Insurgent groups show that they understand this interconnection when they devote as much attention to undermining the government's right, in the eyes of the population, to use force, as to combating that force with force of their own.

The government helps to make elementary social rules effective within the modern state by carrying out all the functions that were outlined in the last section. It is not only by the government that these functions are carried out; individuals and groups other than the state also undertake them. But the role of the government in promoting the effectiveness of elementary social rules is a central one.

(i) The government makes rules – not always in the sense that it invents them or first states them – but in the sense that it fixes upon them society's *imprimatur* or stamp of approval. In the modern state this process of rule-making results in a special set of rules which we refer to as 'the law'. While the making of rules in the modern state is formally the function of the legislature, it is familiar that the rule-making or legislative function is carried out not only by legislatures but by administrative bodies, whose formal function is the translation of law into orders, and judicial bodies, whose formal function is the interpretation of laws rather than the making of them.

(ii) The government helps to communicate the rules to those who are bound by them. The publication of statutes and court records, the actual enforcement of the rules by the prosecution of offenders, the work of the police in apprehending, deterring or punishing offenders, all contribute to the spreading of an awareness of what rules are treated by society as rules of law.

(iii) The government also administers or gives effect to the rules, translating them from general principles into requirements that particular persons do or refrain from doing particular things. This is formally the function of the executive branch, but a specialised branch is not necessarily presupposed by this function, which is in fact normally carried out by other arms of the government as well.

(iv) The government is able to interpret the rules – to resolve uncertainties about the validity of rules, their meaning or their relationship to one another – principally through its judicial arm.

(v) The government is also able to enforce the law through the use, and the threat of the use, of the police and armed forces and through the sanctions imposed by the courts. Particular legal rules may not be backed up by explicit sanctions, but the legal system as a whole is underpinned by the government's coercive power.

(vi) The government can contribute to the legitimisation of the rules, the acceptance of them as valuable in themselves, by the influence it has over education and public information, the powers of persuasion of its own leaders, and its ability to project itself as the symbolic embodiment of the values of the society and to mould the political culture in a manner favourable to acceptance of the rules as legitimate.

(vii) The government may also adapt the rules to changing circumstances and demands by having its legislature repeal or amend old laws and enact new ones, and by having its administrators execute the law and its judges interpret it in such a way as to change its content.

(viii) The government carries out the function of 'protection' of the rules through the political actions it takes to set the social scene in such a way that the rules will continue to operate. The invocation of armed forces to crush a rising or expel a foreign invader exemplifies this 'protection'. So do measures taken by the government to appease political dissatisfaction, to remove social or economic grievances, to suppress irreconcilable agitators or to heal social cleavages or bridge antagonisms that threaten to bring about the breakdown of society.

What these miscellaneous political acts have in common is that they are all directed towards the preservation of order, not by directly upholding or implementing the rules, but by shaping, moulding or managing the social environment in which the rules operate in such a way that they have the opportunity of continuing to do so. They belong to a sphere of action which the rules themselves may not regulate and may even impede, but which their operation nevertheless presupposes.

Order in Primitive Stateless Societies

Order within the modern state is the consequence, among other things, of government; order among states cannot be, for international society is an anarchical society, a society without government. But primitive stateless societies also present this spectacle of 'ordered anarchy', and it is worth considering the resemblances and differences between the ways in which order is created and maintained in the one case and in the other.

Apart from the attention given by political theorists to notional stateless societies, and the largely speculative accounts of them given by historians such as Maine and Maitland, primitive stateless societies were not subject to empirical observation and systematic analysis until they attracted the attention of twentieth-century anthropologists.[2] Primitive societies that have been identified as stateless by the latter include the Nuer, the Western Dinka and the Mandari of southern Sudan, the Tallensi of Northern Nigeria, the Bwamba of Uganda, the Lugbara of Uganda and Congo and the Konkomba of Togoland. All of these societies are without a government in the sense defined above and are, in addition, without central political institutions – legislative, executive or judicial – of any kind. Indeed, it is said of some of them that they contain no specialised political roles at all; while there are persons or bodies within them, such as heads of a family or lineage group or a village, that fulfil political roles, these roles are not formally distinguished from the other roles they have. The distinctions which outside observers draw between the political, the local, the kinship or the ritualistic roles of these persons or groups may have no meaning in the culture of the societies themselves.

At the same time these societies clearly exhibit order in the sense that conduct within them conforms to elementary goals of social coexistence. In the shaping of this conduct rules play a vital part, and their effectiveness depends on the carrying out of the order-maintaining functions of making these rules, communicating, administering, interpreting, enforcing, legitimising, adapting and 'protecting' them. In the absence of any central authority, however, these functions are carried out solely by groups – such as lineage groups and locality groups – into which these stateless societies are divided.

Rules do not emanate from any central rule-making authority but arise out of the practice of lineage or locality groups in their relations with one another, become embodied in 'custom' and are confirmed by moral and religious belief. Custom or established practice is of course also a familiar source of rules in centralised political systems; in primitive stateless societies it is the only source of rules.

Conformity to these rules is brought about by conditioning and inertia, by 'moral' sanctions such as public ridicule and reprobation, and by ritual or supernatural sanctions, such as cursing by the elders of a tribe. In societies that are culturally homogeneous, especially if they are small societies, sanctions such as these will often be sufficient in themselves.

Where such sanctions are insufficient to deter or punish violations of rules, there may be a resort to 'self-help' on the part of groups within the society which take upon their own shoulders the responsibility of determining that there has been a breach of the rules, and of attempting to enforce them. The killing of a member of a lineage or locality group, for example, may lead that group to undertake a retaliatory killing of the guilty party or another member of his group. In circumstances in which the bonds between the groups are very strong, the legitimacy of the retaliation may be accepted on both sides and the matter brought to an end. But in others the legitimacy of the act may be disputed, and a sustained conflict, based on both sides on the exercise of subjectively legitimate self-help, may develop.

Since both groups will be interpreting the rules, and the facts of the case, on their own behalf (or on behalf of one of their members) their judgement is likely to be imperfect. Since, moreover, their ability actually to enforce the rules will depend on the amount of force at their command and their will to use it, the enforcement of the rules is bound to be uncertain. Yet the recourse to self-help does not represent disregard of the rules and the descent of the groups concerned into a Hobbesian state of nature; it represents the operation of a system in which these groups are assuming the functions of interpreting, applying and enforcing the rules. Moreover, in doing so they are confined by rules limiting the activity of self-help itself.

Resort to force by these groups in response to what they judge to be a violation of the rules is accepted throughout these societies as legitimate. There is not a general right to self-help, available to any individual or group within the society; only those groups that are entitled to resort to violence may do so. The force which they employ, if it is legitimate, may only be used in response to a violation of rights. The nature of the force employed, moreover, is limited, for example by the principle that retaliation must be proportionate to the offence.

Acts of self-help in primitive stateless societies, in addition to providing rules with a coercive sanction, also serve two further functions, to which Roger Masters has drawn attention: they 'serve to unite social groups and to maintain legal and moral criteria of right and wrong'.[3] Not only do they help, by galvanising a group in support of violent action against an outside group, to maintain its cohesion, they are also, in addition to being an attempt to enforce a rule against this particular violation, a means of restating the rule itself, of underlining its continued validity and enduring importance.

Primitive anarchical societies clearly have important resemblances to international society in respect of the maintenance of order. In both cases some element of order is maintained despite the absence of a central authority commanding overwhelming force and a monopoly of the legitimate use of it. In both cases, also, this is achieved through the assumption by particular groups – lineage and locality groups in primitive stateless societies, sovereign states in international society – of the functions which, in a modern state, the government (but not the government exclusively) carries out in making rules effective. In primitive anarchical society, as in international society, order depends upon a fundamental or constitutional principle, stated or implied, which singles out certain groups as the sole bodies competent to discharge these political functions. In both societies the politically competent groups may legitimately use force in defence of their rights, while individuals and groups other than these must look to the privileged, politically competent groups for protection, rather than resort to force themselves.

In primitive anarchical societies, as in international society, the relations between these politically competent groups are themselves circumscribed by a structure of acknowledged normative principles, even at times of violent struggle. But in both there is a tendency, during these periods of struggle, for the structure of rules to break down, and the society to fall apart to such an extent that the warring tribes or states are better described as a number of contending societies than as a single society. Finally, in both primitive anarchical society and modern international society there are factors operating, outside the structure of rules itself, inducing the politically competent groups to conform to them. These include the factors of mutual deterrence or fear of unlimited conflict, the force of habit or inertia, the long-term interests they have (consciously rationalised in the modern world, and intuitively felt in primitive society) in preserving a system of collaboration, whatever their short-term interest in destroying it.

However, the differences between international society and primitive stateless societies are also remarkable. In the first place there are crucial differences between the units that are politically competent in the two sorts of society. The state in international society is sovereign in that it has supreme jurisdiction over its citizens and its territory. The lineage or locality groups which exercise political powers in primitive society, by contrast, do not have any such exclusive rights in relation to the persons that make them up, and usually have a less clearly defined relationship to territory.

A given lineage group does not necessarily exercise exclusive authority over the persons of which it is composed. In some stateless societies lineage groups are divided into segments, and within them there is a constant process of segmentation and merging. Segments of a lineage which are units at one level merge into larger segments at others. Whereas at one level these units may be in competition, at higher levels they are united as subordinate parts of a larger segment. These shifting combinations and divisions illustrate what has been called 'the principle of complementary opposition' in primitive stateless societies. Politically competent units in primitive anarchical societies are so related that while any two of them are in conflict for certain purposes they are combined for certain other purposes. Thus, on the one hand, each unit engages in conflict sufficient to generate a sense of identity and maintain its internal cohesion, but on the other hand there is no relationship of conflict between units that is not overlaid with some element of co-operation also.

Nor do politically competent units in primitive anarchical societies possess exclusive jurisdiction over precisely defined territories. The view of Sir Henry Maine that in primitive societies political solidarity arose only out of ties of blood and never out of common possession of a tract of territory has been rejected by modern anthropologists, who contend that primitive societies are based on both blood and territory.[4] But the lineage groups that carry out order-maintaining functions in the stateless societies that have been considered do not have exclusive rights to tracts of territory defined by precise, accepted boundaries.

Because the politically competent groups in primitive stateless societies are not sovereign over persons and territory, but are related less exclusively than is the modern state to the persons that belong to them and to areas of land, they appear to have a less self-sufficient existence and to be less introverted or self-regarding than are the members of the society of states.

A second point of contrast is that whereas modern international society, especially at the present time, is culturally heterogeneous, primitive stateless societies are marked by a high degree of cultural homogeneity. By a society's culture we mean its basic system of values, the premises from which its thought and action derive. All primitive societies appear to depend upon a common culture; stateless societies appear to depend upon it to a special degree. Fortes and Evans-Pritchard came to the tentative conclusion, on the basis of the African systems they studied, that a high degree of common culture was a necessary condition of anarchical structures, while only a central authority could weld together peoples of heterogeneous culture.[5] But the society of sovereign states – or, as it has sometimes been called, the inclusive society, today a political fabric that embraces the whole of mankind – is *par excellence* a society that is culturally heterogeneous.

A third point of contrast is that primitive stateless societies rest not simply on a culture that is homogeneous but also on one that includes the element of magical or religious belief. 'The social system', Fortes and Evans-Pritchard wrote, 'is, as it were, removed to a mystical plane, where it figures as a system of sacred values beyond criticism or revision . . . hence the wars or feuds between segments of a society like the Nuer or the Tallensi are kept within bounds by mystical sanctions.'[6] International society, by contrast, is part of the modern world, the secular world that emerged from the collapse of ecclesiastical and religious authority. The various substitutes that have been brought forward in the last three centuries in the attempt to validate or authenticate the rules of international society – the natural law, the customary practice of states, the interests or 'needs' of states, the law common to 'civilised states' – are all inferior to religious authority in terms of their power to produce social cohesion because they are all subject to question and debate. The moral bases of international society may be less brittle than those of primitive societies, not subject to the shattering impact that was made by Christian and Islamic civilisations on sub-Saharan African and Oceanic systems, more able to absorb new intellectual challenges and preserve some measure of continuity. But they do not approach a magical or religious system of values in terms of their social impact.

Finally, there are gross differences in size between international society and primitive stateless societies. The Nuer, the largest-scale society studied by Fortes and Evans-Pritchard, numbered 300,000 in an area of 26,000 square miles. The society of states embraces all mankind and all the earth.

Together, what is shown by these points of contrast is that the forces making for social cohesion and solidarity are very much stronger in primitive anarchical societies than in international society. The less exclusive and self-regarding nature of the political units of which primitive stateless societies are composed, their cultural homogeneity, the underpinning of their rules by magical and religious belief, and their small and intimate nature, all indicate that though government is lacking in these systems, an impressive degree of social solidarity is not. The maintenance of order in international society has to take place not only in the absence of government but also in the absence of social solidarity of this sort.

Order in International Society

The maintenance of order in world politics depends, in the first instance, on certain contingent facts which would make for order even if states were without any conception of common interests, common rules or common institutions – even if, in other words, they formed an international system only, and not also an international society. A balance of power, for example, may arise in an international system quite fortuitously, in the absence of any belief that it serves common interests, or any attempt to regulate or institutionalise it. If it does arise, it may help to limit violence, to render undertakings credible or to safeguard governments from challenges to their local supremacy. Within international society, however, as in other societies, order is the consequence not merely of contingent facts such as this, but of a sense of common interests in the elementary goals of social life; rules prescribing behaviour that sustains these goals; and institutions that help to make these rules effective.

Common Interests

To say that x is in someone's interest is merely to say that it serves as a means to some end that he is pursuing. Whether or not x does serve as a means to any particular end is a matter of objective fact. But whether or not x is in his interest will depend not only on this but also on what ends he is actually pursuing. It follows from this that the conception of interest is an empty or vacuous guide, both as to what a person does do and as to what he should do. To provide such a guide we need to know what ends he does or should pursue, and the conception of interest in itself tells us nothing about either.

Thus the criterion of 'national interest', or 'interest of state', in itself provides us with no specific guidance ether in interpreting the behaviour of states or in prescribing how they should behave – unless we are told what concrete ends or objectives states do or should pursue: security, prosperity, ideological objectives or whatever. Still less does it provide us with a criterion that is objective, in the sense of being independent of the way state ends or purposes are perceived by particular decision-makers. It does not even provide a basis for distinguishing moral or ideological considerations in a country's foreign policy from non-moral or non-ideological ones: for x can be in a country's interest if it serves as a means to a moral or ideological objective that the country has.

However, the conception of national interest or interest of state does have some meaning in a situation in which national or state ends are defined and agreed, and the question at issue is by what means they can be promoted. To say that a state's foreign policy should be based on pursuit of the national interest is to insist that whatever steps are taken should be part of some rational plan of action; an approach to foreign policy based on the national interest may thus be contrasted with one consisting simply of the uncritical pursuit of some established policy, or one consisting simply of unconsidered reactions to events. A policy based on the idea of the national interest, moreover, may be contrasted with one based on a sectional interest, or one based on the interests of some group wider than the state, such as an alliance or international organisation to which it belongs. To speak of the national interest as the criterion at least directs our attention to the ends or objectives of the nation or state, as against those of some other group, narrower or wider.

The maintenance of order in international society has as its starting-point the development among states of a sense of common interests in the elementary goals of social life. However different and conflicting their objectives may be, they are united in viewing these goals as instrumental to them. Their sense of common interests may derive from fear of unrestricted violence, of the instability of agreements or of the insecurity of their independence or sovereignty. It may have its origins in rational calculation that the willingness of states to accept restrictions on their freedom of action is reciprocal. Or it may be based also on the treatment of these goals as valuable in themselves and not merely as a means to an end – it may express a sense of common values as well as of common interests.

Rules

In international society, as in other societies, the sense of common interests in elementary goals of social life does not in itself provide precise guidance as to what behaviour is consistent with these goals; to do this is the function of *rules*. These rules may have the status of international law, of moral rules, of custom or established practice, or they may be merely operational rules or 'rules of the game', worked out without formal agreement or even without verbal communication. It is not uncommon for a rule to emerge first as an operational rule, then to become established practice, then to attain the status of a moral principle and finally to be incorporated in a legal convention; this appears to have been the genesis, for example, of many of the rules now embodied in multilateral treaties or conventions concerning the laws of war, diplomatic and consular status, and the law of the sea.

The range of these rules is vast, and over much of this range they are in a state of flux. Here we shall mention only three complexes of rules that play a part in the maintenance of international order.

First, there is the complex of rules that states what may be called the fundamental or constitutional normative principle of world politics in the present era. This is the principle that identifies the idea of a society of states, as opposed to such alternative ideas as that of a universal empire, a cosmopolitan community of individual human beings, or a Hobbesian state of nature or state of war, as the supreme normative principle of the political organisation of mankind. It is emphasised elsewhere in this study that there is nothing historically inevitable or morally sacrosanct about the idea of a society of states. Nor does this idea in fact monopolise human thought and action, even in the present phase; on the contrary, it has always had to do battle with competing principles, and does so now. Order on a world scale however, does require that one or another of these basic ideas should be clearly in the ascendancy; what is incompatible with order on a world scale is a discord of competing principles of universal political organisation.

On the one hand, the idea of international society identifies states as members of this society and the units competent to carry out political tasks within it, including the tasks necessary to make its basic rules effective; it thus excludes conceptions which assign this political competence to groups other than the state, such as universal authorities above it or sectional groups within it. On the other hand, the idea of international society identifies the relationship between the states as that of members of a society bound by common rules and committed to common institutions; it thus excludes the conception of world politics as a mere arena or state of war.

This fundamental or constitutional principle of international order is presupposed in ordinary state conduct. The daily actions of states – in arrogating to themselves the rights or competences of principal actors in world politics, and in combining with each other to this end, in resisting the claims of supra-state or sub-state groups to wrest these rights and competences from them – display this principle and provide evidence of its central role. The principle is contained in a number of basic rules of international law. Thus it has been the predominant doctrine that states are the only or the principal bearers of rights and duties in international law; that they alone have the right to use force to uphold it; and that its source lies in the consent of states, expressed in custom or treaty. The principle, however, is prior to international law, or to any particular formulation of international law; it is manifest in a whole complex of rules – legal, moral, customary and operational. It is not a static principle, but is subject to constant development. In the formative stages of international society, it had to meet the challenge of doctrines which proclaimed the right of individuals and of groups other than the state to a place in universal political organisation; and at the present time it faces a similar challenge.

Second, there are what may be called 'the rules of coexistence'. Given the guidance supplied by the constitutional principle as to who are the members of international society, these rules set out the minimum conditions of their coexistence. They include, first of all, the complex of rules which restrict the place of violence in world politics. These rules seek to confine the legitimate use of violence to sovereign states and to deny it to other agents by confining legitimate violence to a particular kind of violence called 'war', and by treating war as violence that is waged on the authority of a sovereign state. Furthermore, the rules seek to limit the causes or purposes for which a sovereign state can legitimately begin a war, for example by requiring that it be begun for a just cause, as maintained by the natural-law doctrines of the formative era of the states system, or by requiring that it be begun only after certain other procedures had been tried first, as insisted by the Covenant of the League of Nations. The rules also have sought to restrict the manner in which sovereign states conduct war, for example by insisting that war be conducted in a way proportionate to the end pursued, or in such a way as to spare non-combatants, or so as to employ no more violence than necessary. In addition, the rules have sought to restrict the geographical spread of a war, by establishing the rights and duties of neutrals and belligerents in relation to one another.

There is a further complex of rules of coexistence which prescribes the behaviour appropriate to sustain the goal of the carrying out of undertakings. The basic rule *pacta sunt servanda*, sometimes seen as a presupposition of the law of nations, and sometimes as a first principle of it, established the presumption on which alone there can be point in entering into agreements at all. Subordinate or qualifying rules concern whether or not good faith need be kept with heretics or infidels, whether or not agreements remain valid in changing circumstances and who is the judge as to whether or not they have changed, whether or not and in what sense agreements are valid that are imposed by force, what the circumstances are in which a party to an agreement can be released from it, what are the principles according to which agreements should be interpreted, whether or not and to what extent a new government succeeds to the obligations of its predecessors, and so on.

The rules of coexistence also include those which prescribe behaviour that sustains the goal of the stabilisation of each state's control or jurisdiction over its own persons and territory. At the heart of this complex of rules is the principle that each state accepts the duty to respect the sovereignty or supreme jurisdiction of every other state over its own citizens and domain, in return for the right to expect similar respect for its own sovereignty from other states. A corollary or near-corollary of this central rule is the rule that states will not intervene forcibly or dictatorially in one another's internal affairs. Another is the rule establishing the 'equality' of all states in the sense of their like enjoyment of like rights of sovereignty.

Third, there is the complex of rules concerned to regulate co-operation among states – whether on universal or on a more limited scale – above and beyond what is necessary for mere coexistence. This includes the rules that facilitate co-operation, not merely of a political and strategic, but also of a social and economic nature. The growth in this century of legal rules concerned with co-operation between states in economic, social, communications and environmental matters exemplifies the place of rules of co-operation and will be considered later (see Chapter 6).

Rules of this kind prescribe behaviour that is appropriate not to the elementary or primary goals of international life, but rather to those more advanced or secondary goals that are a feature of an international society in which a consensus has been reached about a wider range of objectives than mere coexistence. Nevertheless, these rules may be said to play a role in relation to international order, inasmuch as the development of co-operation and consensus among states about these wider goals may be expected to strengthen the framework of coexistence.

This is not the place to expound these three complexes of rules in full, or to examine the problems of interpreting them or reconciling the conflicts between them. Nor is it appropriate here to consider which of them has the status of law, which the status of moral rules, which should be seen as customary or as operational rules, nor to trace the historical evolution through which these rules have passed from one of these embodiments to another, and sometimes back again. It is sufficient to note that the vast and changing corpus of rules and quasi-rules, of which those cited are part of the central core, provide the means whereby international society moves from the vague perception of a common interest to a clear conception of the kind of conduct it requires.

Institutions

In international society it is the members of the society themselves – sovereign states – which are chiefly responsible for performing the functions of helping to make the rules effective; they do so in the absence of either a supreme government, which is able to undertake these functions in the modern state, or the degree of solidarity among themselves that characterises the performance of these functions by politically competent groups in primitive stateless societies. In this sense it is states themselves that are the principal institutions of the society of states.

Thus states undertake the function of making the rules, or legislating, by signifying their consent to them. Rules of general application, like the rules of coexistence, arise out of custom and established practice, and are in some cases confirmed by multilateral conventions. Rules that apply only to particular groups of states may also arise out of custom and established practice – as do the operational rules of crisis avoidance and management now being evolved by the great powers – but they may also be the subject of explicit agreements or treaties.

States communicate the rules through their official words, as when they state that they respect the legal principle of the sovereignty of states, or the moral principle of national self-determination, or the operational rule that great powers should not interfere in each other's spheres of influence. But they also communicate the rules through their actions, when they behave in such a way as to indicate that they accept or do not accept that a particular rule is valid. Because the communication of the rules is in the hands of states themselves, and not of an authority independent of them, the advertisement of the rules is commonly distorted in favour of the interests of particular states.

States administer the rules of international society inasmuch as executive acts ancillary to the rules themselves are performed either by themselves (as when particular states are designated as the depository states for a treaty, or the guarantors of a neutralisation arrangement, or the arbiters of a dispute) or by international organisations which are responsible to them (as when organisations are set up to implement agreements concerning international post and telecommunications, or a host of other matters).

Each state provides its own interpretation of the rules – legal, moral or operational. Even in the case of legal rules, a state relies on its own legal advisers, and there is no conclusive way in which disagreements about interpretation can be settled by an independent authority. The interpretation of moral or of operational rules is even more uncertain.

The enforcement of the rules, in the absence of a central authority, is carried out by states, which may resort to acts of self-help, including acts of force, in defence of their rights under operational, moral or legal rules. Because states are frequently not in a position to carry out effective action in defence of their rights, the enforcement of the rules is uncertain. Because of the low degree of consensus or solidarity among states, actions which the state committing them sees as self-help or rule-enforcement are frequently not viewed as such by international society at large.

States undertake the task of legitimising the rules, in the sense of promoting the acceptance of them as valuable in their own right, by employing their powers of persuasion and propaganda to mobilise support for them in world politics as a whole. At the present time an important means to the legitimisation of rules is to have them endorsed by international assemblies and international organisations.

States undertake the task of changing or adapting operational, moral and legal rules to changing circumstances, but have to do so in the absence of a universal legislative authority competent to rescind old rules and devise new ones, and with the handicap that there is often no consensus as to whether or not, or how, the rules should be changed. States change the rules by demonstrating, through their words or their actions, that they are withdrawing their consent from old rules and bestowing it upon new ones, and thus altering the content of custom or established practice. The operational rules observed by great powers, whereby they respect one anothers' spheres of influence in particular parts of the world, are rescinded or changed when these powers show by what they do or say that they no longer accept them, or regard their boundaries or limiting conditions as having changed. The moral principle of national self-determination – the rule that states should be nation-states – came to displace that of dynastic legitimacy not by enactment of any legislative authority, but by war and revolution. In the changing of legal rules a part is sometimes played by multilateral conventions or treaties, but here also states change the old rules by violating or ignoring them systematically enough to demonstrate that they have withdrawn their consent to them. In other words, while the adaptation of the rules to changed circumstances is part of the process whereby order is maintained, it is itself often accompanied by disorder.

Finally, states undertake the task which, for want of a better term, has been called 'protection' of the rules. The rules which sustain order in international society can operate only if conditions obtain in the international political system that enable them to do so. In particular, they can operate only if that sense of common interests among states, which they seek to translate into a precise guide to conduct, continues to exist. The function of 'protection' of the rules comprises all those things which states may do to create or maintain that state or condition of the system in which respect for the rules can flourish.

The 'protection' of the rules encompasses, first and foremost, those classical acts of diplomacy and war whereby states seek to preserve a general balance of power in the international system (and today a relationship of mutual nuclear deterrence among contending nuclear powers); to accommodate or contain conflicts of ideology; to resolve or moderate conflicts of state interest; to limit or control armaments and armed forces in relation to interests perceived in international security; to appease the demands of dissatisfied states for what they regard as just change; and to secure and maintain the acquiescence of the smaller powers in the assumption by great powers of special rights and responsibilities.

These measures of 'protection' of the rules are not prescribed by the rules of coexistence, or by international law, in which some of the rules of coexistence are stated. Indeed, some of the measures which states take in the course of 'protecting' the rules may bring them into conflict with international law. The activities that go to make up 'protection' of the rules of coexistence are themselves the subject of further bodies of rules, such as those which regulate the balance of power, diplomacy and the special position of the great powers.

In carrying out these functions, states collaborate with one another, in varying degrees, in what may be called the institutions of international society: the balance of power, international law, the diplomatic mechanism, the managerial system of the great powers, and war. By an institution we do not necessarily imply an organisation or administrative machinery, but rather a set of habits and practices shaped towards the realisation of common goals. These institutions do not deprive states of their central role in carrying out the political functions of international society, or serve as a surrogate central authority in the international system. They are rather an expression of the element of collaboration among states in discharging their political functions – and at the same time a means of sustaining this collaboration. These institutions serve to symbolise the existence of an international society that is more than the sum of its members, to give substance and permanence to their collaboration in carrying out the political functions of international society, and to moderate their tendency to lose sight of common interests. The contribution of these institutions to international order, in the past and at present, are considered in Part 2.

Functional and Causal Explanations

A central theme in this study is that the rules and institutions to which reference has been made carry out positive functions or roles in relation to international order. In this study what is meant by statements of this kind is simply that these rules and institutions are part of the efficient causation of international order, that they are among the necessary and sufficient conditions of its occurrence. The present study is not an attempt to apply 'structural-functionalist' explanation, in which terms such as 'function' and 'role' have a different meaning.

In 'structural-functionalist' explanation the statement that these rules and institutions fulfil 'functions' in relation to international order might be taken to imply that international society, for its own survival or maintenance, has certain 'needs', and that the rules and institutions in question are fulfilling those needs. If we can make the additional assumptions that fulfilment of these needs is essential to the survival of international society, and that fulfilment of them cannot be carried out in any other way, then to say that these rules and institutions fulfil these functions is tantamount to endorsing them.

The present study is not intended to provide a rationale for, or justification of, the rules of coexistence in international society or the institutions that help to make them effective. In the first place it is emphasised here that order is not the only value in international politics, nor is it necessarily an overriding one. Thus even if a 'structural-functionalist' explanation were accepted, to the effect that the present rules and institutions of international society are essential to the preservation of order in it, it would not follow from this that they were to be endorsed.

In the second place, whatever merits may lie in the application of 'structural-functionalist' reasoning to other societies, doubts may be entertained about its validity when applied to the society of states. The underlying assumption of the 'structural-functionalist' explanation is that of the wholeness or unity of the society being explained, the primacy of the whole over its parts in accounting for what occurs within it, the possibility of describing the nature and purpose of each part in terms of what it contributes to the 'needs' of the whole.

International society does not display the kind of wholeness or unity that would give point to explanations of this sort. It is emphasised in this study that society is only one of a number of competing elements in international politics; indeed, the description of it as a society at all conveys only part of the truth. An explanation of the rules and institutions of international society that dealt only with the functions they served in relation to international society as a whole would overlook the extent to which international politics is better described as a state of war or as a political field in which individuals and groups other than the state are the principal actors.

In the third place there is room for doubt about the basic validity of 'structural-functional' analysis, even when this is applied to societies displaying more unity than does the society of states. Even in those societies, like modern nation-states or primitive societies marked by a high degree of social consensus and solidarity, there are forces making for anti-social or non-social behaviour which cannot be readily encompassed in a theory which seeks to relate all social events to the working of the social framework as a whole.

4

Order versus Justice in World Politics

Order is not merely an actual or possible condition or state of affairs in world politics, it is also very generally regarded as a value. But it is not the only value in relation to which international conduct can be shaped, nor is it necessarily an overriding one. At the present time, for example, it is often said that whereas the Western powers, in the justifications they offer of their policies, show themselves to be primarily concerned with order, the states of the Third World are primarily concerned with the achievement of justice in the world community, even at the price of disorder. Professor Ali Mazrui, one of the few contemporary writers on international relations to have thought deeply about this question, has said that the Western powers, the principal authors of the United Nations Charter, wrote it in such a way that peace and security are treated as the primary objectives of the organisation, and the promotion of human rights as a secondary objective, whereas the African and Asian states are dedicated to reversing this order of priority.[1]

How far Professor Mazrui is correct in characterising in this way the conflict of policy between the Western powers and the African and Asian states, I shall consider later. My purpose in this chapter is to raise some deeper questions that underlie this contemporary conflict of policy, as they have underlain other such conflicts in the past, concerning the place of order in the hierarchy of human values. In particular I propose to examine the contending claims of order and the other human value most frequently contrasted with it, justice. To this end I shall consider:

(i) What meaning or meanings can we give to the idea of justice in world politics?

(ii) How is order in world politics related to justice? How far are order and justice compatible or mutually reinforcing ends of policy, and how far are they conflicting or even mutually exclusive? (iii) To the extent that order and justice are conflicting or alternative goals of policy, which should have priority?

In the discussion of questions such as these there is a danger of lapsing into subjectivity or policy prescription. Moreover, it would be naive to imagine that such questions, stated in these general terms, could be answered conclusively or authoritatively. But it should be possible, while avoiding subjectivism and the canvassing of solutions, at least to clarify the questions and to achieve a deeper understanding of the considerations that lie behind the various answers to them.

The Meaning of 'Justice'

Unlike order, justice is a term which can ultimately be given only some kind of private or subjective definition. I do not propose to set out any private vision of what just conduct in world politics would be, nor to embark upon any philosophical analysis of the criteria for recognising it. My starting-point is simply that there are certain ideas or beliefs as to what justice involves in world politics, and that demands formulated in the name of these ideas play a role in the course of events.

Clearly, ideas about justice belong to the class of moral ideas, ideas which treat human actions as right in themselves and not merely as a means to an end, as categorically and not merely hypothetically imperative. Considerations of justice, accordingly, are to be distinguished from considerations of law, and from considerations of the dictates of prudence, interest or necessity.

In thinking about justice there are certain distinctions, familiar in theoretical analyses of the idea, which it is helpful to bear in mind.[2] First, there is the distinction between what has been called 'general' justice, justice as identical with virtuous or righteous conduct in general, and 'particular' justice, justice as one species of right conduct among others. The term 'justice' is sometimes used interchangeably with 'morality' or 'virtue', as if to say an action is just were simply another way of saying that it is morally right. It is often argued, however, that ideas about justice constitute a particular sub-category of moral ideas, as we imply when we say that justice should be tempered with mercy, or that states in their dealings with one another are capable of justice but not of charity. It has often been contended that justice is especially to do with equality in the enjoyment of rights and privileges, perhaps also to do with fairness or reciprocity; that, whatever the substance of the rights or privileges in question, demands for justice are demands for the equal enjoyment of them as between persons who are different from one another in some respect but should be treated in respect of these rights as if they were the same.

Demands for justice in world politics are often of this form; they are demands for the removal of privilege or discrimination, for equality in the distribution or in the application of rights as between the strong and the weak, the large and the small, the rich and the poor, the black and the white, the nuclear and the non-nuclear, or the victors and the vanquished. It is important to distinguish between 'justice' in this special sense of equality of rights and privileges, and 'justice' in the sense in which we are using it interchangeably with 'morality'.

A second important distinction is between 'substantive' and 'formal' justice, the former lying in the recognition of rules conferring certain specified rights and duties – political, social or economic – and the latter lying in the like application of these rules to like persons, irrespective of what the substantive content of the rules may be. Demands for 'equality before the law', demands that legal rules be applied in a fair or equal manner to like persons or classes of persons, are demands for 'formal justice' in this sense, although such demands arise in relation to all rules, legal and non-legal: that like groups of people should be treated in a like manner is entailed in the very notion of a rule of any kind. Demands for 'justice' in world politics are frequently demands for formal justice in this sense: that some legal rule, such as that requiring states not to interfere in one another's domestic affairs, or some moral rule, such as that which confers on all nations a right of self-determination, or some operational rule or rule of the game, such as that which requires the great powers to respect one another's spheres of influence, should be applied fairly or equally as between one state and another.

A third distinction is between 'arithmetical justice', in the sense of equal rights and duties, and 'proportionate justice', or rights and duties which may not be equal but which are distributed according to the end in view. Equality may be envisaged as the enjoyment by a class of like persons or groups of the same rights and duties. But it is obvious that equality in this sense will often fail to satisfy other criteria of justice. For one thing, given that persons and groups are sometimes unequal in their capacities or in their needs, a rule that provides them with the same rights and duties may have the effect simply of further underlining their inequality; as Aristotle wrote, 'injustice arises when equals are treated unequally and also when unequals are treated equally'.[3] Marx's principle 'from each according to his capacity, to each according to his need' embodies a preference for 'proportionate' over 'arithmetical' justice in relation to the end of a just distribution of wealth. In world politics certain basic rights and duties, such as the right of states to sovereign independence and the duty of states not to interfere in one another's domestic affairs, generally held to apply equally to all states, exemplify 'arithmetical justice', while the doctrine that the use of force in war or reprisals should be in proportion to the injury that has been suffered may be taken to illustrate 'proportionate justice'.

A fourth distinction, closely connected with the latter, is between 'commutative' or reciprocal justice, and 'distributive' justice, or justice assessed in the light of the common good or common interest of society as a whole. 'Commutative' justice lies in the recognition of rights and duties by a process of exchange or bargaining, whereby one individual or group recognises the rights of others in return for their recognition of his or its own. To the extent that the bargaining strength of individuals and groups is equal, this reciprocal process is likely to result in what we have called 'arithmetical justice' or equal rights. 'Distributive justice', by contrast, comes about not through a process of bargaining among individual members of the society in question, but by decision of the society as a whole, in the light of consideration of its common good or interest. It is clear that 'distributive justice' in this sense may often result in justice which is 'proportionate' rather than 'arithmetical', requiring for example that the rich pay higher taxes than the poor, or that the strong perform more labour than the weak. World politics in the present era is principally a process of conflict and co-operation among states having only the most rudimentary sense of the common good of the world as a whole, and is therefore the domain pre-eminently of ideas of 'commutative' rather than 'distributive' justice. The main stuff of contention about justice in international affairs is to be found in the attempt of sovereign states, through a process of claim and counter-claim, to iron out among themselves what rights and duties will be recognised and how they will be applied. But ideas of 'distributive' justice also play a part in the discussion of world politics, and are exemplified by the idea that justice requires a transfer of economic resources from rich countries to poor.

In applying all these distinctions it is important to consider in what agents or actors in world politics moral rights or duties are taken to be vested. Here one may distinguish what may be called international or interstate justice; individual or human justice; and cosmopolitan or world justice.

International or Interstate Justice

By international or interstate justice I have in mind the moral rules held to confer rights and duties upon states and nations, for example the idea that all states, irrespective of their size or their racial composition or their ideological leaning, are equally entitled to the rights of sovereignty, or the idea that all nations are equally entitled to the rights of national self-determination. The rights of states may of course conflict with the rights of nations, and thus interstate justice is not the same thing as international justice: the principle of national self-determination has been invoked to destroy the sovereign integrity of states and even now threatens a great many of them. But to the extent that there is now a broad consensus that states should be nation-states, and that the official doctrine of most states (even so-called multinational states) is that they are nation-states, there is a measure of harmony between ideas of interstate and of international justice.

Because states are the main agents or actors in world politics, ideas of interstate justice provide the main content of everyday discussion of justice in world affairs. Every state maintains that it has certain rights and duties that are not merely legal in character but moral: it contends that its policy is just in the sense of being morally correct ('general justice'), and demands equality or fairness of treatment as between itself and other states ('particular justice'); it claims a moral right to sovereignty or independence ('substantive justice'), while also claiming that this right should be applied or administered equally to itself as to other states ('formal justice'); it asserts a right of equal treatment as between itself and others, in access to trading opportunities, or in voting at an international assembly ('arithmetical justice'), while also insisting that its financial contribution to an interstate organisation should be determined by the size of its national product ('proportionate justice'); it recognises rights of all kinds that attach to other states, in return for their recognition of its own ('commutative justice'), but it may also, at least in its rhetoric, argue from the idea of the common good of a regional community or of the world community ('distributive justice').

Individual or Human Justice

By individual or human justice I mean the moral rules conferring rights and duties upon individual human beings. In the form of the doctrine of natural law, ideas of human justice historically preceded the development of ideas of interstate or international justice and provided perhaps the principal intellectual foundation upon which these latter ideas at first rested: that is to say, states and nations were originally thought to have rights and duties because individual persons had rights and duties, the rulers of states being persons, and nations being collections of persons. But the ideas of interstate and international justice by the eighteenth century had reached a point of take-off, after which they became independent of the means by which they had become established – as rights and duties were held to attach to the notional personality of a state which was other than its rulers, and the collective personality of a nation which was other than, and on some views more than, the sum of its members.

In this system, in which rights and duties applied directly to states and nations, the notion of human rights and duties has survived but it has gone underground. Far from providing the basis from which ideas of international justice or morality are derived, it has become potentially subversive of international society itself, a position reflected in the doctrine of the positivist international lawyers of the eighteenth and nineteenth centuries that states were the only subjects of international law and that individuals could only be the objects of understandings between states. The basic compact of coexistence between states, expressed in the exchange of recognition of sovereign jurisdictions, implies a conspiracy of silence entered into by governments about the rights and duties of their respective citizens. This conspiracy is mitigated by the practice of granting rights of asylum to foreign political refugees, by declaratory recognition of the moral rights of human beings in such documents as the Atlantic Charter, the United Nations Charter and the Universal Declaration of Human Rights, and by practical co-operation between governments to take account of human rights in such fields as the treatment of prisoners of war and the promotion of economic and social welfare. But the idea of the *duties* of the individual human being raises, in international politics, the question of the duties he has that conflict with his duties to the state – the question that the Nuremberg War Crimes Tribunal raised in relation to German soldiers and political leaders, and which it also raised in relation to the American soldiers and leaders responsible for the prosecution of the Vietnam War.[4] And the idea of the *rights* of the individual human being raises in international politics the question of the right and duty of persons and groups other than the state to which he owes allegiance to come to his aid in the event that his rights are being disregarded – the right of the Western powers to protect the political rights of the citizens of Eastern European countries, of Africans to protect the rights of black South Africans, or of China to protect the right of Chinese minorities in South-east Asia. These are questions which, answered in a certain way, lead to disorder in international relations, or even to the breakdown of international society itself. Thus in the present era the representatives of states, when they discuss the rights or the duties of individual human beings, do so in a muted voice: for if men have rights, which other states or international authorities may champion, there are limits to their own authority; and if men have duties, to causes or movements beyond the state of which they are citizens, the state cannot count on their loyalty.

Cosmopolitan or World Justice

In addition to ideas about interstate or international justice, and about human justice, we need to recognise a third category of ideas which concern what may be called cosmopolitan or world justice. These are ideas which seek to spell out what is right or good for the world as a whole, for an imagined *civitas maxima* or cosmopolitan society to which all individuals belong and to which their interests should be subordinate. This notion of justice as the promotion of the world common good is different from that of the assertion of the rights and duties of individual human beings all over the globe for it posits the idea that these individuals form or should form a society or community whose common interests or common good must qualify or even determine what their individual rights and duties are, just as the rights and duties of individuals within the state have in the past been qualified or determined by notions such as the good of the state, the greatest happiness of the greatest number of its citizens, or the general will. It implies a conception of justice that is 'proportionate' as well as 'arithmetical', 'distributive' as well as 'commutative'.

Such a notion of the world common good concerns not the common ends or values of the society of states, but rather the common ends or values of the universal society of all mankind, whose constituent members are individual human beings. This notion is implicit in a good deal of contemporary discussion, in which men speak or write as if such a cosmopolitan or world society already existed. Thus, in discussions of strategic and arms-control questions, it is not uncommon to speak of a general nuclear war as not simply a disaster for the society of states and an infringement of individual human rights, but also a threat to human life or human civilisation as such. In discussions of the transfer of resources from rich countries to poor, the ultimate object is sometimes taken to be not to make poor countries richer, or to promote the rights of poor individuals to a better life, but to achieve a more equitable distribution of wealth among all individual members of human society, or to achieve minimum standards of wealth or welfare within this society. In discussions of ecological or environmental questions the basic appeal that is being made is not to co-operation among states or to individual human rights and duties, but to the solidarity of all human beings in facing certain ecological or environmental challenges that face them as human beings.

If, in the present condition of world politics, in which states are the principal actors, ideas of interstate or international justice play a dominant part in everyday discussion, and ideas of human justice a smaller part, ideas of cosmopolitan or world justice play very little part at all. The world society or community whose common good they purport to define does not exist except as an idea or myth which may one day become powerful, but has not done so yet. The great mass of political mankind does not have the means of interest articulation and aggregation, of political socialisation and recruitment, which (we are told) are the hallmarks of a political system. In so far as the interests of mankind are articulated and aggregated, and a process of political socialisation and recruitment moulds a universal political system, this is through the mechanism of the society of sovereign states. For guidance as to what the interests of the world as a whole might be, for example with regard to the control of arms, or the distribution of population and resources, or the conservation of the environment, we are forced to look to the views of sovereign states and of the international organisations they dominate.

There is, indeed, no lack of self-appointed spokesmen of the common good of 'the spaceship earth' or 'this endangered planet'. But the views of these private individuals, whatever merit they may have, are not the outcome of any political process of the assertion and reconciliation of interests. In the sense that they are not authenticated by such a political process, the views of these individuals provide even less of an authoritative guide to the common good of mankind than do the views of the spokesmen of sovereign states, even unrepresentative or tyrannical ones, which at least have claims to speak for some part of mankind larger than themselves. Nor do the spokesmen of non-governmental groups (such as bodies of experts on arms control, economic development or environmental matters) possess authority of this kind; they may speak with authority on their particular subject, but to define the interests of mankind is to lay claim to a kind of authority that can only be conferred by a political process.

But if it is chiefly through the views of states, and of states assembled in international organisations, that we have perforce to seek to discover the world common good, this is a distorting lens; universal ideologies that are espoused by states are notoriously subservient to their special interests, and agreements reached among states notoriously the product of bargaining and compromise rather than of any consideration of the interests of mankind as a whole.

The Compatibility of Order and Justice

It is obvious that the existing framework of international order fails to satisfy some of the most deeply felt and powerfully supported of these aspirations for justice. Not only is it true of the contemporary international scene, as noted by Professor Mazrui, that it is marked by conflict between those states that are concerned chiefly to preserve order and those that give priority to the achievement of just change, if necessary at the expense of order; there is also an inherent tension between the order provided by the system and society of states, and the various aspirations for justice that arise in world politics, which is persistently expressed in one way or another.

It is true that justice, in any of its forms, is realisable only in a context of order; it is only if there is a pattern of social activity in which elementary or primary goals of social life are in some degree provided for, that advanced or secondary goals can be secured. It is true *a fortiori*, that international society, by providing a context of order of some kind, however rudimentary, may be regarded as paving the way for the equal enjoyment of rights of various kinds. It is true also that international society at present, through such nearly universal organs as the United Nations and its specialised agencies, is formally committed to much more than the preservation of minimum order or coexistence: it espouses ideas of international or interstate justice, and of individual or human justice, and even takes some account, through its endorsement of the idea of the transfer of resources from rich to poor countries, of goals of world justice; and it facilitates intergovernmental co-operation in many fields to promote the realisation of these ideas.

But, to begin with, the framework of international order is quite inhospitable to projects for the realisation of cosmopolitan or world justice. If the idea of the world common good were to be taken seriously, it would lead to the consideration of such questions as how the immigration policies of states throughout the world should be shaped in the general interest, which countries or which areas of the world have the most need of capital and which the least, how trade and fiscal policies throughout the world should be regulated in accordance with a common set of priorities, or what outcomes of a host of violent civil and international conflicts throughout the world best conformed to the general interests of mankind.

These are of course the very issues over which governments have control, and do not seem likely to be willing to relinquish control, in the absence of vast changes in human society. The position which governments occupy as custodians of the perceived interests of limited sections of mankind imposes familiar obstacles to their viewing themselves simply as so many agencies jointly responsible for the implementation of the world common good. It is sometimes said that the commitment of the donor countries through aid and trade policies to the objective of a minimum level of economic welfare throughout the world implies and presupposes acceptance of the idea of the interests of the community of mankind. Kenneth Boulding, for example, argues that since the transfer of resources from rich to poor countries is wholly one-sided or non-reciprocal it means that the rich see themselves as part of the same community with the poor. 'If A gives B something without expecting anything in return the inference must be drawn that B is "part" of A, or that A and B together are part of a larger system of interests and organisations.'[5] It may be argued that the idea of the community of mankind provides a better rationale for the transfer of resources than others that are sometimes given: better, for example, than the idea sometimes put forward in Western countries that aid to the poor is necessary to promote order or stability (in the sense of a pattern that secures Western-preferred values), or to forestall an incipient revolt of the 'have-nots' against the 'haves' or the idea prominent in the rhetoric of poor countries that it is necessary so that the rich can expiate the guilt of their past wrongs. It is not clear, however, that the idea of the community of mankind does actually underlie the enterprise of the transfer of resources to any important degree; or indeed that the transfer of resources yet has a secure and established position as part of the permanent business of international society, assailed as it is on the one side by the idea that the rich countries should reduce their involvement in the Third World to the minimum, and on the other side by the doctrine that aid is essentially a means of perpetuating domination and exploitation and hence prejudicial to the true interests of the 'have-nots'.

Ideas of world or cosmopolitan justice are fully realisable, if at all, only in the context of a world or cosmopolitan society. Demands for world justice are therefore demands for the transformation of the system and society of states, and are inherently revolutionary. World justice may be ultimately reconcilable with world order, in the sense that we may have a vision of a world or cosmopolitan society that provides for both. But to pursue the idea of world justice in the context of the system and society of states is to enter into conflict with the devices through which order is at present maintained.

The framework of international order is inhospitable also to demands for human justice, which represent a very powerful ingredient in world politics at the present time. International society takes account of the notion of human rights and duties that may be asserted against the state to which particular human beings belong, but it is inhibited from giving effect to them, except selectively and in a distorted way. If international society were really to treat human justice as primary and coexistence as secondary – if, as Professor Mazrui says, this is what the African and Asian states want, i.e. the United Nations Charter were to give pride of place to human rights rather than to the preservation of peace and security – then in a situation in which there is no agreement as to what human rights or in what hierarchy of priorities they should be arranged, the result could only be to undermine international order. It is here that the society of states – including, I should say, despite what Professor Mazrui says, African and Asian states – displays its conviction that international order is prior to human justice. African and Asian states, I believe, like other states, are willing to subordinate order to human justice in particular cases closely affecting them, but they are no more willing than the Western states or the states of the Soviet bloc to allow the whole structure of international coexistence to be brought to the ground.

There is another obstacle to the realisation of human justice within the present framework of international order. When questions of human justice achieve a prominent place on the agenda of world political discussion, it is because it is the policy of particular states to raise them. The world after the First World War heard about the war guilt of the Kaiser, and after the Second World War witnessed the trial and punishment of German and Japanese leaders and soldiers for war crimes and crimes against the peace. It did not witness the trial and punishment of American, British and Soviet leaders and soldiers who *prima facie* might have been as much or as little guilty of disregarding their human obligations as Goering, Yamamoto and the rest. This is not to say that the idea of the trial and punishment of war criminals by international procedure is an unjust or unwise one, only that it operates in a selective way. That these men and not others were brought to trial by the victors was an accident of power politics.

In the same way the world has heard of the human rights of non-European persons in Southern Africa, and may even come to see redress of the wrongs they have suffered, because it is the policy of black African states and others to take up this issue, just as the world once heard of the rights of the Christian subjects of the Sultan of Turkey because it was the policy of certain European powers to uphold them. But the rights of Africans in black African states, or of intellectuals in the Soviet Union, or of Tibetans in China or Nagas in India or communists in Indonesia are less likely to be upheld by international action because it is not the policy of any prominent group of states to protect them. The international order does not provide any general protection of human rights, only a selective protection that is determined not by the merits of the case but by the vagaries of international politics.

There is a further obstacle. Even in cases where, as the consequence of these vagaries of international politics, international society permits action directed towards the realisation of human justice, the action taken does not directly impinge upon individual human beings but takes place through the mediation of sovereign states, who shape this action to their own purposes. Take the case of world economic justice, towards the realisation of which the transfer of resources from the rich to the poor countries is bent. The ultimate moral object of this process is to improve the material standard of life of individual human beings in poor Asian, African and Latin American countries. But the donor countries and international organisations concerned transfer resources not directly to these individuals but to the governments of the countries of which they are citizens. As Julius Stone points out, it is left to these governments to determine the criteria according to which the resources will be distributed to individuals, or indeed to distribute them arbitrarily or not distribute them at all. As he says, the unspoken assumption of the business of transfer of resources is that the actual claimants and beneficiaries of what he calls the 'justice constituency' are not individual human beings but governments.[6] The doubts which donor countries entertain about the way in which the governments of recipient countries distribute or fail to distribute the resources transferred to them of course constitute one of the principal disincentives to foreign aid. Yet one has also to agree with Stone's conclusion that although the transfer of resources, as it takes place at present, necessarily falls short of the realisation of what I have called human justice, it is inevitable, given the present nature of international society, that it should do so: donor countries and organisations cannot determine the way in which recipient governments distribute their resources (although they can sometimes lay down conditions for the distribution of resources transferred) without violating the most fundamental norms of the compact of coexistence.

If international society is quite inhospitable to notions of cosmopolitan justice, and able to give only a selective and ambiguous welcome to ideas of human justice, it is not basically unfriendly to notions of interstate or international justice. The structure of international coexistence, as I have argued, itself depends on norms or rules conferring rights and duties upon states – not necessarily moral rules, but procedural rules or rules of the game which in modern international society are stated in some cases in international law. Whereas ideas of world justice may seem entirely at odds with the structure of international society, and notions of human justice to entail a possible threat to its foundations, ideas of interstate and international justice may reinforce the compact of coexistence between states by adding a moral imperative to the imperatives of enlightened self-interest and of law on which it rests.

Yet international order is preserved by means which systematically affront the most basic and widely agreed principles of international justice. I do not mean simply that at the present time there are states and nations which are denied their moral rights or fail to fulfil their moral responsibilities, or that there is gross inequality or unfairness in their enjoyment of these rights, or exercise of responsibilities. This is of course the case, but it has always been the case, and it is the normal condition of any society. What I have in mind is rather that the institutions and mechanisms which sustain international order, even when they are working properly, indeed especially when they are working properly, or fulfilling their functions – their working is reviewed in Part 2 of this study – necessarily violate ordinary notions of justice.

Consider, for example, the role that is played in international order by the institution of the balance of power. Here is an

institution which offends against everyday notions of justice by
sanctioning war against a state whose power threatens to become
preponderant, but which has done no legal or moral injury; by
sacrificing the interests of small states, which may be absorbed or
partitioned in the interests of the balance; or – in the case of its
contemporary variant, the 'balance of terror' – by magnifying and
exploiting the risk of destruction. Yet this is an institution whose
role in the preservation of order in the international system, in the
past and at present, is a central one.

Or consider the role of another institution: war. War also plays a
central role in the maintenance of international order in the
enforcement of international law, the preservation of the balance
of power and the effecting of changes which a consensus maintains
are just. But war at the same time may be the instrument of
overthrowing rules of international law, of undermining the balance
of power and of preventing just changes or effecting changes that
are unjust. It is at the same time an instrument which once
employed, whether for just or unjust causes, may develop a
momentum of its own so that it ceases to be an instrument of
those who began it, but transforms them and the situation in which
they find themselves beyond recognition.

Consider, again, international law. It is not merely that international law sanctifies the *status quo* without providing for a
legislative process whereby the law can be altered by consent and
thus causes the pressures for change to consolidate behind demands
that the law should be violated in the name of justice. It is also that
when the law is violated, and a new situation is brought about by
the triumph not necessarily of justice but of force, international law
accepts this new situation as legitimate, and concurs in the means
whereby it has been brought about. As Mazrui writes, international
law condemns aggression, but once aggression has been successful it
ceases to be condemned. The conflict between international law and
international justice is endemic because the situations from which
the law takes its point of departure are a series of *faits accomplis*
brought about by force and the threat of force, legitimised by the
principle that treaties concluded under duress are valid.

Moreover, contrary to much superficial thinking on this subject,
it is not as if this tendency of international law to accommodate
itself to power politics were some unfortunate but remediable defect

that is fit to be removed by the good work of some high-minded professor of international law or by some ingenious report of the International Law Commission. There is every reason to think that this feature of international law, which sets it at loggerheads with elementary justice, is vital to its working; and that if international law ceased to have this feature, it would so lose contact with international reality as to be unable to play any role at all.

Or consider the role that is played in the maintenance of international order by the special position of the great powers. Great powers contribute to international order by maintaining local systems of hegemony within which order is imposed from above, and by collaborating to manage the global balance of power and, from time to time, to impose their joint will on others. But the great powers, when they perform these services to international order, do so at the price of systematic injustice to the rights of smaller states and nations, the injustice which has been felt by states which fall within the Soviet hegemony in Eastern Europe or the American hegemony in the Caribbean, the injustice which is written into the terms of the United Nations Charter which prescribe a system of collective security that cannot be operated against great powers, the injustice from which small powers always suffer when great ones meet in concert to strike bargains at their expense.

There is no general incompatibility as between order in the abstract, in the sense in which it has been defined, and justice in any of the meanings that have been reviewed. We may imagine, in other words, a society in which there is a pattern of activity that sustains elementary or primary goals of social life, and also provides for advanced or secondary goals of justice or equality, for states, for individuals and in terms of the world common good. There is no *a priori* reason for holding that such a society is unattainable, or that there is any inconsistency in pursuing both world order and world justice. There is, however, incompatibility as between the rules and institutions that now sustain order within the society of states, and demands for world justice, which imply the destruction of this society, demands for human justice, which it can accommodate only in a selective and partial way, and demands for interstate and international justice, to which it is not basically hostile, but to which also it can provide only limited satisfaction.

The Question of Priority

Given that the framework of international society fails to satisfy these various ideas of justice, what would be the effects upon international order of attempts to realise them? Can justice in world politics, in its various senses, be achieved only by jeopardising international order? And if this is so, which should take priority?

It is possible to distinguish three ideal-typical doctrines which embody answers to these questions. There is first the conservative or orthodox view that recognises an inherent conflict between the values of order and of justice in world politics, and treats the former as having priority over the latter – international society as a society in which 'minimum order' or coexistence is the most that can be expected, and in which demands for 'optimum order' threaten to remove the small area of consensus upon which this coexistence is built.

Second, there is the view of the revolutionary which also is founded upon the idea of an inherent conflict between the present framework of international order and the achievement of justice, but treats the latter as the commanding value: Let justice be done, 'though the earth perish'. The revolutionary, however, does not believe that the earth will perish, but looks forward to the re-establishment of an order that will secure the just changes he wishes to bring about, after a period of temporary and perhaps geographically limited disorder. This has been the doctrine of some black Africans in relation to the African continent, of Arab nationalists in relation to the Arab lands, and of the early Bolsheviks and later of China in relation to the world as a whole.

Third, there is the liberal or progressivist view that has always represented one important strand in thought about foreign policy in the West, that (perhaps without denying it altogether) is reluctant to accept that there is any necessary conflict between order and justice in world politics, and is constantly seeking after ways of reconciling the one with the other. It is inclined, for example, to see the righting of injustices as the true means to the strengthening of international order: the removal of *apartheid* or of 'the last vestiges of colonialism' as the way in which the black African states can best be integrated into the system of 'peace and security', the provision of economic justice for the poor peoples of the world as the means of avoiding an otherwise inevitable violent confrontation of 'haves' and 'have-nots'. It is inclined to shy away from the recognition that justice in some cases cannot be brought about through processes of consent or consensus, to argue that attempts to achieve justice by disrupting order are counter-productive, to cajole the advocates of 'order' and of 'justice' into remaining within the bounds of a moral system that provides for both and permits an adjustment that can be mutually agreed.

It is clear that demands for the preservation of order and for the promotion of just change in world politics are not mutually exclusive, and that there is sometimes scope for reconciling the one with the other. Any regime that provides order in world politics will need to appease demands for just change, at least to some degree, if it is to endure; and thus an enlightened pursuit of the goal of order will take account also of the demand for justice. Likewise the demand for just change will need to take account of the goal of order; for it is only if the changes that are effected can be incorporated in some regime that provides order, that they can be made secure.

It is sometimes possible, moreover, to bring about a change agreed to be just with the consent of the parties affected, and in this case there may be no injury to the foundations of international order. The liberation of African and Asian peoples from European empires has been accompanied by violence and disorder, and those who fought for it consciously subordinated order to justice. But some part was played also in the process by the orderly transfer of power by metropolitan governments to subject nations. It is clear also that even where there is not consent by all the parties affected, but there is overwhelming evidence of a consensus in international society as a whole in favour of a change held to be just, especially if the consensus embraces all the great powers, the change may take place without causing other than a local and temporary disorder, after which the international order as a whole may emerge unscathed or even appear in a stronger position than before. It can scarcely be doubted that an international society that has reached a consensus not merely about order, but about a wider range of notions of international, human and perhaps world justice, is likely to be in a stronger position to maintain the framework of minimum order or coexistence than one that has not.

The conflict between international order and demands for just change arises in those cases where there is no consensus as to what justice involves, and when to press the claims of justice is to re-open questions which the compact of coexistence requires to be treated as closed.

If, for example, there were a consensus within the United Nations, including all the great powers, in favour of military intervention in Southern Africa to enforce national self-determination for black majority populations and to uphold black African political rights, it might be possible to regard such intervention as implying no threat to international order, or even as strengthening international order by confirming a new degree of moral solidarity in international society. In the absence of such a consensus, demands for external military intervention imply the subordination of order to considerations of international and human justice. The argument that has been advanced by black African states in the United Nations Security Council since 1963 to the effect that *apartheid* is not merely a violation of human rights but a threat to the peace, whatever merits it may have as a construction of the law of the Charter or as a political tactic, obscures the position: it is the proponents of intervention who wish to threaten the peace, and they are moved by considerations not of peace but of justice.

The military action taken by India in wresting Goa from Portugal in 1961 and by Indonesia in West Irian in 1962 also represents the breaking of the peace for the sake of a change conceived to be just. It is interesting that in these cases, as in relation to the proposed military intervention in Southern Africa, the justifications provided related to order as well as to justice: in the Goan case Krishna Menon defended India's action in terms of the need to respond to Portugal's aggression of 1510, since when there had been 'permanent aggression'. Similarly, the Indian intervention in East Pakistan in 1971 was defended, *inter alia,* as a response to 'demographic aggression'. Thus the revolutionaries accommodate themselves to the prevailing modalities of the system.

When, then, demands for justice are put forward in the absence of a consensus within international society as to what justice involves, the prospect is opened up that the consensus which does exist about order or minimum coexistence will be undone. The question then has to be faced whether order or justice should have priority.

In the present study I have sought to avoid giving a 'persuasive definition' to the term 'order' that would prejudge the question of the value of order as a human goal. On the other hand, I do in fact hold that order is desirable, or valuable in human affairs, and *a fortiori* in world politics.

Order in social life is desirable because it is the condition of the realisation of other values. Unless there is a pattern of human activities that sustains elementary, primary and universal goals of social life, it will not be possible to achieve or preserve objectives that are advanced, secondary or the special goals of particular societies. International order, or order within the society of states, is the condition of justice or equality among states or nations; except in a context of international order there can be no such thing as the equal rights of states to independence or of nations to govern themselves. World order, or order in the great society of all mankind, is similarly the condition of realisation of goals of human or of cosmopolitan justice; if there is not a certain minimum of security against violence, respect for undertakings and stability of rules of property, goals of political, social and economic justice for individual men or of a just distribution of burdens and rewards in relation to the world common good can have no meaning.

Thus, not only is order in world politics valuable, there is also a sense in which it is prior to other goals, such as that of justice. It does not follow from this, however, that order is to be preferred to justice in any given case. In fact ideas of both order and justice enter into the value systems, the justificatory or rhetorical stock-in-trade of all actors in world politics. The advocate of revolutionary justice looks forward to the time when a new order will consolidate the gains of the revolution. The proponent of order takes up his position partly because the existing order is, from his point of view, morally satisfactory, or not so unsatisfactory as to warrant its disturbance. The question of order *versus* justice will always be considered by the parties concerned in relation to the merits of a particular case.

When the merits of any particular case are considered, moreover, the priority of order over justice cannot be asserted without some assessment of the question whether or not or to what extent injustice is embodied in the existing order. Why do we regard the existing order as valuable? Mazrui writes that 'the importance of peace is, in the ultimate analysis, *derivative*. Taken to its deepest roots, peace is important because "the dignity and worth of the human person" are important.'[7] Those who are unwilling to jeopardise international order for the sake of anti-colonial or racial or economic justice reach their conclusions because of the assessments they make about justice as well as order, whether the former are acknowledged or not.

Furthermore, to the extent that the framework of international order is a strong one, it is able to withstand the shock of violent assaults carried out in the name of 'justice'. At the present time, for example, the nuclear peace has made the world safe for just wars of national liberation, carried out at the sub-nuclear level, and the international or interstate peace has made the world safe for just internal or civil violence.

We have also to bear in mind that whether or not there is a consensus in favour of a just change may be uncertain, and that violent assaults on the existing order aimed at just change may have the effect of altering what the existing consensus is. Sometimes it is the struggle for just change itself that creates a consensus in favour of this change that did not exist when the struggle was first undertaken. Today, for example, it may be argued that there is a consensus in international society that the sovereignty of colonial powers over their subject territories is not legitimate, and that violence waged against such powers for the aim of national liberation is just. But this consensus did not exist in the early decades of the anti-colonial struggle, and if indeed it exists today, it is a consequence of that struggle. Thus, while order in world politics is something valuable, and a condition of the realisation of other values, it should not be taken to be a commanding value, and to show that a particular institution or course of action is conducive of order is not to have established a presumption that that institution is desirable or that that course of action should be carried out.

Part 2

Order in the Contemporary International System

5

The Balance of Power and International Order

In this chapter I propose to deal with the following questions:

(i) What is the balance of power?

(ii) How does the balance of power contribute to international order?

(iii) What is the relevance of the balance of power to the maintenance of international order at present?

The Balance of Power

We mean here by 'the balance of power' what Vattel meant: 'a state of affairs such that no one power is in a position where it is preponderant and can lay down the law to others'.[1] It is normally military power that we have in mind when we use the term, but it can refer to other kinds of power in world politics as well. The state of affairs of which Vattel speaks can be realised in a number of different ways.

First, we have to distinguish a simple balance of power from a complex one, that is to say a balance made up of two powers from one consisting of three or more. The simple balance of power is exemplified by the clash of France and Habsburg Spain/Austria in the sixteenth and seventeenth centuries, and by the clash of the United States and the Soviet Union in the Cold War. The complex balance of power is illustrated by the situation of Europe in the mid-eighteenth century, when France and Austria, now detached from Spain, were joined as great powers by England, Russia and Prussia. It is also illustrated by world politics at the present juncture, when the United States and the Soviet Union have been joined by China as a great power, with Japan as a potential fourth great power and a combination of Western European powers as a potential fifth. However, no historical balance of power has ever been perfectly simple or perfectly complex. Situations of a simple balance of power have always been complicated by the existence of some other powers, whose ability to influence the course of events may be slight but is always greater than zero.[2] Situations of a complex balance of power are capable of being simplified by diplomatic combinations, as for example, the six-power balance of the pre-First World War period was resolved into the simple division of the Triple Alliance and the Triple Entente.

Whereas a simple balance of power necessarily requires equality or parity in power, a complex balance of power does not. In a situation of three or more competing powers the development of gross inequalities in power among them does not necessarily put the strongest in a position of preponderance, because the others have the possibility of combining against it.

In a simple balance of power the only means available to the power that is falling behind is to augment its own intrinsic strength (say, in the eighteenth century its territory and population; in the nineteenth century its industry and military organisation; in the twentieth century its military technology). Because in a complex balance of power there exists the additional resource of exploiting the existence of other powers, either by absorbing or partitioning them, or by allying with them, it has usually been held that complex balances of power are more stable than simple ones.[3]

Second, we must distinguish the general balance of power, that is the absence of a preponderant power in the international system as a whole, from a local or particular balance of power, in one area or segment of the system. In some areas of the world at present, such as the Middle East or the Indian subcontinent or South-east Asia, there may be said to be a local balance of power; in others, such as Eastern Europe or the Caribbean, there is a local preponderance of power. Both sorts of situation are consistent with the fact that in the international system as a whole there is a general balance of power.

The distinction between the general balance and local balances should not be confused with that between the dominant balance and subordinate balances. At the present time the Soviet-American balance of power (sometimes called the 'central balance') is the dominant balance in the world, and the local balances of the Middle East, the Indian subcontinent and South-east Asia are subordinate to it, in the sense that it affects them much more than they affect it. The powers that make up the dominant balance in some cases directly participate in a subordinate balance, as the Soviet Union and the United States are now elements in the Middle East balance. Burke uses this distinction between dominant and subordinate balances when he speaks of the relationship of Britain, France and Spain in the late eighteenth century as 'the great middle balance' of Europe, which qualified the operation of 'the balance of the north', 'the balance of Germany' and 'the balance of Italy'.[4] The dominant balance, however, is still only a particular balance, and is not to be identified with the general balance or equilibrium of the system as a whole.

Third, one should distinguish a balance of power which exists subjectively from one that exists objectively. It is one thing to say that it is generally believed that a state of affairs exists in which no one state is preponderant in military strength; it is another to say that no one state is in fact preponderant. It is sometimes generally believed that a rough balance of military strength exists between two parties when this does not reflect the 'true' position as revealed by subsequent events; in Europe in the winter of 1939–40, for example, it was widely held that a military balance existed between the Allies and Germany, but a few weeks' fighting in the spring showed that this was not the case. A balance of power in Vattel's sense requires that there should be general belief in it; it is not sufficient for the balance to exist objectively but not subjectively. If (to take the case of a simple balance of power) one state is in fact in no position to secure an easy victory over another, but is generally believed to be in this position, then it can (in Vattel's terms) 'lay down the law' to the other. The problem of maintaining a balance of power is not merely one of ensuring that a military balance exists, it is also a problem of ensuring that there exists belief in it. The main significance of a victory in the field of battle may be not what it does to affect the outcome of future battles, but what it does to affect beliefs about their outcomes. In this sense the German victory in Western Europe in 1940 did not show that the balance of power that had previously been thought to exist did not 'really' exist; it created a new situation in which what had been a balance of power was replaced by German preponderance.

But if the subjective element of belief in it is necessary for the existence of a balance of power, it is not sufficient. If a power is in fact in a position to gain an easy victory over its neighbour, even though it is generally thought to be balanced by it, this means that the beliefs on which the balance of power rests can quickly be shown to be false, and a new subjective situation brought about. A balance of power that rests not on the actual will and capacity of one state to withstand the assaults of another, but merely on bluff and appearances, is likely to be fragile and impermanent.

Fourth, we must distinguish between a balance of power which is fortuitous and one which is contrived. A fortuitous balance of power is one that arises without any conscious effort on the part of either of the parties to bring it into being. A contrived balance is one that owes its existence at least partly to the conscious policies of one or both sides.

The distinction between a balance that is fortuitous and one that is contrived should not be confused with that between policies of contriving a balance that are 'freely chosen' and those that are 'determined'. Many writers who have conceived of the balance of power as something that is consciously brought about have been insistent that states threatened by a potential dominant power have the option of failing to counterbalance it. For example, writers like Burke, Gentz and Heeren, who lived under the shadow of the possible collapse of the European balance of power due to the expansion of Revolutionary and Napoleonic France, and who urged policies of resistance to France, had a strong sense of the possibility that the rest of Europe would fail to provide a counterpoise, just as the ancient world had failed to provide a counterpoise to Rome.[5] These writers may be contrasted with those – like Rousseau and Arnold Toynbee – who view balances of power as the consequence of some historical law of challenge and response, which ensures that whenever a threat to the balance arises, some countervailing tendency will be brought into being to check it.[6] But while the former group of thinkers emphasises the possibility that a challenge to the balance of power will fail to produce a response, and the latter asserts a historical tendency for a response to arise, both view the balance of power as something that is contrived rather than fortuitous.

A purely fortuitous balance of power we may imagine to be simply a moment of deadlock in a struggle to the death between two contending powers, each of which aims only at absolute aggrandisement. The element of contrivance presupposes that at least one of the parties, instead of pursuing the goal of absolute expansion of its power, seeks to limit it in relation to the power of the other. It forms an estimate of the military strength of the opponent, and takes this into account in determining the level of its own military strength – whether it seeks a level higher, equal or lower than that of the opponent. This is the normal position of any state that is acting 'rationally' (that is, that is acting in a way that is internally consistent and consistent with given goals) within the system of power politics. The concept of a contrived balance of power, however, embraces a spectrum of possibilities.

The most elementary form of contrived balance of power is a two-power balance in which one of the parties pursues a policy of preventing the other from attaining military preponderance. A more advanced form is a three-power balance in which one power seeks to prevent any of the others from attaining preponderance, not merely by augmenting its own military strength, but also by siding with whatever is the weaker of the other two powers: the policy known as 'holding the balance'. This form of balance-of-power policy was familiar in the ancient world, as David Hume argues, relying mainly on Polybius's celebrated account of the policy of Hiero of Syracuse, who sided with Carthage against Rome.[7]

It is a further step from this to the policy of preserving a balance of power throughout the international system as a whole. This is a policy which presupposes an ability to perceive the plurality of interacting powers as comprising a single system or field of forces. It presupposes also a continuous and universal system of diplomacy, providing the power concerned with intelligence about the moves of all the states in the system, and with means of acting upon them. The policy of preserving a balance throughout the international system as a whole appears to have originated only in fifteenth-century Italy, and to have developed along with the spread of resident embassies. It became firmly implanted in European thought only in the seventeenth century, along with the notion that European politics formed a single system.[8]

It is a further step again to the conception of the balance of power as a state of affairs brought about not merely by conscious policies of particular states that oppose preponderance throughout all the reaches of the system, but as a conscious goal of the system as a whole. Such a conception implies the possibility of collaboration among states in promoting the common objective of preserving the balance, as exemplified by the successive grand alliances of modern times against potentially dominant powers. It implies also that each state should not only act to frustrate the threatened preponderance of others, but should recognise the responsibility not to upset the balance itself. It implies self-restraint as well as the restraint of others. The idea that preservation of the balance of power throughout the international system as a whole should be the common goal of all states in the system was one that emerged in Europe in the seventeenth and early eighteenth centuries, especially as part of the coalitions against Louis XIV, and which came to fruition in the preamble to the Treaty of Utrecht in 1713.

Functions of the Balance of Power

Preservation of a balance of power may be said to have fulfilled three historic functions in the modern states system:

(i) The existence of a general balance of power throughout the international system as a whole has served to prevent the system from being transformed by conquest into a universal empire;

(ii) The existence of local balances of power has served to protect the independence of states in particular areas from absorption or domination by a locally preponderant power;

(iii) Both general and local balances of power, where they have existed, have provided the conditions in which other institutions on which international order depends (diplomacy, war, international law, great power management) have been able to operate.

The idea that balances of power have fulfilled positive functions in relation to international order, and hence that contrivance of them is a valuable or legitimate object of statesmanship, has been subject to a great deal of criticism in this century. At the present time criticism focuses upon the alleged obscurity or meaninglessness of the concept, the untested or untestable nature of the historical generalisations upon which it rests, and the reliance of the theory upon the notion that all international behaviour consists of the pursuit of power. Earlier in the century, especially during and after the First World War, critics of the doctrine of the balance of power asserted not that it was unintelligible or untestable, but that pursuit of the balance of power had effects upon international order which were not positive, but negative. In particular, they asserted that the attempt to preserve a balance of power was a source of war, that it was carried out in the interests of the great powers at the expense of the interests of the small, and that it led to disregard of international law. I shall deal with these latter criticisms first.

Attempts to contrive a balance of power have not always resulted in the preservation of peace. The chief function of the balance of power, however, is not to preserve peace, but to preserve the system of states itself. Preservation of the balance of power requires war, when this is the only means whereby the power of a potentially dominant state can be checked. It can be argued, however, that the preservation of peace is a subordinate objective of the contrivance of balances of power. Balances of power which are stable (that is, which have built-in features making for their persistence) may help remove the motive to resort to preventive war.

The principle of preservation of the balance of power has undoubtedly tended to operate in favour of the great powers and at the expense of the small. Frequently, the balance of power among the great powers has been preserved through partition and absorption of the small: the extraordinary decline in the number of European states between 1648 and 1914 illustrates the attempt of large states to absorb small ones while at the same time following the principle of compensation so as to maintain a balance of power. This has led to frequent denunciation of the principle of the balance of power as nothing more than collective aggrandisement by the great powers, the classic case being the partition of Poland in 1772 by Austria, Russia and Prussia. Those who, like Gentz and Burke, argued that the partition of Poland was an aberration and a departure from the true principles of the balance of power, which enjoined respect for the independence of all states, large and small alike, took as their starting-point an idealised and legalistic conception of the balance-of-power doctrine which misconstrues its essential content. The partition of Poland was not a departure from the principle of balance of power but an application of it. (The matters discussed here are considered further in Chapter 9.)

From the point of view of a weak state sacrificed to it, the balance of power must appear as a brutal principle. But its function in the preservation of international order is not for this reason less central. It is part of the logic of the principle of balance of power that the needs of the dominant balance must take precedence over those of subordinate balances, and that the general balance must be prior in importance to any local or particular balance. If aggrandisement by the strong against the weak must take place, it is better from the standpoint of international order that it should take place without a conflagration among the strong than with one.

It is a paradox of the principle of balance of power that while the existence of a balance of power is an essential condition of the operation of international law, the steps necessary to maintain the balance often involve violation of the injunctions of international law. It is clear that situations in which one state has a position of preponderance are situations in which that state may be tempted to disregard rules of law; preponderant powers are, as Vattel perceives, in a position to 'lay down the law to others'. The most basic of the rules of international law – those dealing with sovereignty, non-intervention, diplomatic immunity and the like – depend for their effectiveness on the principle of 'reciprocity'. Where one state is preponderant, it may have the option of disregarding the rights of other states, without fear that these states will reciprocate by disregarding their rights in turn. It is this feeling that there must be some security for the observance of rules of international law other than the mere hope that a preponderant state will choose to be law-abiding that leads international lawyers like Oppenheim to the conclusion that 'the first and principal moral that can be deduced from the history of the development of the law of nations is that a law of nations can exist only if there be an equilibrium, a balance of power between the members of the family of nations'.[9]

But while international law depends for its very existence as an operating system of rules on the balance of power, preservation of the latter often requires the breaking of these rules. Rules of international law where they allow the use or threat of force at all do so only, in Grotius's phrase, 'to remedy an injury received'. Before a state may legitimately resort to force against another state there must first be a violation of legal rights which can then be forcibly defended. Preservation of the balance of power, however, requires the use or threat of force in response to the encroaching power of another state, whether or not that state has violated legal rules. Wars initiated to restore the balance of power, wars threatened to maintain it, military interventions in the internal affairs of another state to combat the encroaching power of a third state, whether or not that state has violated legal rules, bring the imperatives of the balance of power into conflict with the imperatives of international law. The requirements of order are treated as prior to those of law, as they are treated also as prior to the interests of small powers and the keeping of peace.

It is noticeable that while, at the present time, the term 'balance of power' is as widely used as at any time in the past in the every day discussion of international relations, in scholarly analyses of the subject it has been slipping into the background. This reflects impatience with the vagueness and shifting meaning of what is undoubtedly a current cant word; doubts about the historical generalisations that underlie the proposition that preservation of a balance of power is essential to international order; and doubts about its reliance on the discredited notion that the pursuit of power is the common denominator to which all foreign policy can be reduced.

The term 'balance of power' is notorious for the numerous meanings that may be attached to it, the tendency of those who use it to shift from one to another and the uncritical reverence which statements about it are liable to command.[10] It is a mistake, however, to dismiss the notion as a meaningless one, as von Justi did in the eighteenth century and Cobden in the nineteenth, and some political scientists are inclined to do now.[11] The term is not unique in suffering abuses of this kind, and as with such other overworked terms as 'democracy', 'imperialism' and 'peace', its very currency is an indication of the importance of the ideas it is intended to convey. We cannot do without the term 'balance of power' and the need is to define it carefully and use it consistently.

But if we can make clear what we mean by the proposition that preservation of the balance of power functions to preserve international order, is it true? Is it the case that a state which finds itself in a position of preponderant power will always use it to 'lay down the law to others'? Will a locally preponderant state always be a menace to the independence of its neighbours, and a generally preponderant state to the survival of the system of states?

The proposition is implicitly denied by the leaders of powerful states, who see sufficient safeguard of the rights of others in their own virtue and good intentions. Franklin Roosevelt saw the safeguard of Latin America's rights in U.S. adherence to the 'good-neighbour policy'. The United States and the Soviet Union now each recognise a need to limit the power of the other, and assert that this is a need not simply of theirs but of international society at large. But they do not admit the need for any comparable check on their own power.

One form of this view is Kant's idea that the constitutional state or *Rechtsstaat,* which has its own internal checks on the power of rulers, is capable of international virtue in a way in which the absolutist state is not. Thus he is able to recommend the formation of a coalition of *Rechtsstaaten,* which through accretion may come eventually to dominate international politics, without any sense that this coalition will abuse its power.[12] In the early 1960s doctrines of an Atlantic Community, built upon the coalition of North American and West European power, followed the Kantian pattern: they were put forward without any sense that such a coalition would seem or would be menacing to other states, or that these latter would have a legitimate interest in developing a counterpoise to it.

Against this we have to set Acton's view that power itself corrupts, that no matter what the ideology or the institutions or the virtue or good intentions of a state in a position of preponderance, that position itself contains a menace to other states which cannot be contained by agreements or laws but only by countervailing power.[13] States are not prevented from falling foul of this by constitutional systems of checks and balances; the corrupting effects of power are felt not merely by the rulers but by the political system as a whole. Rulers who cling to their virtue in situations where possibilities of vice abound tend to be replaced by rulers who do not. Fénelon puts this point well:

Il n'est pas permis d'espérer, parmi les hommes, qu'une puissance supérieure demeure dans les bornes d'une exacte modération, et qu'elle ne veuille dans sa force que ce qu'elle pourrait obtenir dans la plus grande faiblesse. Quand même un prince serait assez parfait pour faire un usage si merveilleux de sa prospérité, cette merveille finirait avec son règne. L'ambition naturelle des souverains, les flatteries de leurs conseillers et la prévention des nations entières ne permettent pas de croire qu'une nation qui peut subjuger les autres s'en abstienne pendant les siècles entiers.[14]

Criticism of the doctrine that the balance of power functions to maintain international order sometimes derives from the idea that this is part of a theory of 'power politics', which presents the pursuit of power as the common and overriding concern of all states in pursuing foreign policy. On this view the doctrine we have been discussing involves the same fallacies as the 'power-political' theory of which it is part.

Doctrines which contend that there is, in any international system, an automatic tendency for a balance of power to arise do derive from a 'power-political' theory of this kind. The idea that if one state challenges the balance of power, other states are bound to seek to prevent it, assumes that all states seek to maximise their relative power position. This is not the case. States are constantly in the position of having to choose between devoting their resources and energies to maintaining or extending their international power position, and devoting these resources and energies to other ends. The size of defence expenditure, the foreign-aid vote, the diplomatic establishment, whether or not to play a role in particular international issues by taking part in a war, joining an alliance or an international organisation, or pronouncing about an international dispute – these are the matters of which the discussion of any country's foreign policy consists, and proposals that have the effect of augmenting the country's power position can be, and frequently are, rejected. Some states which have the potential for playing a major role – one thinks of the United States in the inter-war period and Japan since her economic recovery after the Second World War – prefer to play a relatively minor one. But the doctrine I have been expounding does not assert any inevitable tendency for a balance of power to arise in the international system, only a need to maintain one if international order is to be preserved. States may and often do behave in such a way as to disregard the requirements of a balance of power.

The Present Relevance of the Balance of Power

It is clear that in contemporary international politics there does exist a balance of power which fulfils the same functions in relation to international order which it has performed in other periods. If any important qualification needs to be made to this statement it is that since the late 1950s there has existed another phenomenon which in some respects is a special case of the balance of power but in other respects is different: mutual nuclear deterrence. In a final section of this chapter I shall consider the meaning of mutual nuclear deterrence and its relation to the balance of power.

There clearly does now exist a general balance of power in the sense that no one state is preponderant in power in the international system as a whole. The chief characteristic of this general balance is that whereas in the 1950s it took the form of a simple balance (though not a perfectly simple one), and in the 1960s was in a state of transition, in the 1970s it takes the form of a complex balance. At least in the Asian and Pacific region China has to be counted as a great power alongside the United States and the Soviet Union; while Japan figures as a potential fourth great power and a united Western Europe may in time become a fifth. However, the statement that there is now a complex or multilateral balance of power has given rise to a number of misunderstandings, and it is necessary to clear these away.

To speak of a complex or multiple balance among these three or four powers is not to imply that they are equal in strength. Whereas in a system dominated by two powers a situation of balance or absence of preponderance can be achieved only if there is some rough parity of strength between the powers concerned, in a system of three or more powers balance can be achieved without a relationship of equality among the powers concerned because of the possibility of combination of the lesser against the greater.

Moreover, to speak of such a complex balance of power is not to imply that all four great states command the same kind of power or influence. Clearly, in international politics moves are made on 'many chess-boards'. On the chess-board of strategic nuclear deterrence the United States and the Soviet Union are supreme players, China is a novice and Japan does not figure at all. On the chess-board of conventional military strength the United States and the Soviet Union, again, are leading players because of their ability to deploy non-nuclear armed force in many parts of the world, China is a less important player because the armed force it has can be deployed only in its own immediate vicinity, and Japan is only a minor player. On the chess-boards of international monetary affairs and international trade and investment the United States and Japan are leading players, the Soviet Union much less important and China relatively unimportant. On the chess-board of influence derived from ideological appeal it is arguable that China is the pre-eminent player.

However, the play on each of these chess-boards is related to the play on each of the others. An advantageous position in the international politics of trade or investment may be used to procure advantages in the international politics of military security; a weak position on the politics of strategic nuclear deterrence may limit and circumscribe the options available in other fields. It is from this interrelatedness of the various chess-boards that we derive the conception of over-all power and influence in international politics, the common denominator in respect of which we say that there is balance rather than preponderance. Overall power in this sense cannot be precisely quantified: the relative importance of strategic, economic and politico-psychological ingredients in national power (and of different kinds of each of these) is both uncertain and changing. But the relative position of states in terms of overall power nevertheless makes itself apparent in bargaining among states, and the conception of over-all power is one we cannot do without.

Furthermore, to speak of the present relations of the great powers as a complex balance is not to imply that they are politically equidistant from one another, or that there is complete diplomatic mobility among them. At the time of writing a *détente* exists between the United States and the Soviet Union, and between the United States and China, but not between the Soviet Union and China. Japan, while it has asserted a measure of independence of the United States and improved its relations with both the Soviet Union and China, is still more closely linked both strategically and economically to the United States than to any of the others. While, therefore, the four major powers have more diplomatic mobility than they had in the period of the simple balance of power, their mobility is still limited, especially by the persistence of tension between the two communist great powers so considerable as to preclude effective collaboration between them.

We have also to note that the complex balance of power that now exists does not rest on any system of general collaboration or concert among the great powers concerned. There is not any general agreement among the United States, the Soviet Union, China and Japan on the proposition that the maintenance of a general balance of power is a common objective, the proposition proclaimed by the European great powers in the Treaty of Utrecht. Nor is there any general agreement about a system of rules for avoiding or controlling crises, or for limiting wars. (These matters are discussed further in Chapter 9.)

The present balance of power is not wholly fortuitous in the sense defined above, for there is an element of contrivance present in the 'rational' pursuit by the United States, the Soviet Union and China of policies aimed at preventing the preponderance of any of the others. It may be argued also that there is a further element of contrivance in the agreement between the United States and the Soviet Union on the common objective of maintaining a balance between themselves, at least in the limited sphere of strategic nuclear weapons. There is not, however, a contrived balance of power in the sense that all three or four great powers accept it as common objective – indeed, it is only the United States that explicitly avows the balance of power as a goal. Nor is there any evidence that such a balance of power is generally thought to imply self-restraint on the part of the great powers themselves, as distinct from the attempt to restrain or constrain one another.

The United States and the Soviet Union have developed some agreed rules in relation to the avoidance and control of crises and the limitation of war. There is not, however, any general system of rules among the great powers as a whole in these areas. Neither in the field of Sino-Soviet relations nor in that of Sino-American relations does there exist any equivalent of the nascent system of rules evolving between the two global great powers. In the absence of any such general system of rules, we cannot speak of there being, in addition to a balance among the great powers, a concert of great powers concerned with the management of this balance.

Finally, the present complex balance of power does not rest on a common culture shared by the major states participating in it, comparable with that shared by the European great powers that made up the complex balances of the eighteenth and nineteenth centuries (to be discussed further in Chapter 13). In the European international system of those centuries one factor that facilitated both the maintenance of the balance itself and co-operation among the powers that contributed to it was their sharing of a common culture, both in the sense of a common intellectual tradition and stock of ideas that facilitated communication, and in the sense of common values, in relation to which conflicts of interest could be moderated. Among the United States, the Soviet Union, China and

Japan there does exist, as will be argued later, some common stock of ideas, but there is no equivalent of the bonds of common culture among European powers in earlier centuries.

All five of the misunderstandings that have been mentioned arise from the fact that in present-day thinking the idea of a balance of power tends to be confused with the European balance-of-power system, particularly that of the nineteenth century. The latter system is commonly said to have been characterised by rough equality among the five principal powers (Britain, France, Austria-Hungary, Russia and Prussia-Germany); by comparability in the kind of power available to each, which could be measured in terms of numbers of troops; by political equidistance among the powers and maximum diplomatic mobility; by general agreement as to the rules of the game; and by an underlying common culture.

Whether or not the European system of the last century in fact possessed all these qualities might be disputed. Thus there were substantial inequalities between the five powers at different times. It was never possible to reduce British sea power and financial power, and continental land power, to a common denominator. There were ideological inhibitions to diplomatic mobility arising from associations such as the Holy Alliance, the *Dreikaiserbund* and the 'Liberal Alliance' of Britain and France. We do have to recognise, however, that the European balance of the nineteenth century was only one historical manifestation of a phenomenon that has occurred in many periods and continents, and that in asserting that there exists a complex balance of power at the present time we are not contending that this embodies every feature of the European model of the last century.

This presently existing balance of power appears to fulfil the same three functions in relation to international order that it has performed in earlier periods, and that were mentioned in the last section. First, the general balance of power serves to prevent the system of states from being transformed by conquest into a universal empire. While the balance continues to be maintained, no one of the great powers has the option of establishing a world government by force (see Chapter 11).

Second, local balances of power – where they exist – serve to protect the independence of states in particular areas from absorption or domination by a locally preponderant power. At the present time the independence of states in the Middle East, in the Indian subcontinent, in the Korean peninsular and in peninsula South-east Asia is assisted by the existence in these areas of local balances of power. By contrast, in Eastern Europe where there is a Soviet preponderance and in Central America and the Caribbean, where there is a U.S. preponderance, local states cannot be said to be independent in the normal sense. It would be going too far to assert that the existence of a local balance of power is a necessary condition of the independence of states in any area. To assert this would be to ignore the existence of the factor of a sense of political community in the relations between two states, the consequence of which may be that a locally preponderant state is able, up to a point, to respect the independence of a weaker neighbour, as the United States respects the independence of Canada, or Britain respects the independence of Eire. We have also to recognise that the independence of states in a particular area may owe less to the existence or non-existence of a balance among the local powers than to the part played in the local equilibrium by powers external to the region: if a balance exists at present between Israel and her Arab neighbours, for example, this balance owes its existence to the role played in the area by great powers external to it.

Third, both the general balance of power, and such local balances as exist at present, help to provide the conditions in which other institutions on which international order depends are able to operate. International law, the diplomatic system, war and the management of the international system by the great powers assume a situation in which no one power is preponderant in strength. All are institutions which depend heavily on the possibility that if one state violates the rules, others can take reciprocal action. But a state which is in a position of preponderant power, either in the system as a whole or in a particular area, may be in a position to ignore international law, to disregard the rules and procedures of diplomatic intercourse, to deprive its adversaries of the possibility of resort to war in defence of their interests and rights, or to ignore the conventions of the comity of great powers, all with impunity.

Mutual Nuclear Deterrence

Since the 1950s there has existed another institution or quasi-institution which is in some respects a special case of the balance of power and in other respects different: mutual nuclear deterrence. In this final section I shall consider the following:

(i) What is the balance of terror or relationship of mutual nuclear deterrence?

(ii) How is mutual nuclear deterrence related to the balance of power?

(iii) How does mutual nuclear deterrence function in relation to international order?

In dealing with the first of these questions we shall begin by considering the meaning of deterrence; then consider the meaning of mutual deterrence; and finally set out what is involved in the special case with which we are concerned, mutual nuclear deterrence.

To say that Country A deters Country B from doing something is to imply the following:

(i) That Country A conveys to Country B a threat to inflict punishment or deprivation of values if it embarks on a certain course of action;

(ii) That Country B might otherwise embark on that course of action;

(iii) That Country B believes that Country A has the capacity and the will to carry out the threat, and decides for this reason that the course of action is not worthwhile.

All three of these conditions have to be fulfilled if we are to speak of deterrence. To take the first, there has to be a threat conveyed by the deterrer to the deterred. If, for example, the Soviet Union desisted from attacking the United States because it believed that the United States would inflict intolerable punishment in retaliation, but the United States had not in fact conveyed any such threat of punishment, we could not say that the United States had deterred a Soviet attack. There has to be the conveying of a threat if the deterrer is to take credit for the result.

To take the second condition, there has to be some possibility that the country that is the object of the threat will undertake the course of action from which the deterrer wishes it to desist. If there is, in fact, no possibility that the Soviet Union will attack the United States in any circumstances, then even though the United States has conveyed threats of punishment and the Soviet Union has desisted from attacking the United States, we cannot say that the Soviet Union has been deterred from doing so. We should note, however, that policies of deterrence may have a rationale independently of whether the country at which they are aimed has a present intention to initiate an attack. It may be argued, for example, that U.S. policies aimed at deterrence of Soviet attack are justified by the objective of creating a feeling of security from attack within the United States, or by the objective of discouraging the emergence within the Soviet Union of an intent to attack, even though there is no evidence of any present intent.

To take the third condition, the country threatened with punishment is not deterred unless it believes that the country making the threat has the capacity and the will to carry it out, and decides for this reason that the course of action it would otherwise follow is not worthwhile. The threat that is conveyed by the deterrer has to be 'credible' to the country deterred; and it has to be judged by the latter to render the course of action contemplated unacceptable or not worthwhile. Whether or not the punishment threatened (assessed in terms of the probability of it as well as the extent of it) renders the course of action unacceptable will of course vary with circumstances: what the country (or particular leaders of it) hopes to gain from doing the thing in question or to lose by not doing it, what importance it attaches to the values of which the deterrer threatens to deprive it, and so on. It is for this reason that there is no absolute 'level of damage' which is necessary and sufficient to deter a country from doing something.

Deterrence of attacks by other powers has always been one of the objects for which states have sought to use their military forces. What is novel about deterrence in the age of nuclear weapons is that states have been driven to elevate it to the status of a prime object of policy by their reluctance to use nuclear weapons in actual war. The policies or strategies of deterrence that have been evolved vary along three separate dimensions: the range of actions from which it is hoped to deter the adversary; the priority accorded to deterrence in the scheme of policy; and the force threatened to produce deterrence.

Thus in the United States the object of policy has been envisaged as to deter the Soviet Union from a nuclear attack on the United States; from any attack on the United States; from a nuclear attack on the United States or its allies; and from any attack on the United States and its allies. These contrasts have sometimes been referred to in terms of a choice between 'finite deterrence' and 'extended deterrence'.

Deterrence has been envisaged, as in the 1957 U.K. Defence White Paper, as the sole object of policy for nuclear weapons ('deterrence only'), or 'deterrence plus defence', or, as in the later years of Robert McNamara's Secretaryship of Defence, in terms of a combination of deterrence and other objectives, such as 'damage limitation'.

The force required to achieve deterrence has not only been seen in terms of nuclear weapons, but also in terms of a combination of nuclear and conventional weapons: in terms of a single massive threat or a series of graduated threats (Siessor's 'the great deterrent' *versus* Buzzard's 'graduated deterrents', or Dulles's 'massive retaliation' *versus* McNamara's 'flexible response').[15]

Mutual deterrence is a state of affairs in which two or more powers deter each other from doing something. In the broadest sense it may be a state of affairs in which the powers deter each other from a wide range of actions by a wide range of kinds of threat. These actions and threats need not be nuclear in nature, nor military at all. Nor need the threat conveyed by the deterrer constitute retaliation in kind; powers may be deterred from a chemical weapons attack by a threat of retaliation with conventional or nuclear weapons, or they may be deterred from military attacks by threats of economic reprisals. Here, however, I wish to focus upon the special case of mutual nuclear deterrence: a state of affairs in which two or more powers deter one another from deliberate nuclear attack by the threat of nuclear retaliation.

As with the state of affairs we have called a 'balance of power', a situation of mutual nuclear deterrence may be realised in a simple, two-power relationship or in a more complex relationship of three or more powers. At the present time there is a relationship of mutual nuclear deterrence between the United States and the Soviet Union, and one growing up also between China and the Soviet Union and between China and the United States. Some would claim that Britain and the Soviet Union and France and the Soviet Union are also in this relationship. A three- (or more) power relationship of mutual nuclear deterrence is the sum of the bilateral relationships involved, not (as in the case of the balance of power) the product of these relationships as a whole. As in the case of the balance of power, again, mutual nuclear deterrence might in principle be realised either generally or locally. If the spread of nuclear weapons proceeded so far as to enable every state to deter every other state from nuclear attack – or if (to take a more likely hypothesis) all states were consolidated under one or another existing 'nuclear umbrella' – there might arise a general situation of mutual nuclear deterrence, the state of affairs which Morton Kaplan calls a 'unit veto system' (discussed further in Chapter 11).[16] At present there are only particular or local relationships of mutual nuclear deterrence.

As in the case of the balance of power, again, situations of mutual nuclear deterrence may in principle arise fortuitously or as the result of contrivance. The Soviet-American relationship of mutual nuclear deterrence arose in the late 1950s as the results of efforts on the part of each to deter the other, if not to gain a strategic nuclear ascendancy over the other. A central idea of advocates of arms control has been that the situation which arose thus fortuitously could be preserved only by conscious, collaborative efforts to bring this about: that left to its own logic or momentum, strategic nuclear competition between the super powers could lead to the undermining of mutual nuclear deterrence, and that collaboration in the field of arms control had therefore to be directed towards preserving the stability of the relationship of mutual nuclear deterrence.[17]

Mutual Nuclear Deterrence and the Balance of Power

The idea of a contrived relationship of mutual nuclear deterrence is in some respects similar to that of a contrived balance of power, but in other respects different. First, a relationship of mutual nuclear deterrence between two powers is only part of the relationship of balance of power between them, the latter being made up of all the ingredients of national power, of which the exploitation of nuclear force is only one. Where, in a two-power situation, one of the powers has the ability to strike at the other with nuclear weapons, the creation of a relationship of mutual nuclear deterrence is a necessary condition of a balance of power between them. But it is not a sufficient condition. At the present time, as we have noted, there appears to be developing a relationship of mutual nuclear deterrence between the Soviet Union and China and between the United States and China, and some would argue that there is mutual nuclear deterrence between France and the Soviet Union and between Britain and the Soviet Union. But no one would argue that in any of these relationships the two states concerned were equal in power.

Second, whereas in a simple or two-power situation a balance requires equality or parity in military strength, a relationship of mutual deterrence does not; it requires only that each power has sufficient nuclear striking power for the purpose of deterring a nuclear attack. For each power there is a threshold level of damage with which it needs to be able to threaten the other; a degree of nuclear strength that cannot threaten this level of damage will be insufficient for the purpose of deterrence, and a degree of strength that can threaten more than this level will be redundant for this purpose, although it may still be justified by other strategic criteria such as the need to limit damage, to 'extend' deterrence so as to cover allies, or to fortify the country's diplomatic position for purposes of crisis bargaining.

The irrelevance of equality or parity to mutual nuclear deterrence in a two-power situation can be seen in the case of the United States and the Soviet Union. From the time when the relationship of mutual nuclear deterrence first arose between the two super powers, at the earliest in the mid-1950s, until the end of the 1960s the United States had a clear superiority over the Soviet Union in all of the relevant indices of strategic nuclear strength: total numbers of strategic nuclear delivery vehicles (ICBMS, SLBMs and long-range bombers), total megatonnage of nuclear stockpiles, and total numbers of deliverable nuclear warheads. By the end of the 1960s the Soviet Union had achieved 'parity' in some of these indices. The United States' loss of strategic 'superiority', it may be argued, has deprived it of an important diplomatic advantage, and has contributed to a shift in the balance of power away from the United States and towards the Soviet Union. But it has not in itself undermined the relationship of mutual deterrence, which persists independently of fluctuations in the balance of strategic nuclear strength.

In a complex balance of power involving three or more states, as argued above, maintenance of the balance does not require equality or parity because inequalities can be corrected by alliance agreements. In a complex situation of mutual nuclear deterrence such as the three-sided relationship now emerging between the Soviet

Union, the United States and China, alliance arrangements or *ad hoc* combinations may also play a role. It is conceivable, for example, that joint Soviet-American threats directed against China could undermine the credibility of Chinese threats of nuclear retaliation in a way that neither the United States nor the Soviet Union could accomplish singly. Similarly joint American-Chinese threats directed at the Soviet Union might serve to establish China's deterrent *vis-à-vis* the Soviet Union at a time when the ability of China herself to deter Soviet attack was in doubt. A French theorist, André Beaufre, at one time argued that the West's ability to deter Soviet attack was strengthened by the fact that there existed three separate centres of nuclear decision in the West – Washington, London and Paris.[18] But alliance combinations in a many-sided relationship of mutual nuclear deterrence have a different function from those that take place to maintain a complex balance of power: they are still concerned with providing a deterrent that is sufficient for the purpose in hand, rather than with adding the military strength of one country to another in such a way as to ensure that no power is preponderant.

Third, whereas the balance of power is essentially an objective phenomenon, the relationship of mutual deterrence is essentially subjective. The state of affairs we call a 'balance of power', it was argued above, is defined by the actual absence of any preponderant power, and not merely by belief that no power is preponderant. Mutual nuclear deterrence, by contrast, is essentially a state of belief: the belief on each side that the other has the will and the capacity to retaliate to a sufficient level. In principle two powers could deter each other from nuclear attack by bluff both as to their will and as to their capacity.

Robert McNamara has argued strongly that the deterrent policy of the United States can be effective only if there is an actual will to carry out threatened nuclear retaliation, together with actual capacity to achieve 'assured destruction'.[19] It seems likely that this is the actual policy of the United States, and it may well be that any attempt to base nuclear deterrence on bluff as to will or capacity carries great risks that the bluff will be called. Nevertheless, an actual will and capacity to retaliate is not part of the definition of mutual deterrence. McNamara's doctrine on this point, even if it is correct, shows only that the actual will and capacity to retaliate is essential to producing the adversary's belief in it.

Fourth, whereas the balance of power has as its primary functions the preservation of the international system and the independence of states, and has the preservation of peace as only an incidental consequence, the preservation of mutual nuclear deterrence has (as we shall see) the preservation of nuclear peace as its primary function.

The Functions of Mutual Nuclear Deterrence

The relationship of mutual nuclear deterrence, which so far exists unambiguously only between the United States and the Soviet Union, may be said to have fulfilled the following functions.

(i) It has helped to preserve the nuclear peace, at least between the United States and the Soviet Union, by rendering deliberate resort to nuclear war by either one of them 'irrational' as an instrument of policy.

(ii) It has also served to preserve peace between the two leading nuclear powers, which are reluctant to enter directly into non-nuclear hostilities with one another, for fear of expansion of the conflict; and peace between states that are allies of these two powers, because of the restraint exercised by the latter upon them.

(iii) It has contributed to the maintenance of a general balance of power in the international system by helping to stabilise the dominant balance, that is, the balance between the two global great powers. Thus, indirectly, the relationship of mutual nuclear deterrence has contributed to the functions fulfilled by the general balance of power: maintenance of the system of states, of the independence of states and of the conditions under which other institutions concerned with international order can operate effectively.

It is important to understand the limitations within which the preservation of mutual nuclear deterrence may be said to carry out its major function of contributing to the preservation of the nuclear peace. First, mutual nuclear deterrence can make deliberate resort to nuclear war 'irrational' as an instrument of policy only so long as it is stable, that is, it has a built-in tendency to persist. 'The balance of terror' is not created by the mere existence of nuclear weapons in the hands of two adversaries, nor does it persist automatically while these weapons continue to be available. In principle a relationship of mutual deterrence may be upset by one or both of two technological developments: the acquisition by one side or both of an effective defence of cities and populations against strategic nuclear attack; or the development by one side or both of an effective means of disarming the other's strategic nuclear retaliatory forces before they are brought into action. It is also vulnerable in principle to change in the political and psychological dimensions of mutual nuclear deterrence: in the will or resolve of the deterrer to carry out his threat, in the ability of the deterrer to cause the deterred to believe that he can and will do so and in the assessment which the deterred makes as to whether or not the risks that the threat will be carried out are worth incurring.

Second, while the relationship of mutual nuclear deterrence persists, and deliberate resort to nuclear war is rendered irrational there are still dangers of nuclear war arising by accident or miscalculation, which the relationship of mutual nuclear deterrence by itself does nothing to assuage. It is beyond our present task to consider the steps that have been taken and might be taken to deal with these possibilities; the only point here is that the measures which the nuclear powers take, unilaterally or jointly, to reduce the likelihood of war by 'accident' or miscalculation, or to control it if it occurs, lie outside the field of actions taken to preserve mutual nuclear deterrence.

Third, mutual nuclear deterrence, while it persists and helps to make nuclear war unlikely in itself, does nothing to solve the problem of limiting or controlling a nuclear war that has broken out. Unilateral strategic policies of 'deterrence only' have long been criticised for failing to answer the question: 'what if deterrence fails?' Arms-control arrangements founded upon the idea that mutual nuclear deterrence is a self-sufficient goal in the strategic nuclear field are open to the same criticism. 'Deterrence only' is an insufficient goal in both strategy and arms control, and proposals drawn up in terms of it may have the effect not merely of failing to insure against the possibility that nuclear war will break out, but of obstructing the business of controlling it if it does.

Fourth, the idea of mutual nuclear deterrence as a source of the nuclear peace places a tremendous burden upon the supposition that men can be expected to act 'rationally'. When we say that action is rational all we mean is that it is internally consistent and consistent with given goals. There is no such thing as 'rational action' in the sense of action dictated by 'reason' as against 'the passions', a faculty present in all men and enjoining them to act in the same way. When we say that it is 'irrational' for a statesman deliberately to choose to bring about the destruction or devastation of his own country, all we mean is that such an action is not consistent with the goals which statesmen are normally expected to pursue. This does not mean that they will not act in this way or have not done so in the past.

Fifth, to say that mutual nuclear deterrence carries out this function in relation to preservation of peace is not to endorse the proposition that international security is enhanced by the presence of nuclear weapons on both sides in international conflicts. Elsewhere I have argued that if it were possible to return to the world that existed before the development of nuclear technology (which it is not), international security would be enhanced, even if this meant that wars, though less potentially catastrophic, were more likely.[20] I have also argued against the notion that international security is enhanced by the spread of nuclear weapons.[21] But in an international system in which nuclear technology is ineradicably present, and in which possession of nuclear weapons has spread beyond the original custodians of them, one must recognise the positive functions performed by relationships of mutual nuclear deterrence among the nuclear powers.

Sixth, the preservation of mutual nuclear deterrence obstructs the long-term possibility of establishing international order on some more positive basis. The preservation of peace among the major powers by a system in which each threatens to destroy or cripple the civil society of the other, rightly seen as a contemporary form of security through the holding of hostages, reflects the weakness in international society of the sense of common interest. It is for this reason that some theorists of arms control have been drawn to advocate the attempt to base strategic arms policy and strategic arms understandings on defence rather than deterrence, and that the global great powers, even in reaching understandings (like the Moscow Agreements of May 1972) that tend to confirm the relationship of mutual nuclear deterrence, are reluctant to state explicitly that this is the basis of their understanding.

6

International Law and International Order

In this chapter I propose to consider the following questions:

(i) What is international law, and what bearing does it have on international behaviour?

(ii) What is the role of international law in relation to international order?

(iii) What is the role of international law in relation to international order in the special circumstances of the present time?

The Nature of International Law

International law may be regarded as a body of rules which binds states and other agents in world politics in their relations with one another and is considered to have the status of law. This is a definition which some authorities would challenge and which therefore requires further elucidation.

The definition I have put forward identifies international law as a particular kind of *body of rules*. Some international lawyers reject the conception of international law as a body of rules and instead define it as a particular kind of social process. This is a point of view which originated with the American school of 'legal realism' and is at present associated with the work of the Yale school of international law, especially that of Myres S. McDougal.[1] McDougal and his school insist that law should be regarded as a social process, more particularly as a process of decision-making that is both authoritative and effective. They reject the idea of law as a 'body of rules' because they hold that this process of authoritative and effective decision-making does not consist simply of the application of a previously existing body of rules, but is shaped by social, moral and political considerations as well. They also hold that these social, moral and political goals should play a central part in legal decision-making. The conception of law as a 'body of rules' they see as one which restricts the scope of social, moral and political considerations in legal, and especially judicial, decision-making.

Rules are general imperative propositions; a *body* of rules is a group of such general imperative propositions that are linked logically to one another in such a way as to have a common structure. To assert the validity of a rule of international law (or of municipal law, or of morality, or of a game) is to say that it meets some test that is laid down by another rule. Reasoning about international law, therefore, like reasoning about any other body of rules, is reasoning on a normative plane and not on an empirical or factual one.

But to the extent that rules of international law actually influence behaviour in world politics, they are part of social reality. Indeed, a body of rules which had no such existence in social reality, which existed only on a normative plane, would be unlikely to interest us. In this sense the view of the Yale international lawyers and others that law is 'a social process' is a correct one. It may be conceded, furthermore, that the actual social process of legal decision-making, in the international as in the municipal setting, is not a pure process of the application of existing legal rules, but reflects the influence of a variety of factors 'extraneous' to legal rules themselves, such as the social, moral and political outlook of judges, legal advisers and legal scholars. Moreover, there is a proper place in legal decision-making for social, moral and political principles that do not derive from the law itself.

But without reference to a body of rules the idea of law is quite unintelligible. On the normative plane, reasoning about the validity of law may legitimately encompass considerations other than the content of the legal rules, but if the latter were to be dispensed with all legal reasoning would be meaningless. On the factual plane, if we are to recognise legal decision-making as a distinct social process and distinguish it from other processes of decision-making, it can only be by recognising that it is a process whose central and distinguishing feature is the attempt to shape decisions in relation to an agreed body of legal rules.

The definition of international law that has been put forward describes international law as a body of rules governing the mutual interaction not only of states but of *other agents* in international politics. In the last century it was commonly held that only states were subjects of international law, and that whatever part might actually be played in international politics by agents other than states – for example, by individual human beings, by groups other than states, or by international or intergovernmental organisations – these could figure in international law only as objects of it and not as subjects. At the present time, however, many international lawyers consider that individual human beings, groups other than states, and international organisations are subjects of international law in the same sense that states themselves are – that is to say, that they are not merely affected by the rules of international law but have duties and rights conferred upon them by these rules.

International law, in the definition that has been given, is taken to be a body of rules which is considered to have *the status of law*. That there are rules which states and other agents in international politics regard as binding on one another, there can be no doubt. It is by virtue of this fact that we may speak of the existence of an international society. But whether or not these rules, or some of them, have the status of law, is a matter of controversy.

Throughout modern history there has been a tradition of thought which has sought to deny that international law is 'law' properly so-called, on the grounds that an essential feature of law is that it is the product of sanctions, force or coercion. The origins of this tradition lie in the view of Hobbes that, 'where there is no common power, there is no law'.[2] It received its most celebrated statement in the doctrine of John Austin that law is 'the command of the sovereign', and that since there exists no sovereign in international society (no 'determinate human persons, to whom the bulk of society pay habitual obedience, and who do not habitually obey any other person'), international law is not 'law' properly so-called but is merely 'positive international morality'.[3] The Austinian view of law is powerfully maintained, although with important modifications, in the contemporary doctrine of Hans Kelsen that law is distinguished from other kinds of social order (for example, from religious orders based on supernatural sanctions, and from moral orders based on voluntary obedience) by its character as a 'coercive order'.[4] The essential feature of a rule of law, in Kelsen's view, is that it stipulates that a delict (or violation of a norm) ought to be followed by a sanction (or threatened evil).

Whatever the difficulties of the Austinian view, it does help to bring out the fact that international law, whether or not it is 'law' properly so-called, differs from municipal law in one central respect: whereas law within the modern state is backed up by the authority of a government, including its power to use or threaten force, international law is without this kind of prop.

It does not follow from this, however, that international law does not deserve the name 'law'. This conclusion is resisted by two groups of theorists: those who argue that international law, though operating in the absence of a world government, nevertheless does rest on sanctions, force or coercion; and those who accept that international law does not rest on coercion, but question the assumption that law has to be defined in terms of coercion.

An important representative of the former group is Hans Kelsen himself. Kelsen accepts the basic Austinian notion of law as a 'coercive order'. He argues, furthermore, that it is a characteristic of law that it establishes a 'force monopoly of the community', in the sense that where there is a legal order the use of force is either a violation of the law, or is an enforcement action carried out on behalf of the community. He argues, however, that international law is a 'coercive order' which rests on decentralised sanctions rather than centralised ones.

Within the state, according to Kelsen, the law is enforced by a central authority entrusted with this task. In international society, by contrast, sanctions are applied by individual members of the society according to the principle of self-help. The sanctions include reprisals and war. They may be undertaken not only by the state that is the immediate victim of a violation of the law, but also by other states which come to its assistance. Acts of reprisal or war that are carried out in order to enforce the law represent action on behalf of the community.

Kelsen's contention is that in international law, as in certain systems of primitive law in which sanctions are authorised by general acceptance of the principle of 'blood revenge', the essential element of coercion is present by virtue of the willingness and the ability of individual members of the society to enforce their rights by resort to self-help. The principle of self-help, he argues, is present also in national or municipal society, inasmuch as while the enforcement of the law rests primarily on the 'centralised' enforcement mechanism of the state, individual citizens do retain certain elementary rights of self-defence. Kelsen recognises also that international society may contain some elements of a centralised enforcement mechanism, such as that provided for it in the collective security mechanisms of the League and the United Nations. The contrast between municipal law and international law, therefore, is between a legal order that is 'relatively centralised' and one that is 'relatively decentralised'. In both kinds of legal order, however, there is a 'force monopoly of the community'.[5]

The efficacy of international law in international society does in fact depend on measures of self-help. In the absence of a central authority with preponderant power, some rules of international law are in fact upheld by measures of self-help, including the threat and use of force, by individual states. When a state is subject to attack or threat of attack and its right to independence placed in jeopardy, and it resorts to force in self-defence, we may recognise not only that it is enforcing its rights under the law but also that these rights cannot be upheld in any other way. While it is not the case that every rule of international law depends for its effectiveness on coercive acts of self-help, the system of international law as a whole may depend on some such resort to self-help. It is for this reason that there exists an intimate connection between the effectiveness of international law in international society and the functioning of the balance of power (see Chapter 5). It is only if power, and the will to use it, are distributed in international society in such a way that states can uphold at least certain rights when they are infringed, that respect for rules of international law can be maintained.

But while resort to reprisals and war by states often has the effect that the law is upheld, this is not to say that what principally motivates states which resort to reprisals and war in these cases is the desire to enforce the law. States resort to force for a variety of motives that are political in nature: the hope of material gain; the fear of other states; and the desire to make them conform to a faith or a doctrine (see Chapter 8). The belief that the rights of the state have been infringed, and that they should be set right by remedial or punitive action, may not be present at all among these motives;

and where it is present, it may be only one of a number of motives, and not the strongest.

Moreover, even in cases where, it may be argued, resort to force by a state does have the effect of vindicating rights held under international law, or of asserting the authority of the law, it may be difficult to find evidence that this is how the matter is viewed in international society at large. The central difficulty of Kelsen's position is that, in particular cases, international society is not able to reach a consensus as to which side in a war represents the lawbreakers and which side the international community. In Kelsen's view, war, when it breaks out, must be either a delict or a sanction. Only if this is so can it be said that in international society there is a 'force monopoly of the community'. But whether or not legal analysis can always show that war is either a breach of the law or an act of law enforcement, the fact is that international society can seldom, if ever, be mobilised behind such an interpretation. The typical case is that in which states are not agreed as to which side in a conflict, if either, possesses a just cause. There may be deep disagreement among states as to which side represents the community and which the lawbreakers, or there may be general concurrence in treating the war as purely political in nature. The view of the nineteenth-century positivist international lawyers, that the law did not seek to distinguish between just and unjust causes of war, was one which was founded upon recognition of the actual lack of solidarity in international society in this regard. The idea of international law as a coercive order based on a system of sanctions which is decentralised is a fiction which, when applied to reality, strains against the facts.[6] An alternative way of defending the view that international law is truly 'law' is to question the doctrine of Hobbes and his successors that law necessarily involves sanctions, force or coercion. The conception of legal rules as rules backed up by sanctions is one derived from municipal law. It may be argued that sanctions are not a necessary feature of legal rules as such; indeed, it maybe questioned whether the conception of law as a coercive social order can be strictly applied even to systems of municipal law.

H. L. A. Hart, for example, contends that the conception of law as 'orders backed by threats' is inapplicable to municipal law in a number of respects. Although a criminal-law statute, of all varieties of law, comes closest to resembling orders backed by threats, such a statute nevertheless differs from orders in that it commonly applies to those who enact it and not merely to others. Varieties of municipal law which confer legal powers to adjudicate or legislate, or which create or vary legal relations, cannot be regarded as orders backed by threats. There are legal rules which differ from orders in their mode of origin, because they are not brought into being by anything analogous to prescription. Finally, Hart argues that the analysis of law in terms of the sovereign habitually obeyed, and necessarily exempt from all legal limitation, fails to account for the continuity of a modern legal system.[7]

Hart argues that what distinguishes a legal system is not the presence of a sovereign able to back up rules with force, but 'the union of primary and secondary rules'. Primary rules are those which require human beings to do or abstain from certain actions: examples are the rules restricting violence, requiring the keeping of promises or protecting property. Secondary rules are rules about rules: they do not so much impose duties, as confer powers on human beings 'to introduce new primary rules, to extinguish or modify old ones, or in various ways determine their incidence or control their operations'.[8] Such rules are those, for example, which establish legislative, executive or judicial powers.

Hart notes that it is possible to imagine a society which exists by primary rules alone, and that studies of primitive societies claim that this possibility is realised. He remarks, however, that such a structure of purely primary or 'unofficial' rules is bound to have certain defects, and that the remedy for these defects lies in supplementing the simple structure of primary rules with secondary rules, or rules about rules.

Where there are only primary rules, 'the rules by which the society lives will not form a system, but will simply be a set of separate standards, without any identifying or common mark, except of course that they are the rules which a particular group of human beings accept'.[9] Hence, if doubts arise as to what the rules are, there is no procedure for settling this doubt. This defect, the defect of *uncertainty,* is remedied by what Hart calls 'rules of recognition'. These 'will specify some feature or features possession of which by a suggested rule is taken as a conclusive affirmative indication that it is a rule of the group to be supported by the social pressure it exerts'.[10] This feature may be no more than an authoritative list or text of the rules, to be found in some written document or carved on some monument; or, in a complex society, the characteristic may be their having been enacted by a specific body, or their long acceptance in customary practice, or their relation to judicial decisions. It is by virtue of the presence of this rule or standard of recognition (the equivalent, in Hart's theory, of the 'basic norm' in Kelsen's jurisprudence) that we may speak of a set of rules as forming together a legal system.

When there is merely a set of primary rules, moreover, these rules will have a *static* character; there will be no means of deliberately adapting the rules to changing circumstances, by eliminating old rules or introducing new ones.

> The only mode of change in the rules known to such a society will be the slow process of growth, whereby courses of conduct once thought optional become first habitual or usual, and then obligatory, and the converse process of decay, when deviations, once severely dealt with, are first tolerated and then pass unnoticed.[11]

The remedy for this defect lies in another kind of secondary rule, 'rules of change', which empower individuals or bodies to introduce new primary rules and to eliminate old ones.

A third defect of the simple form of social life in which primary rules are present is 'the *inefficiency* of the diffuse social pressure by which the rules are maintained'. Disputes as to whether or not a particular rule has been violated occur in all societies; but in the absence of any means of authoritatively settling the matter, such disputes are likely to continue interminably. The remedy for this defect is another kind of secondary rule, 'rules of adjudication', which empower individuals to make authoritative determinations of the question whether, on a particular occasion, a primary rule has been broken, and lay down the procedures that are to be followed.

Hart's conception of law as the union of primary and secondary rules is one which enables us to dispense with the notion of law as necessarily involving sanctions or coercion. It is still a conception, however, that leaves us in some doubt as to whether international law is properly called 'law'. For what is called international law is clearly what Hart calls a set of primary rules. Within international society there are rules, generally believed to have the status of law, requiring states and other actors to do and refrain from doing certain things. But it is impossible to find rules of recognition, establishing beyond doubt those rules which are, and which are not, part of the system and what relation these rules have to each other within the system. It is impossible to find rules of change, empowering any body to alter the rules in relation to changing circumstances. And it is not possible to find rules of adjudication, empowering any body to lay down authoritatively whether or not, in a particular case, there has been a violation of the rules.

Hart himself does not draw the conclusion that for this reason international law should be denied the status of law. He does not seek to use his concept of law as the union of primary and secondary rules to establish a conclusive definition legislating the way in which the term should be used, but is content to accept the view of Bentham, the originator of the term 'international law', that the latter rules are 'sufficiently analogous' to law to justify application of the term.[12]

The views of those who reject the claims of international law to the status of law, do help to illuminate some of the special features of international law, and especially the respects in which it differs from municipal law (and resembles the law of certain primitive societies). However, the view that international law is 'law' properly so-called is one that has important practical consequences, and the debate that has raged about this question is no idle or sterile one. International law as a practical activity does in fact have a great deal in common with municipal law. The language and procedure of the one are closely akin to those of the other. The modern legal profession is one that embraces international law as well as the municipal law of particular countries. The activity of those who are concerned with international law, public and private – statesmen and their legal advisers, national and international courts, and international assemblies – is carried on in terms of the assumption that the rules with which they are dealing are rules of law. If the rights and duties asserted under these rules were believed to have the status merely of morality or of etiquette, this whole corpus of activity could not exist. The fact that these rules are believed to have the status of law, whatever theoretical difficulties it might involve, makes possible a corpus of international activity that plays an important part in the working of international society.

The Efficacy of International Law

Having defined international law we have now to consider what bearing it has on the actual behaviour of states. Rules by themselves are mere intellectual constructs. If we are to speak of the rules of international law as a factor seriously affecting the life of international society, we must establish that they have a degree of efficacy; that is to say, that there is some degree of resemblance as between the behaviour prescribed by the rules, and the actual behaviour of states and other actors in international politics.

In order to establish the efficacy of the rules of international law, it is not necessary to establish an *identity* as between actual and prescribed behaviour; that is to say, that there are no cases in which the rules are disregarded. It is not true of any system of legal rules that it is never disregarded; indeed, in cases where conformity between actual and prescribed behaviour can be regarded as a forgone conclusion, there can be no point in having rules at all. It is for this reason that societies do not develop rules requiring their members to breathe, eat and sleep, which they may be relied upon to do, but do develop rules requiring them not to kill, steal or lie, which some of them are likely to do, whether there are rules prohibiting this kind of behaviour or not.

The question is whether the rules of international law are observed to a sufficient degree (it is not possible to specify precisely to what degree) to justify our treating them as a substantial factor at work in international politics, and, in particular, as a means of preserving international order. There has always been a school of thought which, whether or not it rejects the claims of international law to the term 'law', regards these rules as a non-existent or at most a negligible factor in the actual conduct of international relations.

There is no doubt that there exists a substantial degree of co-incidence as between actual international behaviour and the behaviour prescribed by the rules of international law. If it were possible or meaningful to conduct a quantitative study of obedience to the rules of international law, it might be expected to show that most states obey most agreed rules of international law most of the time. Any state which lives at peace with at least one other state, which is involved in diplomatic relations with it, which exchanges money, goods and visitors with it, or which enters into agreements with it, is involved constantly in obedience to rules of international law.

In particular cases, rules of law are violated or disregarded; but these cases do not in themselves provide evidence that international law as such is without efficacy. In the first place, violation of a particular rule usually takes place against the background of conformity to other rules of international law, and indeed of conformity even to the rule that is being violated, in instances other than the present one. When, for example, Germany in 1914 invaded Belgium, in violation of the treaty of 1839 (neutralising Belgium) and of the rule of international law that treaties should be honoured, it continued to respect other principles of international law and to base its relations with other countries upon them. Moreover, in cases other than that of the treaty providing for the neutrality of Belgium, it continued to proclaim and to practise the rule of the sanctity of treaties.

In the second place, the violation is sometimes in itself of such a nature as to embody some element of conformity to the rule that is being violated. The distinction between violation of a rule and conformity to it is not always a sharp one; the decision of an authority as to whether or not a violation has occurred is always, in the end, yea or nay, but the processes of argument whereby this decision is arrived at may contain uncertain and arbitrary elements, both in the interpretation of the rule and in the construction of the facts. In reality the behaviour of a state in relation to the particular rule of international law is best thought of as finding its place in a spectrum of positions stretching from clear-cut conformity at one extreme to a clear-cut violation at the other. The violation of an agreement may be a measured response to some action of another party, designed to preserve some part of the agreement or to keep alive the possibility of restoring it.

In the third place, where a violation takes place the offending state usually goes out of its way to demonstrate that it still considers itself (and other states) bound by the rule in question. In some cases the state in question may deny that any violation has taken place, arguing, for example, as Nazi Germany did in remilitarising the Rhineland in 1936, that the agreement being disregarded had already lapsed because of previous violations by other parties, or that it was invalid in the first place. In other cases, such as Germany in violating Belgian neutrality in 1914, or the

United States in admitting violation of Soviet air space by the U2 aircraft in 1960, the offending state may admit that a rule has been broken but appeal to some conflicting principle of overriding importance. Even when the appeal is to a principle such as 'necessity' or 'vital interests', at least there is acceptance of the need to provide an explanation.

What is a clearer sign of the inefficacy of a set of rules is the case where there is not merely a lack of conformity as between actual and prescribed behaviour, but a failure to accept the validity or binding quality of the obligations themselves – as indicated by a reasoned appeal to different and conflicting principles, or by an unreasoning disregard of the rules. An unreasoning disregard of the rules – a failure to respond to them because of lack of knowledge of what they are, lack of understanding of them or lack of acceptance of the premises from which they derive – is characteristic of the behaviour of groups not recognising any common international society; for historical examples of it we have to look to encounters between member states of international society and political entities outside it (some examples are discussed in Chapter 2). What does from time to time occur in the history of modern international society is a reasoned rejection of its legal rules, or of certain of them, by states committed to revolutionary change, such as Bolshevik Russia (for example, in relation to the law of succession) or certain contemporary African and Asian states (for example, in relation to the legitimacy of colonial sovereignty and foreign property rights). But these examples of reasoned rejection of rules of international law have represented the temporary and local breakdown of these rules, not the general breakdown of the international legal system as a whole.

The denigrators of international law, however, while they are wrong when they claim that international law is without efficacy, are right to insist that respect for the law is not in itself the principal motive that accounts for conformity to law. International law is a social reality to the extent that there is a very substantial degree of conformity to its rules; but it does not follow from this that international law is a powerful agent or motive force in world politics.

States obey international law in part because of habit or inertia; they are, as it were, programmed to operate within the framework of established principles. In so far as their conformity to law derives from deliberation or calculation, it results from motives of three sorts. First, obedience may be the consequence of the fact that the action enjoined by the law is thought to be valuable, mandatory or obligatory, apart from its being legally required, either as an end in itself or as part of, or a means to, some wider set of values. Rules that are carried out primarily for this sort of reason are sometimes spoken of as 'the international law of community'. Second, obedience may result from coercion, or the threat of it, by some superior power bent on enforcing the agreement. Agreements that are observed chiefly for reasons of this sort are sometimes spoken of as 'the international law of power', and are exemplified by the acceptance of peace treaties by vanquished states at the time of their defeat and for as long a period thereafter as they remain too weak to challenge the verdict of war. Third, obedience may result from the interest a state perceives in reciprocal action by another state or states. Agreements and principles resting on this sense of mutual interest are sometimes called 'the international law of reciprocity'. These are exemplified by the most central principles of international law, such as mutual respect for sovereignty, the keeping of promises and the laws of war.[13]

The argument that states obey the law only for ulterior motives, or that they do so only when they consider it is in their interests to do so, is sometimes put forward as if it somehow disposed of the claims of international law to be taken seriously. Of course, it does not. The importance of international law does not rest on the willingness of states to abide by its principles to the detriment of their interests, but in the fact that they so often judge it in their interests to conform to it.

The Contribution of International Law to International Order

What is the role of law in relation to international order? The first function of international law has been to identify, as the supreme normative principle of the political organisation of mankind, the idea of a society of sovereign states. This is what was called in Chapter 2, the fundamental or constitutional principle of world politics in the present era. Order in the great society of all mankind has been attained, during the present phase of the modern states system, through general acceptance of the principle that men and territory are divided into states, each with its own proper sphere of authority, but linked together by a common set of rules. International law, by stating and elaborating this principle and by excluding alternative principles – such as the Hobbesian notion that international politics is an arena in which there are no rules restricting states in their relations with one another, or the notion that mankind is properly organised as a universal state based on cosmopolitan rights, or as a universal empire founded on the supremacy of a particular nation or race – establishes this particular realm of ideas as the determining one for human thought and action in the present phase, and so precludes the opening of questions without end and the eruption of conflicts without limit.

It is emphasised elsewhere in this study that order in the great society of all mankind might in principle be attained in many other ways than through a society of sovereign states which is neither historically inevitable nor morally sacrosanct. If in fact mankind were organised as a cosmopolitan state, or a universal empire, or according to some other principle, law might play a part in identifying this other principle as the supreme and seminal one. What, however, is incompatible with order on a global scale is a welter of competing principles of universal political organisation, such as existed in Europe during the period of the wars of religion. The first function of law in relation to order in world politics is thus to identify one of these principles of universal political organisation and proclaim its supremacy over all competitors.

The second function of international law in relation to international order has been to state the basic rules of coexistence among states and other actors in international society. These rules, which have been discussed above, relate to three core areas: there are rules relating to the restriction of violence among states and other actors; rules relating to agreements among them; and rules relating to sovereignty or independence (see Chapters 1 and 3).

The third function of international law is to help mobilise compliance with the rules of international society – both the basic rules of coexistence, illustrated above, the rules of co-operation, discussed in Chapter 2, and others. We have seen that while the actual behaviour of states does in some measure conform to the prescriptions of international law, respect for international law is not the principal motive force accounting for this conformity. It follows from this that it is erroneous to view the principal contribution of international·law to international order as lying in its imposition of restraints on international behaviour. Governments have a degree of respect for legal obligations; they are reluctant to acquire a reputation for disregarding them, and, in relation to most of the agreements into which they enter, they calculate that their interests lie in fulfilling them. But when their legal obligations and the interest they perceive in being known as governments that fulfil them come into conflict with their major interests and objectives, instead of being confirmed by them, these obligations are often disregarded.

However, it is not only through imposing restraints on international behaviour that international law helps to secure compliance with the basic rules of international society; the basic factors making for compliance with international law – acceptance by the parties of the ends or values underlying the agreement, coercion by a superior power, and reciprocal interest – exist independently of legal commitments, and without their operation legal commitments are ineffective. But the framework of international law serves to mobilise and channel these factors in the direction of compliance with agreements. In particular, international law provides a means by which states can advertise their intentions with regard to the matter in question; provide one another with reassurance about their future policies in relation to it; specify precisely what the nature of the agreement is, including its boundaries and limiting conditions; and solemnise the agreement in such a way as to create an expectation of permanence.

The Limitations of International Law

While the above functions are those which international law fulfils in relation to international order, it is important to take account of the limitations within which they are carried out. First, it is not the case that international law is a necessary or essential condition of international order. The functions which international law fulfils are essential to international order, but these functions might in principle be carried out in other ways. The idea of a society of states might be identified and its centrality proclaimed, the basic rules of coexistence might be stated, and a means provided for facilitating compliance with agreements, by a body of rules which has the status of moral rules or supernatural rules. Some past international societies – the Greek city-state system, the system of Hellenistic kingdoms that arose after the death of Alexander, the ancient Indian system of states – were without the institution of international law. That modern international society includes international law as one of its institutions is a consequence of the historical accident that it evolved out of a previous unitary system, Western Christendom, and that in this system notions of law – embodied in Roman law, divine law, canon law and natural law – were pre-eminent. The place of international law in our present international society gives it a distinctive stamp. Because the central rules of this society are considered to have the status of law, and not merely of morality, the sense of their binding force is an especially strong one, and the notion that there does exist in principle a single authoritative definition of the meaning of the rules (however difficult it may be, owing to the lack of authoritative 'rules of adjudication' to discover what they are) is a deeply entrenched one.

Second, international law is not by itself sufficient to bring about international order. International law cannot fulfil any of the functions that have been ascribed to it unless other conditions, not guaranteed by international law itself, are present. International law cannot identify the idea of international society as the supreme normative principle unless an international society in some measure already exists, and is receptive to the treatment of this principle as the supreme one. International law can contribute to international order by stating the basic rules of coexistence among states only if these rules have some basis in the actual dealings of states with one another. International law can mobilise the factors making for compliance with rules and agreements in international society only if these factors are present. Still less is it the case that international law by itself can be an instrument for the strengthening of order or peace, as is implied by programmes for 'world peace through law', or 'world peace through world law'. The multiplication or 'strengthening' of international legal restraints and prohibitions may play a part in strengthening international order in cases where it serves to mobilise or dramatise other factors at work in the situation, but attempts to legislate order or peace in the absence of these factors serve only to bring international law into discredit without advancing the prospects of peace.

In the third place, international law, or some particular interpretation of international law, is sometimes found actually to hinder measures to maintain international order. A classic case is the clash between international law and measures deemed necessary to maintain a balance of power. The clash between imperatives deriving from international law, and imperatives deriving from the principle that a balance of power should be maintained, can be traced at several points. One point is the question of preventive war. Most expositions of international law contend that preventive war is illegal; in cases where no legal injury has been done by one state to another, the latter cannot legally make war. The imperatives of the balance of power, however, as we noted in Chapter 5, point to the possible need to make war against a state which has not done legal injury to any other, but whose relative power is growing in such a way as to threaten the balance.

Another point of clash between these two sets of imperatives is the question of sanctions against aggressive war. At the time of the Italian invasion of Ethiopia, it was widely held by international lawyers that Italy had gone to war in disregard of its obligations under the League Covenant, and that, the League having called for sanctions against Italy, Britain, France and other member states should apply them. From the point of view of the balance of power, however, the effect of sanctions against Italy was simply that Italy would be driven into the arms of Germany, and the efforts of Britain and France to maintain a balance in relation to Germany placed in jeopardy. The same clash of imperatives was repeated at the time of the Russian invasion of Finland in 1939, when Britain and France again had to choose between taking action against Russia as an 'aggressor', and preserving the option of co-operation with Russia against Germany.

A final point of clash between the imperatives of international law and of the balance of power concerns the question of intervention. Most expositions of international law contend that states are bound to refrain from forcible or dictatorial intervention in one another's internal affairs (though on some views they may intervene on the invitation of a local government in order to resist intervention by another power). It is often argued, however, that considerations of the balance of power require intervention in the internal affairs of a state in order to establish a great power's influence in it, or resist the influence of another great power, because of wider considerations of the distribution of power in international society at large.

There have been various attempts to resolve this clash of imperatives between international law and the balance of power. One is to seek to absorb the principle of the balance into international law itself. Another is to adopt a restrictive view of the sphere of validity of international law, and assign the question of the balance of power, along with other imperatives deriving from devices for the maintenance of order, to a sphere of 'power politics' that law does not attempt to regulate. Here I do not seek to consider whether or not, or how, this clash could be resolved, but only to draw attention to it as a basic limitation of the contribution of international law to international order.

Fourth, it should be noted that international law is a vehicle or instrumentality of purposes other than international order, and which may indeed be opposed to it. Legal instrumentalities are sometimes used, for example, to promote justice in world politics – international justice, human justice or cosmopolitan justice – and this is an objective which can be disruptive of international order (see Chapter 4). Law is an instrumentality of political purposes of all kinds, and the promotion of order is only one of them.

Contemporary International Law

What contribution does international law make to international order in the special circumstances of the present time? The period since the end of the Second World War has been one of great change in international law, so we are told by specialists in that subject. The changes that have taken place relate to the subjects of international law – or whom the law seeks to regulate; the scope of international law – or what it regulates; the processes by which the law is made; and the role of the international lawyer.

As regards the subjects of international law, opinion appears to have moved decisively against the doctrine of the nineteenth-century positivists that international law (in Oppenheim's words) is a 'law between states only and exclusively'.[14] It is widely held that individual human beings are subjects of international law, on the evidence of such instruments as the charters of the Nuremberg and

Tokyo War Crimes Tribunals, the Universal Declaration of Human Rights of 1948, the Covenant on Civil and Political Rights and the Covenant on Economic, Social and Cultural Rights of 1966, and the European Convention on Human Rights of 1950. The status of subjects of international law is also accorded by many authorities to groups other than states: the United Nations and other universal or near-universal intergovernmental organisations; regional inter-governmental organisations, international non-governmental organisations such as professional and scientific associations, non-profit-making foundations and multinational economic organisations.[15]

Some authorities contend that because states have ceased to be the sole subjects of international law and now take their place alongside individuals and other groups, this heralds a change that is taking place from what previously has been international or interstate law to what is, or is in process of becoming, the law of the world community. Thus Philip Jessup has written of a transition from international law to 'transnational law', or law which regulates all actions or events that transcend national frontiers, whether the actions involved are those of states, individuals, international organisations, corporations or other groups.[16] C. Wilfred Jenks has written of the emergence of 'the common law of mankind' and Percy Corbett of the change from international law to 'world law'.[17]

As regards the change in the scope of international law, it is clear that since the Second World War there has been an enormous growth in that part of international law which regulates economic, social, communications and environmental matters – as distinct from political and strategic affairs, with which international law in earlier periods had been primarily concerned. The extension of the state's activities in these fields, together with the rising importance in world politics of actors other than the state, has had as its consequence an increase in the attention paid by international law to economic matters, as reflected in the activities of the United Nations Economic and Social Council, UNCTAD, the World Bank, the International Monetary Fund, the Food and Agriculture Organisation, and other bodies; to social matters, as illustrated by the work of the World Health Organisation and UNESCO; to the regulation of transport and communications, as evidenced by the International Telecommunications Union or the International Civil

Aviation Organisation; and more recently to the regulation of international aspects of man's relationship to the human environment.

This expansion of the scope of international law has led B. V. A. Röling to speak of a transition that is taking place from a traditional 'international law of liberty' towards a contemporary 'international law of welfare'. The 'international law of liberty', in Röling's view, was made by a small group of prosperous European states, concerned to reconcile the freedom of the one with the freedom of the other, in accordance with the pattern of the liberal state. The 'international law of welfare', by contrast, reflects the extension of the state's intervention in economic life, as well as the impact on international society of the majority of states that are neither prosperous nor European, and are concerned to challenge the law of liberty in an international equivalent of the class struggle. 'The world community', he writes, 'is bound to become a welfare community, just as the nation-state became a welfare state'.[18] Wolfgang Friedmann has written, in terms that are to some extent comparable, of a transition from 'the international law of coexistence' to 'the international law of cooperation', reflecting both the 'horizontal' expansion of international law to incorporate new states outside the European tradition, and its 'vertical' expansion to regulate new fields of international activity.[19]

It is also widely held that changes have taken place in the processes by which international law is made, or the sources from which it derives. Since the nineteenth century the predominant doctrine among international lawyers has been that the only true source of international law is the consent of states – either their express consent, as in that part of international law that is contained in international conventions or treaties, general or particular, or their implied consent, as in international customary law. Article 38 of the Statute of the International Court of Justice states that there are four sources of international law: international conventions, whether general or particular, establishing rules expressly recognised by the consenting states; international custom, as evidence of a general practice accepted as law; the general principles of law recognised by civilised nations; and the judicial decisions and the teachings of the most highly qualified publicists of the various nations, as subsidiary means for the determination of rules of law.

The third and fourth of these sources listed appear to allow some scope for the treatment, as a valid part of international law, of rules to which the states contesting an issue before the Court have not given their consent – or in relation to which it may be difficult to demonstrate that these states have given their consent. Nevertheless, the fourth source is treated by the Statute as merely a 'subsidiary' means of determining the law; the other three sources, which must be taken to be the principal sources identified by the Statute, firmly ground international law in the actual practice of states; and the Statute of the International Court of Justice itself represents, on the positivist view, an instrument whose validity derives from the express consent of signatories of it.

The doctrine that valid international law derives only from the consent of states has always had to contend with that school of thought, which from the sixteenth century until the eighteenth represented the mainstream of opinion, according to which international law derived from natural law also. The twentieth century has seen a number of attempts, for example by Brierly and Lauterpacht, to revive the idea of natural law as a source of international law.[20] And it has also witnessed a proliferation of theories which have sought, while avoiding the now unfashionable doctrine of natural law, to find some other basis for arguing that there are sources of international law other than the consent of states. Of these the most important and influential at the present time are those which may be called the 'solidarist' theories. Their distinctive mark is that, while on the one hand they seek to avoid embracing natural law, and argue that the sources of law should be found in the actual practice of states, they hold that valid international law derives not merely from those rules to which states have consented, but also from those rules in relation to which international society as a whole has achieved solidarity or consensus, even though consent to the rules is withheld by some states.

Thus Richard A. Falk argues that 'there is discernible a trend from consent to consensus as the basis of international legal obligations' where consensus means 'an overwhelming majority, a convergence of international opinion, a predominance, to something more than a simple majority but something less than unanimity or universality'.[21] The principal example Falk has in mind is the consensus displayed in the United Nations General Assembly in relation to questions of colonialism and racism. Falk argues that international society, if it is to function effectively, should be provided with a legislative authority to translate such a consensus into rules of law despite the opposition of a few sovereign states; in particular, he argues that the International Court of Justice should confirm the role of consensus as a source of international law.[22] His position, however, is not simply that a switch from consent to consensus as the source of international legal obligation would be desirable, but that this is a present trend.

A crucial issue for the solidarist point of view is that of the legal standing of resolutions of the political organs of the United Nations, especially the General Assembly, in which the chief evidence of emerging solidarity or consensus in international society is thought to lie. The traditional positivist theory maintains that resolutions of the General Assembly are recommendations only, and are not legally binding. The solidarist seeks to show that these resolutions have legal standing or significance of some kind. It is unusual to argue that the General Assembly is a world legislature any of whose resolutions enacts universal law. But it is often argued that the status of law attaches to resolutions that are passed repeatedly by overwhelming majorities; or to those which have a special solemnity; or to those which are backed (as is sometimes argued by Soviet writers) by states of the two main socio-economic systems and the three main political groups.[23] More moderate statements of this point of view claim not that any of these resolutions has legally binding status *per se,* but rather that they are significant for the law-making process, or help to shape it. Rosalyn Higgins, in her seminal study of *The Development of International Law Through the Political Organs of the United Nations,* contends that resolutions of the General Assembly, taken as a whole, provide 'a rich source of evidence about the development of customary law'.[24] The solidarist thesis is stated most clearly by C. Wilfred Jenks, who maintains that the basis of obligation in international law is now 'the will of the international community'.[25] Jenks maintains that agreement about the sources of binding international law has been elusive in the past because 'the law is only now reaching a stage in its development at which we can rationalise from experience, and from the potentialities which are opening up before us, an analysis of the basis of obligation which is historically, logically and above all teleologically, satisfactory'.[26] In our own times, he thinks, the will of the international community has developed to the point at which it can be recognised as the basis of international legal obligation.

Finally, a change has taken place in the role of international lawyers, as that role is seen by at least an important part of the international legal profession. The traditional positivist point of view, which still predominates in Britain and Western Europe, is that the role of the judge, the legal adviser and the legal scholar is to state what the rules of international law are, and to do this accurately and objectively without choosing among non-legal values, such as moral, social and political values, that are at stake in the issue in hand. The traditional point of view does not deny that the interpretation of the law has moral, social and political implications or that the consideration of these implications is important. But it does hold that the choice between alternative moral, social and political doctrines should not determine the international lawyer's exposition of the content of existing law.

It is now, however, the doctrine of a very influential body of international lawyers, principally but not exclusively in the United States, that the international lawyer both is and should be 'policy-orientated' in the sense that he explicitly seeks to choose between moral, social and political values. The starting-point of those who embrace this doctrine is the perception of the earlier school of 'legal realists', that in the actual exposition by judges, legal advisers and legal scholars of the content of the law, so-called 'non-legal considerations' do in fact always play a part. The advocates of a 'policy-orientated jurisprudence' therefore see themselves as calling simply for the recognition of an aspect of international legal decision-making that is in any case present.[27] They also argue, however, that by thus making explicit the role of the international lawyer as a maker of law rather than a mere applier or interpreter of it – and so, to use Richard A. Falk's words, liberating the law from 'the myths of logical and doctrinal restraint' – they place him in a position to make a constructive and creative contribution to the development of international law.[28] The law, they say, must be seen in its social context and not in abstraction; to respond to changes in that social context it must be dynamic and not static. Given the absence in international society of any legislative authority competent to change the law, it is encumbent on the professional international lawyer to take account of changing values in expounding the law.

These four changes that have taken place in international law since the end of the Second World War are connected with one another and tend to reinforce one another. They lead some international lawyers to the conclusion that there has been not merely change in international law, but progress: progress away from a law that binds states only towards a law of the world community; from a law concerned only with coexistence among these states towards one concerned with economic, social and environmental co-operation among men in the world community; from a law in which particular, recalcitrant states, by withholding their consent, can defy the consensus of the world community, to a law in which that consensus has become the source of binding obligation; from a law which is interpreted statically and mechanically, and is therefore necessarily out of touch with the changing values of the world community (reflecting, as Röling says, *das Nützliche von Gestern*), to a law which is expounded dynamically and creatively and can keep abreast of these changing values.

But has this 'progress' of international law been reflected in any strengthening of the role played by international law in relation to international order? Martin Wight has pointed out that the periods in which the claims made for international law are most extravagant and inflated are also the periods in which actual international practice is most marked by disorder, while in periods in which actual international relations are relatively orderly, the claims made for international law are most modest:

international theory (at least in its chief embodiment as international law) sings a kind of descant over against the movement of diplomacy. . . . When diplomacy is violent and unscrupulous international law soars into the regions of natural law; when diplomacy acquires a certain habit of cooperation, international law crawls in the mud of legal positivism.[29]

Is the 'progress' of international law in our own times, perceived by the international lawyers, anything more than its heightened protest against the facts of international politics? However this question is answered, it is doubtful whether these recent changes in international law have brought with them any increase in the role played by international law in relation to international order.

Subjects of International Law

The spread of the doctrine that states are not the only subjects of international law would be likely to represent a strengthening of the contribution of international law to international order only if it were accompanied by agreement among states as to what the rights and duties of these other subjects are, comparable at least to the minimal agreement that exists among states about their own rights and duties. It was the inability of states to agree about the rights and duties of individual human beings and about organisations such as the Papacy and the Empire that led them in the formative years of European international society to the conclusion that order was best founded on a system of international law of which states alone were subjects, and from which the divisive issues of the rights and duties of individuals and groups other than the state were excluded.

The tentative steps that have been taken in our own times towards establishing the rights and duties of individuals in international law do not in fact reflect agreement as to what these rights and duties are and how they can be upheld. In these circumstances the discussion of human rights and duties is a consequence, as it is also a cause, of tension among states: the discussion of them that led to the Nuremberg and Tokyo War Crimes Tribunals was part of the tension between the Allied powers and the Axis; the discussion of human rights in the Soviet Union part of the Cold War; the discussion of the rights of black Africans in South Africa part of the struggle between the anti-imperialist states and their opponents.

Carried to its logical extreme, the doctrine of human rights and duties under international law is subversive of the whole principle that mankind should be organised as a society of sovereign states. For, if the rights of each man can be asserted on the world political stage over and against the claims of his state, and his duties proclaimed irrespective of his position as a servant or a citizen of that state, then the position of the state as a body sovereign over its citizens, and entitled to command their obedience, has been subject to challenge, and the structure of the society of sovereign states has been placed in jeopardy. The way is left open for the subversion of the society of sovereign states on behalf of the alternative organising principle of a cosmopolitan community. Similarly, the proposition that international or so-called supranational bodies are subjects of international law carries with it the seeds of subversion of the society of sovereign states in favour of an organising principle in which an international or supranational body, or a series of such bodies, has displaced sovereign states as the chief repositories of rights and duties on the world political stage.

To take this point of view is not to argue that the attempt to establish human rights and duties in international law is unfortunate or undesirable; this would be to commit the error of treating order as the only or the commanding value (see Chapter 4). It is simply to observe that in our own times the international discussion of human rights and duties in international law is more a symptom of disorder than of order.

Scope of International Law

The expansion of the scope of international law to encompass economic, social, communications and environmental matters represents a strengthening of the contribution of international law to international order in the sense that it provides a means of coping with new threats to international order. The growing impact of the policies of states on each other in these fields is a source of conflict and disorder among them which international legal regulation serves to contain. If international law had not responded to these developments by expanding its scope, the threats to international order arising from the growth of interdependence in the economic, social, communications and environmental fields would be greater than they are.

But the growth of international legal regulation in these areas does not in itself imply that any strengthening has taken place in the contribution of international law to its traditionally central area of concern. The idea that progress has taken place from an 'international law of coexistence' to an 'international law of co-operation' carries with it the implication that the former has become more firmly established since the latter has been able to build on it. If we look at the contemporary state of the 'international law of coexistence' it is clear that this is not the case.

Let us consider only that part of the 'international law of coexistence' that deals with the restriction of violence. The notion that in recent times there has been a strengthening of the role of international law in restricting international violence rests principally on the doctrine of the United Nations Charter that the use or threat of force by states is illegal. A typical statement of this view has been made by Ian Brownlie:

> The outstanding feature of the last half a century is the decisive change from a legal regime of indifference to the occasion for war, in which it was regarded primarily as a duel, a means of settling a private difference, to a legal regime which has placed substantial limitations on the competence of states to resort to force. After 1928 the cumulative effect of the Kellogg-Briand Pact, the Saavedra Lamas Pact, the Stimson doctrine, the state practice in the period 1928 to 1942, the war of sanction conducted against the Axis, the Nuremberg Charter, the principles of which were subsequently affirmed by the General Assembly of the United Nations, and the Charter of the United Nations, was to establish an emphatic prohibition of the use of force for selfish ends.[30]

Because of the introduction into positive international law in this century of a number of restrictions – of which those contained in the United Nations Charter are the latest – on the right of states to resort to force, the legal situation is undoubtedly different from what it was in the nineteenth century – although the difference is not so great if we reflect that states at that time considered themselves subject to moral restrictions on their right to resort to force, and that the interpretation of the present legal restrictions on resort to force is hardly less uncertain and subjective than the interpretation of the older, moral principles.

However, it is obvious that the principal factors inhibiting states from resort to war lie outside international law, in the rising costs of war (especially, for those exposed to it, the risk of nuclear destruction) and the declining gains to be expected from it (see Chapter 8). The law restricting resort to force by states may be said to help mobilise these factors making against resort to force: by adhering to prohibitions like those contained in the United Nations Charter, states are advertising their intentions not to resort to force, reassuring each other with regard to their intentions in this respect, specifying the boundaries and limitations and solemnising their renunciation of the older doctrine of a sovereign state's prerogative right to resort to force.

However, the contribution made by the present law to mobilising the factors making against resort to force is severely limited. The rule is clearly at loggerheads with actual international practice, especially if we consider that it inhibits not only the use of force – which, while it occurs frequently, at least does so only in particular areas of the world for limited periods – but also the threat of force, which in contemporary international relations is ubiquitous and continuous. The contradiction between the imperatives of international law and imperatives deriving from other devices for the maintenance of order is nowhere clearer than in the United Nations Charter's prohibition of that threat of force by states which, in the form of the relationship of mutual nuclear deterrence, has provided the principal basis of general peace in the present era. Moreover, the rule is so vague and imprecise as to provide little guidance. The prohibition, for example, is widely taken to be subject to the exceptions that force may be used in self-defence, in defence of other states, when authorised by a competent international organ, at the invitation of a state requesting intervention in a civil war, and for a variety of other reasons.[31] While the United Nations Charter may be read as providing a broad prohibition of the use or threat of force except for purposes of defence or in fulfilment of the United Nation's own collective-security procedures, it is also the doctrine of most members of the United Nations, especially of the communist and Third World states, that force may legitimately be used in a war that is not defensive if it is a just 'war of national liberation'.

If the restrictions which contemporary international law imposes on the resort to force by states are only of limited value, in other respects there is evidence of actual decline in the contribution made by international law to the restriction of violence. As noted above, international law has sought to restrict violence in international society by confining resort to legitimate violence to sovereign states. In our own times, however, it is clear that the monopoly of legitimate international violence long enjoyed by sovereign states is being challenged on the one hand by non-state political groups employing so-called 'low-level' or 'terrorist' violence on an international scale, and on the other hand by the assumption by international organisations of a right to use violence.

It was noted also that international law has traditionally sought to restrict the manner in which war is conducted – for example, by insisting that it be commenced with a declaration of war, that it be ended with a peace agreement, and that the violence employed in it should not be directed against non-combatants. It is notorious that these traditional principles – although something of them survives in the Red Cross Conventions – have been so far neglected in our own times that the law and the practice of war are utterly remote from each other. The prospects that wars will be limited in their conduct now rest with tacit conventions and unilateral limitations in strategic policy in which the traditional legal limitations have little or no place. As regards the protection provided by international law to violence directed against diplomatic agents, while the law itself has been strengthened by the Vienna Conventions on Diplomatic and Consular Relations of 1961 and 1963, their coming into force ushered in a period remarkable for a very high incidence of actual violation of diplomatic immunities.

Sources of International Law

The alleged shift from consent to consensus as the basic source of international law is one that at first sight contains great promise for the strengthening of the contribution of international law to international order. What it promises is that when there is overwhelming solidarity in international society in favour of the view that a particular rule or course of action has the status of law, then recognition of its legal status cannot be averted merely because a particular recalcitrant state or group of states withholds its consent. If the view of an overwhelming majority or preponderance of states may be taken to represent 'the will of the international community', this appears to open the way for the strengthening of the international law of coexistence, and indeed of other branches of international law also.

The issues raised by the conflicting doctrines of consent and consensus are too complex to be discussed in full here. Some basic points, however, may be made. Those rules which in this study have been called the rules of coexistence serve to sustain order in an international society in which a consensus does not exist in normal circumstances about much else besides these rules. The rules governing the use of force, for example, serve to contain and limit war in a situation in which a consensus does not exist as to which side in the war represents the just cause. The rules governing international agreements are designed to secure respect for undertakings in a situation in which there is not a consensus in international society as to whether or not a particular agreement is desirable. The rules upholding the sovereign jurisdiction of each state against forcible intervention by other states in its internal affairs are an attempt to secure the mutual respect of states for one another's sovereignty in a situation in which they cannot normally achieve a consensus in distinguishing just interventions from unjust ones.

If in fact international society were to achieve such basic moral and political solidarity that a consensus – in the sense of the agreement of the overwhelming majority – could normally be achieved about the justice of a war, a treaty or an act of intervention, then the contribution of international law to international order might be strengthened by acceptance of the doctrine of consensus. The interests of order are not served, however, if in the situation in which no such consensus actually exists, and the international society is divided into contending groups, one of these groups claims to represent the consensus and acts as if it does. The result in this case is not that the rules deriving from the assumption of consensus are upheld, but simply that the traditional rules which assume a lack of consensus are undermined.

We may take, as an example, the rules relating to the restriction of violence. These, as noted above, seek to limit the place of violence in international relations by confining it to sovereign states, restricting their right to resort to it, restricting the manner in which they conduct it, and restricting its spread beyond the initial belligerents. The Grotian or solidarist doctrine, however, according to which international law distinguishes just from unjust causes of war, and treats war as a contest between the law-enforcers and the law-breakers, has as its primary purpose not the limitation of war but the triumph in war of the party representing the just cause. Where, as in the Abyssinian crisis and the Korean War, there is not in fact an overwhelming consensus as to which side represents the just cause, but at the same time one side claims to represent international society as a whole and sees its opponents as violators of the law, the consequence is not the triumph of the former over the latter, but simply the weakening of the rules restricting violence.

The crucial question, in relation to each particular claim that an international consensus establishes the legal status of a rule or a course of action, is whether or to what extent such a consensus actually exists. The doctrine that the source of international law is the consensus or solidarity of states is one which, like the doctrine of consent, does seek to ensure that international law is closely related to the actual practice of states, and does not merely express some arbitrarily derived moral protest against it. Indeed, on some interpretations the doctrine of consensus is not very different from the doctrine of consent. If – as is sometimes maintained by exponents of the consent theory, concerned to deal with the case of new states which have not signified their consent, or with the case of states whose consent to a particular rule is difficult to prove, or was given previously but has been withdrawn – consent is taken to include 'implied consent', then states may be bound by rules to which they cannot be shown to have explicitly consented;[32] and if, as some proponents of the consensus doctrine proclaim, the consensus of states is a source of law only if there is an overwhelming majority of states, representing a preponderance of power and the solidarity of the main political and economic groups, and if the existence of this consensus is demonstrated by the evidence, then the consensus theory is not likely to have the result of intensifying conflicts between major sections of international society.

It must be recognised, however, that to some international lawyers the attraction of the consensus doctrine lies in the opportunities it offers to develop international law not in relation to the actual practice of states, but in conformity to their own views as to what international order or international justice requires. In this form the doctrine that international law derives from the consensus of states or 'the will of the international community' represents not an attempt to amplify positive international law, but the desire, as it were, to allow natural law to enter by the back door.

The Role of the International Lawyer

The doctrine that the role of the international lawyer is to provide an interpretation of the law that is not static and mechanical but dynamic and creative also appears at first sight one that promises to strengthen the contribution of international law to international order. If judges, legal advisers and legal scholars do not feel that their role is simply to state objectively the international law of yesterday but are free to adapt it in relation to changing social, moral and political values, does this not mean that international law is becoming a more effective instrument for the promotion of international order? But if international lawyers become so pre-occupied with the sociology, the ethics or the politics of international relations that they lose sight of what has been in the past their essential business, that is the interpretation of existing legal rules, the only result must be a decline in the role of international law in international relations.

It may be conceded that the work of judges, legal advisers and legal scholars in interpreting existing legal rules is in fact always influenced by their views on social, moral and political questions. It may be conceded also that it is not only inevitable, but also desirable, that international lawyers take account of these non-legal considerations in interpreting the law. Very often it is not possible to choose between two conflicting interpretations of the law using legal criteria alone; as Rosalyn Higgins points out, such appeal to non-legal principles is not extraneous to the law but is 'part of the legal process'.[33] It is true, also, that in international law as in municipal law, judges, legal advisers and scholars will sometimes have the opportunity, by exercising the discretion available to them in interpreting the law in such a way as to take account of changing social, moral and political beliefs, to help adapt the law to changing circumstances.

But if a distinction is not preserved between those rules of international conduct which have the status of law and those which do not, international law cannot survive as a distinct normative system at all. If the international legal profession were to cease to regard the exposition and interpretation of existing legal rules as its main task, and to give itself over to the discussion of the sociology, the ethics or the politics of international relations, international lawyers would cease to have anything distinctive to contribute.

In some areas of the contemporary international legal profession there is in fact a trend in this direction. The doctrine that international law is not a system of rules, but can be viewed as 'a process of authoritative decision', or 'a tool of social engineering', is one which deprives international law of its essential focus and leads to its disappearance as a distinct branch of international studies. It is the logical consequence of this trend that the choice between one interpretation of the law and another is reduced to the choice between one authority's moral and political values and those of another – for example, between Myres S. McDougal's 'cold war' values and Richard A. Falk's radical global salvationism.[34]

The recent changes in international law that have been reviewed do not suggest that a strengthening has taken place in the contribution of international law to international order. The growing place accorded to individual human rights and duties in international law is a sign of the contraction of consensus, not of its expansion. The growth of a new 'international law of co-operation' is based not on a strengthened 'international law of coexistence' but on a weakened one. The trend, among some international lawyers, to treat consensus rather than consent as the source of international law reflects the drift of international legal theory away from the standard of actual state practice. The tendency of part of the international legal profession to eschew the interpretation of existing law in favour of the promotion of non-legal values embodies a trend whose logical conclusion is the disappearance of international law as a distinct social science.

The achievement of international law in our own times may be not to have brought about any strengthening of the element of order in international society, but rather to have helped to preserve the existing framework of international order in a period in which it has been subject to especially heavy stress. In our own times the area of consensus in international society has shrunk as the consequence of the ideological split between communist and non-communist states, and as a consequence of the expansion of international society beyond its originally European or Western base. The adherence of both communist and non-communist states, and of states both within and beyond the European cultural tradition, to some common terms of international law, symbolised above all by the great world conventions on the law of the sea, diplomatic and consular relations, and the law of treaties, has helped to maintain, in a period of inevitably contracting consensus, some elements of a common framework. The international law to which, in some measure, all states in the global international system give their formal assent still serves to carry out its traditional functions of identifying the idea of a society of states as the operational principle of world politics, stating the basic rules of coexistence and facilitating compliance with those and other rules.

7

Diplomacy and International Order

In this chapter I propose to consider the following questions:
(i) What is diplomacy?
(ii) How does diplomacy contribute to international order?
(iii) What is the relevance of diplomacy to international order at present?

Diplomacy

Three important senses of the term 'diplomacy' should be distinguished:

(i) The conduct of relations between states and other entities with standing in world politics by official agents and by peaceful means. This is the widest sense of the term and is what is meant by it here.

(ii) Such conduct of relations by professional diplomatists. This, for example, is part of the Oxford English Dictionary definition, used by Sir Harold Nicolson: 'Diplomacy is the management of international relations by negotiation; the method by which these relations are adjusted by ambassadors and envoys; the business or art of the diplomatist.'[1] At a time when the role of ambassadors and envoys in the conduct of international relations has greatly shrunk, this definition is unduly constricting.

(iii) Such conduct of relations between states that is carried out in a manner which is, in the everyday sense of the term, 'diplomatic', that is, tactful or subtle. An example of this use is the first part of Sir Ernest Satow's celebrated definition: 'Diplomacy is the application of intelligence and tact to the conduct of relations between the governments of independent states, extending sometimes also to

156

their relations with vassal states; or, more briefly still, the conduct of business between states by peaceful means.'² This, of course, is a statement of what Satow thinks diplomacy should be rather than of what it is: diplomatists can be unintelligent and tactless, but they do not thereby cease to be diplomatists.

The preferred definition above confines our attention to such conduct of relations in world politics as is carried out by persons authorised to act in the name of a particular state or other recognised political entity. When a private individual seeks to play a role in the relationships between states – as Bertrand Russell did when he sent cables to President Kennedy and Chairman Khrushchev during the Cuban missile crisis – this may or may not affect the course of events but it is not diplomacy. Diplomacy is the conduct of international relations by persons who are official agents; hence the importance in diplomacy of letters of credence or other tokens of representative or symbolic status. War also exemplifies the conduct of international relations by official agents; diplomatists differ from soldiers in that they confine themselves to peaceful means.

We must apply the term diplomacy to the official relations not only of states but also of other political entities with standing in world politics. The agents of the United Nations, of other general international organisations such as the International Labour Organisation, and of regional international organisations, may be said to engage in diplomacy. Political groups which are not widely recognised as states – for example, at the time of writing, groups dedicated to national liberation – but which enjoy standing in world politics, sometimes appoint agents which enter into negotiation with states and with other such groups. Satow's definition recognises the possibility that vassal states may conduct diplomacy, and clearly diplomacy has taken place in the past between European states and a host of entities not recognised by the former as being states.

The core of traditional diplomacy has resided in the official relationships between sovereign states. Great uncertainty still surrounds the application to diplomatic relationships, involving entities other than the sovereign state, of rules and procedures evolved in interstate diplomacy – an uncertainty reflected in the decision of the Vienna Conference on Diplomatic Intercourse and Immunities, which met in 1961 to codify world diplomatic practice, to confine its attention to traditional interstate diplomacy rather than face the problems that would arise in the attempt to take account of the diplomatic relations of international organisations.[3] Yet it is clear that entities other than states have standing as actors in world politics, and that they are engaged in diplomacy *vis-à-vis* states and one another.

One writer, seeking to get away from definitions of diplomacy which confine it to relations between states, has taken it to be 'the conduct, through representative organs and by peaceful means, of the external relations of any given subject of international law with any other such subject or subjects'.[4] The difficulty with this is that there is widespread disagreement as to what are the subjects of international law. Moreover, a political entity may have standing in world politics even though it is not generally regarded as a subject of international law. Sometimes a political entity achieves standing in world politics because states recognise that it enjoys a position of power, or because states support its aspirations to achieve such a position of power.

The pristine form of diplomacy is the transmitting of messages between one independent political community and another. Ragnar Numelin, in his study of the diplomatic forms and institutions of primitive or prehistoric communities, contends that the most elementary form of diplomacy is the sending of a messenger or herald, bearing his message stick or other equivalent of letters of credence from one primitive tribe or group to a neighbouring tribe.[5] In thinking about diplomacy we need today to bear in mind the following distinctions.

(1) Diplomacy includes both the formulation of a state's external policy and its execution. The formulation of policy includes the gathering and assessment of information about the international environment and the weighing of alternative lines of policy. Execution comprises the communication to other governments and peoples of the line of foreign policy that has been decided, attempts to explain and justify this policy to them and, where appropriate, to secure their co-operation or neutralise their opposition in carrying it out – by reason and persuasion if possible, but sometimes by threats of force or other kinds of coercion.

(2) Diplomatic relations are either bilateral or multilateral. Bilateral relationships formally link one state or government with another, but in present practice they are also links between one

'people' or political system and another. Just as at one time an ambassador represented his sovereign in the court of another, now an ambassador is taken – in conformity with the prevailing doctrine that all legitimate states are nation-states – to represent his people. Moreover, the ambassador takes it upon himself, within the limits imposed by the duty of non-interference in the host country's domestic affairs, to influence in desired directions not only the government to which he is accredited but the 'people', that is, the active elements of the country's political life.

Multilateral diplomacy may take the form of conferences of two or more states, or of permanent conferences, that is, international organisations. Much of the importance of conferences and international organisations lies not in the multilateral diplomacy to which they give rise but in the opportunities they provide for bilateral diplomacy. Genuinely multilateral diplomacy is the conduct of business among three or more states seeking to resolve an issue together, as in the United Nations General Assembly. Diplomatic links between a state and an international organisation to which it belongs involve an element which is neither bilateral nor multilateral but is not lateral either. The British Ambassador to the United Nations is conducting business not only with other states represented in the United Nations, but with the United Nations itself, through its Secretariat and other organs. If the United Nations or other international bodies came to occupy a commanding position in world politics, such that a state's links with it were more important than its lateral links with other states – as a mediaeval German prince's links with the Holy Roman Emperor were more important than his links with other princes – this would be a sign of the disappearance of the system of states and its supersession by a different kind of universal political order.

(3) Diplomacy may be either *ad hoc* or institutionalised. Some diplomatic contacts, like the first encounters of Europeans with the original peoples of the Americas, arise purely out of the need to deliver a particular message or transact a particular piece of business, without any implication of permanent relationship, or of mutually agreed rules and conventions. Present-day diplomatic contacts among sovereign states are institutionalised in the sense that they are maintained independently of particular items of business that arise, that they take place against the background of a permanent relationship among the parties involved, and that

they are conducted on the basis of well-understood rules and conventions, in some cases having the status of law.

It is clear from Ragnar Numelin's account, to which reference has been made, that diplomatic contacts even among primitive peoples are often highly institutionalised in this sense, the exchange of messages and the conduct of negotiations conforming to elaborate rules backed up by magical or religious sanction. Important stages in the institutionalisation of diplomatic relations in the modern international system were the emergence of resident embassies in Italy in the fifteenth century, spreading throughout Europe as a whole in the sixteenth; legal recognition of the extraterritoriality of ambassadors by foreign services in the period of Louis XIV; emergence of the diplomatic corps in the eighteenth century; the agreement of the European powers at the Congress of Vienna in 1815 on a system of determining precedence among diplomatic missions consistent with the doctrine of the equality of states; the incorporation of Turkey, China, Japan, Korea and Siam into the European diplomatic mechanism during the late nineteenth century; and the 1961 Vienna Convention, which codified traditional state-to-state diplomatic practice on a world-wide scale, and secured the consent of the new states that emerged from the break up of European empires.

(4) Finally, we should distinguish between the 'diplomatic' and the consular branches of the conduct of international relations. The basis of this distinction is that the former is concerned with the relations of the governments of two countries, and the latter with the relations of private citizens, both with the government of another country and its private citizens. The distinction is, however, not always easy to draw, and at present it is complicated by the fact that diplomatic missions often perform consular functions, while consulates perform 'diplomatic' functions on a local scale – for example, they are used widely as listening posts to test the local political mood of a country. Whereas in the last century and early this century many nations maintained separate consular services, the present tendency is for diplomatic and consular services to be merged.

It is obvious that diplomacy presupposes the existence of an international system, that is, of two or more states interacting as a set of parts. If the world consisted of political communities completely isolated from one another, no question of diplomatic relations could arise. Equally, if the different parts of the world, although they were in contact with one another, were subordinated to a central authority, there could be no question of diplomatic relations among the parts; the crucial political relationships would be those between each of the parts and the centre, and those would be relations of subordination.

It is also obvious that diplomacy, at least in the highly institutionalised form in which it exists now, presupposes that there exists not only an international system but also an international society. The exchange of diplomatic missions is made possible by the acceptance by the states concerned of complex rules and conventions. The sending country accepts the principle that its diplomatists will not interfere in the internal affairs of the receiving country. The receiving country accepts the immunity of the diplomatist, his staff, his mission and communications from constraint, and accepts the duty to protect the mission from molestation by others and to assist it in its work.

But if the diplomatic institutions of today presuppose an international society, international society does not presuppose them in the same way. These diplomatic institutions developed slowly and uncertainly and have been quite different in form at different stages in the evolution of international society. The growth of resident embassies, for example, had to await the appearance of certain conditions. As Butler and Maccoby write:

> For this does postulate a group of powerful and independent states, free externally from grave danger of barbarian conquest, and internally secure from the establishment of any universal monarchy. It postulates also a similarity of religion, institutions and language, together with political and commercial relations of the closest kinds.[6]

The principle that ambassadors should not interfere in the politics of the receiving country, now so central, was not established in the early stages of resident diplomacy, but emerged only as interference by ambassadors was challenged by the receiving government, as by Elizabeth's expulsion of the Spanish envoy D'Espes in 1572 and the ambassador Mendoza in 1584. Even in the eighteenth century there were numerous cases of fomentation of resistance and revolt by ambassadors. 'The action which these incidents did as a rule provoke', Butler and Maccoby write, 'should be taken as evidence not so much that a contrary convention existed as that the conception of correct procedure was the fruit of gradual growth'.[7]

The most important general analysis of diplomacy and its place in international society remains that of Callières, who was in the service of Louis XIV, and whose *De la manière de négocier avec les souverains* was published in 1716.[8] Callières's ideas were formulated at the moment of the emergence of a complex balance after the checking of Louis XIV's bid for European hegemony, and of the coming together of parts of the European international system that had previously been largely unaffected by one another.

It is not surprising, then, that one of Callières's central ideas is the need for negotiation (he did not call it 'diplomacy') which is continuous and universal. Each prince, he thought, had a need for continual negotiation in the form of permanent embassies in all great states, far or near, in time of peace as well as war.

> To understand the permanent use of diplomacy, and the necessity for continual negotiations we must think of the states of which Europe is composed as being joined together by all kinds of necessary commerce, in such a way that they may be regarded as members of one Republic, and that no considerable change can take place in any one of them without affecting the condition, or disturbing the peace, of all the others. The blunder of the smallest of sovereigns may indeed cast an apple of discord among all the greatest powers, because there is no state so great which does not find it useful to have relations with the lesser states and to seek friends among the different parties of which even the smallest state is composed.[9]

Callières held that negotiation should not only be continuous and universal, but also professional. He noted the rarity of good negotiators, by comparison with good soldiers, and the lack of fixed rules for those in the foreign service. Negotiators, he held, were not best drawn from the ecclesiastical profession (because of its divided allegiance between church and sovereign), from the profession of arms (because the negotiator should be a man of peace), or from the law (because the methods of the law excluded faculties of suppleness and flexibility). The art of the negotiator is a profession in itself. 'It demands all the penetration, all the dexterity, all the suppleness which a man can well possess. It requires widespread understanding and knowledge, and above all a correct and piercing discernment.'[10]

For Callières this professional diplomacy plays a constructive and creative role, not merely in relation to the purposes of the prince or sovereign, but also in relation to the 'one Republic' of which all European princes are part. This role is one of helping to ensure that the interests of rulers triumph over their passions, and not their passions over their interests. He criticises the view of Rohan (in *De l'interest des princes et des estats de la chrestiente*, 1638) that sovereigns rule the people, and interest rules the sovereign, arguing that 'the passions of princes and of their ministers often overrule their interests'.[11] The task of the negotiator is, by means of reason and persuasion, to bring princes to act on a true appreciation of their interests, rather than a mistaken one, and to recognise common interests, where these exist.

The notion of the 'ideal ambassador' as a person governed by his reason rather than his passions, and seeking to subordinate the latter to the former in the conduct of foreign policy, is bound up with the emergence of rationalism in the seventeenth century, and especially with the notion that the proper objective of states was the pursuit of their interests rather than of their honour or their faith. The idea that states or nations have 'true' or objective interests, as distinct from perceived interests, and that men are endowed with a faculty of reason that enables them to see what these objective interests are, is one that is rejected elsewhere in this book (see Chapter 3). But there is such a thing as rationality in the sense of action that is internally consistent and consistent with given goals. Diplomatic theory presents the role of the 'ideal ambassador' in terms of adherence to canons of rationality in this sense, and the modern diplomatic tradition embodies an attempt to sustain behaviour on this model.

The Functions of Diplomacy

The functions which diplomacy has fulfilled in relation to order within the modern states system are as follows.

First, diplomacy facilitates communication between the political leaders of states and other entities in world politics. Without communication there could be no international society, nor any international system at all. Thus the most elementary function of diplomatists is to be messengers; as a condition of their performing this function effectively, there arises the most elementary diplomatic convention or institution, perhaps the only one that is common to all historical international societies, the immunity of the envoy from being killed or constrained by the receiving state.

A second function of diplomacy is the negotiation of agreements. Without the negotiation of agreements, international relations would be possible but they would consist only of fleeting, hostile encounters between one political community and another. Agreements are possible only if the interests of the parties, while they may be different, overlap at some point, and if the parties are able to perceive that they do overlap. The art of the diplomatist is to determine what this area of overlapping interests is, and through reason and persuasion to bring the parties to an awareness of it. The extent to which diplomacy can play any role or serve any function in the international system is therefore bound up with the extent to which states visualise foreign policy as the rational pursuit of interests of the state which at least in principle at some points overlap with the interests of other states. Diplomacy can play no role where foreign policy is conceived as the enforcement of a claim to universal authority, the promotion of the true faith against heretics, or as the pursuit of self-regarding interests that take no account of the interests of others.

A third function of diplomacy is the gathering of intelligence or information about foreign countries. Each country's external policies have to be based on information about developments in the world outside. While each country seeks to deny other countries some information about itself, it also wishes to impart some information. Thus, just as Byzantine practice was at one time to blind fold foreign envoys on their journey to the capital city, and there to incarcerate them in fortresses where they could not learn anything, but also to impress them with displays of military might, great powers today seek to deny their enemies access to information about their military capacities, but at the same time to impress them with selected military information, for the sake of 'deterrence'. Diplomatists have always played an important part in the gathering of intelligence, and the reciprocal interests of states in permitting access to information on a selective basis is nowhere better illustrated than in the institution of the military attaché which began to be formalised in the early part of the nineteenth century.[12] The development in the late seventeenth and early eighteenth centuries of the idea of international politics as a single field of forces, and especially of the idea of the balance of power as a perennial concern of statesmen, implied a constant flow of information about events in all countries, the continuous and universal diplomacy on which Callières places such stress.

A fourth function of diplomacy is minimisation of the effects of friction in international relations. Friction is the chafing or rubbing together of things in proximity. Given the juxtaposition of different political communities, each with its own values, preoccupations, prejudices and sensibilities, friction in international relations is always present, even between states and nations that perceive a wide area of common interests and whose relations are close and amicable. Such friction is a constant source of international tension and discord that may be unrelated to the 'true' interests of the parties concerned.

To minimise this kind of friction, and to contain its effects where it takes place, is one of the main functions of diplomacy. It is this function which prompts Satow's definition of diplomacy in terms of 'the application of intelligence and tact', and which accounts for our use of the world 'diplomatic' to describe the handling of human situations in everyday life in a manner that is tactful or subtle.

The diplomatist, or at all events the 'ideal diplomatist', helps to minimise friction through the conventions he observes in dealing with foreign officials, and also through his influence upon his own state's policy. In dealing with the representatives of other states, he observes conventions of language. In advancing or defending his own state's interests he seeks always to keep his objective in view, and use only those arguments that will promote the end in view, avoiding arguments that are intended to give vent to feelings or to satisfy his own or his country's pride or vanity. He seeks always to reason or persuade rather than to bully or threaten. He tries to show that the objective for which he is seeking is consistent with the other party's interests, as well as with his own. He prefers to speak of 'rights' rather than of 'demands', and to show that these rights flow from rules or principles which both states hold in common, and which the other state has already conceded. He tries to find the objective for which he is seeking in a framework of shared interest and agreed principle that is common ground between the parties concerned.

While there is force in the contention of Nicolson and others that diplomatists, in order to build up confidence and trust, should seek to be truthful, it is also the case that the business of minimising friction requires the diplomatist to avoid explicit recognition of stark realities, to refrain from 'calling a spade a spade'. It is for this reason that there is an inherent tension between the activity of being a diplomatist and the activity of academic inquiry into international politics.

Finally, diplomacy fulfils the function of symbolising the existence of the society of states. Diplomatists, even in the pristine form of messengers, are visible expressions of the existence of rules to which states and other entities in the international system pay some allegiance. In the developed form of the diplomatic corps that exists in every capital city they are tangible evidence of international society as a factor at work in international relations.

The Present Relevance of Diplomacy

If diplomacy has fulfilled the above functions in relation to international order in the past, does it continue to do so at present? Taking the term in the first, broadest sense in which it was defined at the beginning of this chapter, no one would argue that diplomacy has ceased to contribute to international order. This is, however, sometimes said of diplomacy in the second sense, the conduct of relations between states by professional diplomatists.

Those who argue in this way may point out that in a number of respects there has been a decline, since the First World War, in the role played in international politics by professional diplomacy, or at least by professional diplomacy on the nineteenth-century pattern. First, the role of the resident ambassador and his mission has declined in relation to that of other conductors of international business. The resident ambassador has been bypassed by heads of government and other ministers, who meet frequently in direct encounters; by special missions from the civil service of his home country, which visit the country to which he is accredited to deal with their opposite numbers; and in some cases by other permanent missions from his own country, whose work he is not able to control. The U.S. ambassador in some countries, for example, has working alongside him not only his own diplomatic staff but an economic-aid mission, a military assistance advisory group, representatives of the Central Intelligence Agency, the Treasury, the Peace Corps and many other branches of the home government, and the personnel of U.S. military bases or installations.

Some observers foresee that in cases where the volume of business between two states is very large and their relations very close and intimate – as between Britain and the United States – the institution of the resident diplomatic mission may in due course disappear. In the past the absence of diplomatic relations between two states has tended to signify one of two things: either that the business between them is slight or unimportant, or that their relations are so hostile as to make the exchange of ambassadors impossible. Diplomatic relations, in other words, have presupposed a certain minimum of business between the states concerned. If dealings with the British and U.S. governments ceased to be channelled through their respective ambassadors in Washington and London (or rather, if the fiction that they are so channelled were dropped), it may be argued that no great change would result.

A corollary of this argument is that resident embassies will continue to serve a function where a relationship does not involve more business than can be channelled through them, or where this relationship is still marked by a degree of hostility. On this argument, while the British embassy in Washington may be expected to become superfluous, the British embassy in Moscow, saving great changes in the nature of Anglo-Soviet relations, will not. Johan Galtung and Mari Ruge take this argument a step further when they write that bilateral, government-to-government diplomacy will be considerably reduced, and mainly used between antagonists, and that 'there may come a time when entering bilateral diplomacy may be a sign of hostility, not of friendship'.[13] Second, in this century bilateral diplomacy has declined in relation to multilateral diplomacy, principally as a consequence of the proliferation of international organisations. Particularly among the advanced countries of the Western world many important diplomatic questions are dealt with at least in part in a multilateral context: defence questions in the framework of NATO, trade and development assistance questions in that of the O.E.C.D. or the World Bank, monetary questions in the framework of the Group of

Ten, the economic relations of the E.E.C. countries with each other and with the outside world through the machinery of that association.

Of course, growth in the relative importance of multilateral diplomacy does not in itself imply a decline in the role of the professional diplomatist. For one thing, as noted above, conferences and international organisations provide opportunities for bilateral diplomacy as well as for genuinely multilateral diplomacy, and it is often the former that are the more important; for another the conduct of genuinely multilateral diplomacy is often in the hands of professional diplomatists. To a large extent the growth of multilateral diplomacy represents a change in the character of the professional diplomatist's work rather than a decline in his role. But it also reflects another change which will now be considered.

This third change is that in international politics as a whole since the First World War there has been a decline in that central preoccupation of professional diplomacy which Callières calls 'negotiation' and Satow calls the 'conduct of business': the attempt, through the 'application of intelligence and tact', to identify the interests of states and bring about conciliation between them where possible. On the one hand, the intelligent and tactful conduct of business has given place to 'political warfare', 'loudspeaker diplomacy' or 'diplomacy by insult'. On the other hand, it has given place to what may be called 'international technical management', an activity in which there is room for intelligence and tact, but in which the central concern is not conciliation of the different interests of states but collaboration to maximise a common interest.

The supplanting of diplomacy in Satow's sense of the conduct of business between states by 'political warfare' is a normal feature of periods of low consensus in international society. Its present phase dates from the First World War, more specifically from 1917 when the United States, in entering the war, and the Soviet Union, in the first flush of revolution, alike demanded an end to the Old Diplomacy. When two men meet to conduct business, two things are noticeable. One is that they are dealing with each other: when one speaks it is the other whom he is addressing. The other thing is that they both assume at least the possibility that they have some common interests. Their interests are of course different, and each is concerned only to advance his own interests. But they do both consider that there is, or at all events that there may be, some common ground between them that it is their purpose to explore. Very frequently, when the representatives of states meet at the present time neither of these conditions is present. Whereas the parties concerned appear to be addressing each other, they are in fact directing their remarks to third parties, whose support each is trying to enlist in the struggle. And they are quite unconscious of any common ground between them, each conceiving the achievement of his own aims as requiring that he inflict a total defeat on the adversary. Such persons are not conducting business but, as Nicolson points out, are engaged in an oratorical contest, like the envoys of the Greek city-states.

Nicolson's writings present the view that the decline of the Old Diplomacy has been a deplorable development.[14] He sees the principle that there should be 'open covenants' as an advance upon the Old Diplomacy, in so far as it makes possible parliamentary control of foreign policy and provides a safeguard against secret treaties of the sort that were concluded before and during the First World War. But the principle that covenants should be 'openly arrived at' he holds to rule out all negotiation, which is inherently secret or confidential, and to have led directly to the era of confrontations between the fascist and communist powers and their opponents, in which diplomacy gives place to 'political warfare'.

The difficulty with Nicolson's view is that it does not take account of the changes in general conditions of international life that have made the New Diplomacy a necessary instrument of foreign policy for any state. One of these changes, of which Nicolson noted one expression in the intrusion of public opinion and democratic legislatures into the sphere of foreign policy, is the political activisation of previously inert masses of people in most of the countries of the world, making the public justification or rationalisation of foreign policy mandatory for all governments, to both domestic and international audiences. The other change is the breakdown of that consensus among the European great powers whereby each of them, while sometimes locked in bitter rivalries with one or more of the others, at least accepted their right to exist. Given international conflicts that are not moderated by any sense of a continuing comity of states within which all have their rightful place, and given the imperative under which all governments have laboured of mobilising mass opinion or feeling in support of their policies, 'forensic diplomacy' is an efficient or functional instrument of policy, a consequence rather than a cause of the more general decline of the conditions of international order.

While in some areas of international relations diplomacy has given place to political warfare, in others it has given place to international technical management. Diplomacy is an activity appropriate to the situation in which the states or other political entities concerned are pursuing different interests, but also have some common interests. It is undermined not only by the growth of situations in which states can perceive no common interest, but also by situations in which states regard their interests as being identical. In these situations, states seek to advance their interests not by negotiating or bargaining with each other but by co-operating to maximise their common interest. Their common problem is not the political or diplomatic one of reconciling different interests or demands but the technical one of finding the most efficient means of achieving a given end.

It is difficult to find examples of international relationships in which international technical management has wholly driven out the diplomatic approach. Moreover, it should not be assumed that international problems are always best approached as problems of international technical management rather than as problems of diplomacy. The presentation of international problems as problems of technical management often merely obscures the true position, which is that states have different interests, and that common interests have first to be identified by a process of bargaining before any question of maximisation of them can arise.

Nevertheless, the perspective of technical management has intruded into international life in a number of areas. Examples are the discussion of strategic or security objectives in NATO, the discussion of international development assistance among the advanced countries, and the discussion of economic affairs within the European Economic Community.[15] It is clear that much of the present discussion of the ecological or environmental problem of mankind is discussed as a technical problem of maximising the interests of the human species rather than as a problem of reconciling different interests.

The consequence of all this is that in a number of areas of international discussion the conciliator or negotiator has given place to the technical expert – military, economic, social, educational, scientific, ecological. International organisations which, because of their permanence, reflect the willingness of states to accept and not to question the existence of a community of interests in a particular area, confirm this tendency.

In the third place, diplomatic institutions – the rules and conventions that make diplomatic intercourse possible and facilitate its working – have declined in this century. It is true that the central institutions of diplomacy have managed to survive the international turbulence of the twentieth century; and indeed, on a narrowly legal view it could be said that they have been strengthened. The diplomatic system has witnessed the number of states in the world grow to 140, while incorporating them all; none has formally repudiated the mechanism. The Cold War and the struggle of the anti-imperialist nations against the West have taken place without any general collapse of the system, and even without its total collapse as between the main blocs in these conflicts. At the same time the 1961 Vienna Convention on Diplomatic Relations and the 1963 Vienna Convention on Consular Relations, both signed and ratified by states from all the main political blocs, constitute an important legal advance in so far as they codify and formalise many rules that were previously rules only of customary law, and at the same time secure the adherence of many states outside the European tradition, whose acceptance of the rules of customary law might have been subject to doubt, in so far as the history out of which these rules evolved was not theirs.

But this strengthening and broadening of the legal forms in which the rules or institutions of diplomacy are expressed has gone along with a decline in their observance. The diplomatic relations between Western and communist nations during the Cold War were marked by frequent abuse by diplomatists of their privileges, especially for purposes of espionage, resulting in competitive resort to the declaration of a diplomatist as *persona non grata*. Receiving states have failed to respect the principle *ne impediatur legatio,* as embassies have been bugged, 'spontaneous' demonstrations organised and police protection not provided. In communist states restrictions have been imposed on the free movement of diplomatists. During the period of the Cold War consular relations between Western and communist countries disappeared, almost entirely. Many pairs of antagonistic states have broken off diplomatic relations, or have been unable to enter into them. The 1960s witnessed an upsurge of physical attacks, sometimes leading to their total destruction, on diplomatic missions, most notably in Indonesia and in China during the Cultural Revolution. The decade also saw the development of diplomatic kidnapping as a new hazard of diplomatic life, in which the foreign diplomatist's life was placed in jeopardy by political struggles within the receiving country.

The above indications of a decline in the role of professional diplomacy, or of a change in its character, do not establish that it has ceased to make a central contribution to the maintenance of international order. The decline of professional diplomacy may prove to be both a cause and a result of a wider decline in the conditions of international order in this century. If we consider the functions that diplomacy fulfils in relation to international order that were enumerated above, it is clear that all of them could in principle be fulfilled in other ways than by a mechanism of professional diplomacy of the sort we have now. But it is also clear that this traditional mechanism which is now the common property of all states in the world, and which continues to flourish despite some elements of decline, is well-adapted to fulfil them.

Communication

Communication between the political leaderships of states and other actors in world politics takes place constantly without the mediation of professional diplomatists. As we have seen, there is communication through direct meetings of political leaders of different states, and through the meetings of officials and special agents other than diplomatists. Messages can also be exchanged without any kind of personal intermediary by letter, cable, radio, telephone or teleprinter. Before the advent of postal services, cables, radio and television, the herald or messenger was a *sine qua non* of communication between separate political communities. This is no longer the case. In the 1960s the proliferation of 'hot lines' between the heads of a number of important states took place in the belief that rapid, direct communication in times of crisis was preferable to communication between specialised intermediaries.

But there is more to communication than the exchange of messages; messages have to be understood and interpreted. They have to convey moods and intentions as well as information. Their meaning depends on their context: the persons who send them and receive them, the circumstances in which they are sent, the previous history of exchanges on the subject. The significance of a message may lie in what it omits as well as in what it includes, in the choice of one phrase rather than another in conveying an idea.

Diplomatists are specialists in precise and accurate communication. They are more than mere couriers or heralds; they are experts in detecting and conveying nuances of international dialogue, and are equipped not merely to deliver a message but to judge the language in which it should be couched, the audience to whom and the occasion at which it should be presented. Modern diplomatists have been assisted by the fact that at any one time there has been one language which, more than any other, has been the language of diplomacy: until the middle of the eighteenth century, Latin; from then until the end of the First World War, French; since that time, principally English. Apart from language itself, diplomatists are assisted in the work of communication by certain conventions of phrase and emphasis which are the common currency of their profession, and which serve to minimise misunderstanding. Because diplomatists are familiar with the personalities between whom messages are exchanged and the contexts in which they find themselves, they are expert in the proper wording of a message that is sent and the construction of one that is received.

Negotiation

The negotiation of agreements between states can and does take place without the mediation of professional diplomatists. We have seen how the resident ambassador, for example, has been bypassed in this role by direct meetings of the political leaders or foreign ministers of states, and by meetings of officials other than diplomatists, such as technical experts negotiating agreements on some technical subject.

It would be mistaken, however, to conclude that the role of professional diplomatists in the negotiation of agreements was not still a vital one. The conclusion of agreements by heads of state or foreign ministers is often only the climax of a long process of reconnoitre, probing, testing of proposals and preliminary negotiation, carried out by professional diplomatists. The diplomatic profession, moreover, is a repository of specialist skills and techniques in the business of negotiation. The negotiation of agreements, as we have seen, presupposes a situation in which two parties perceive themselves as having different interests, but in which also they recognise the possibility that these interests overlap at some point. The art of the negotiator is to determine what this area of common interests is, and through reason and persuasion to bring the parties to an awareness of it. The exercise of this art requires knowledge of the parties concerned, and of how they perceive their interests, as distinct from what their interests are. It requires imagination in conceiving proposals, and skill and experience in formulating and propounding them. It requires precise and accurate communication. The task of negotiation is greatly facilitated if it can be undertaken in private, without the intrusion of competing preoccupations and loyalties, and if the negotiators are all members of the same profession, between whom there is confidence and mutual respect.

Information

As regards the function of gathering and assessing information about foreign countries, the diplomatist is only one of many persons engaged in this task. Whereas in some historical situations the resident ambassador was the only or at least the principal source of information about a foreign country, at present information may also be provided by the press and other mass media, by scholars and writers, by exchanges of private visitors, as well as through specialist intelligence agents and by technical means such as aerial and satellite photography. It is often remarked that diplomatic reporting from some countries is inferior to the reports of journalists or is lacking the depth of scholarly analyses; this underlies the complaint sometimes now made about the redundancy and excessive bulk of diplomatic reporting.

   Nevertheless, the professional diplomatist is uniquely skilled in gathering a particular kind of information that is essential to the conduct of international relations. This is information about the views and policies of a country's political leadership, now and in the near future. It is knowledge of personalities rather than of the forces and conditions which shape a country's policy over the long term. It is knowledge of the current situation and how it is likely to develop rather than of the pattern of past regularities. It derives from day-to-day personal dealings with the leading political *strata* in the country to which a diplomatist is accredited, sometimes to the detriment of his understanding of society at large in that country.

Such knowledge by itself can be misleading. Foreign offices need to supplement it with understanding of a foreign society as a whole, as distinct from its leading political elements, and with knowledge of basic continuities and long-term trends, as distinct from assessments of the current scene. For these latter kinds of knowledge, professional diplomatists are not the best source. But the day-to-day conduct of international business depends upon information and advice about the personalities in a foreign government, the ebb and flow of their political fortunes, the combinations and rivalries among them, and this the professional diplomatist is sometimes best able to supply.

Minimisation of Friction

The function of minimising friction in international relations might in principle be carried out without modern diplomatic institutions; persons other than diplomatists are capable of applying intelligence and tact in international exchanges, just as diplomatists are capable of failing to do so. But the diplomatic profession has sought to adapt itself to this role and embodies traditions and conventions that equip it uniquely for performing the role.

The long tradition of tracts that have been written in modern times on the qualities of 'the ideal ambassador' often stress those which appear to be required for the fulfilment of this function of the minimisation of friction. When we read in Callières that the ideal negotiator should have an equable humour, a tranquil and patient nature, and an address always open, genial and civil, or, in Nicolson, that he should have calm, self-control, patience and good temper, these vacuous recommendations that fail to tell us under what conditions diplomatists should have these virtues, or what objects they serve, can be read as a description of the kind of behaviour that fulfils the function of minimisation of friction; the striking thing is how little over the centuries the recommendations have changed.

Symbolic Function

The function of symbolising the existence of the society of states, and beyond it of the element of unity in the political organisation of mankind, is fulfilled not only by organised diplomacy but also by universal international organisations, especially the United Nations. The symbolic function carried out by the diplomatic mechanism is, however, an important one.

Diplomatic relations between states are not a source of the mutual recognition by states of one another's sovereignty, equality, independence and other rights, but they presuppose such a mutual recognition of rights and provide tangible evidence of its existence. The presence in capital cities of a diplomatic corps is a sign not only of the existence of foreign states and nations, but of organised international society as a whole, providing the host government and people with a reminder of this factor which must qualify their policies.

The diplomatic profession itself is a custodian of the idea of international society, with a stake in preserving and strengthening it. R. B. Mowat has written of the 'collegiality' of the diplomatic profession: the common outlook that binds diplomatists working together in foreign cities, in isolation from their country and in close communion with other foreign diplomatists.[16] The solidarity of the diplomatic profession has declined since the mid-nineteenth century, when diplomatists of different countries were united by a common aristocratic culture, and often by ties of blood and marriage, when the number of states was fewer and all the significant ones European, and when diplomacy took place against the background of 'the international of monarchs' and the intimate acquaintance of leading figures through the habit of congregating at spas. But in the global international system in which states are more numerous, more deeply divided and less unambiguously participants in a common culture, the symbolic role of the diplomatic mechanism may for this reason be more important. (The concept of a 'diplomatic culture' is discussed in Chapter 13.) The remarkable willingness of states of all regions, cultures, persuasions and stages of development to embrace often strange and archaic diplomatic procedures that arose in Europe in another age is today one of the few visible indications of universal acceptance of the idea of international society.

8

War and International Order

It may be argued that it is perverse to treat war as an institution of the society of states, but in the sense that it is a settled pattern of behaviour, shaped towards the promotion of common goals, there cannot be any doubt that it has been in the past such an institution, and remains one. In this chapter I propose to consider:

(i) What is war?

(ii) What functions has it fulfilled in relation to international order in the historical modern states system?

(iii) What, if any, are the functions of war in international politics at the present time?

War

War is organised violence carried on by political units against each other. Violence is not war unless it is carried out in the name of a political unit; what distinguishes killing in war from murder is its vicarious and official character, the symbolic responsibility of the unit whose agent the killer is. Equally, violence carried out in the name of a political unit is not war unless it is directed against another political unit; the violence employed by the state in the execution of criminals or the suppression of pirates does not qualify because it is directed against individuals.

We should distinguish between war in the loose sense of organised violence which may be carried out by any political unit (a tribe, an ancient empire, a feudal principality, a modern civil faction) and war in the strict sense of international or interstate war, organised violence waged by sovereign states. Within the modern states system only war in the strict sense, international war, has been legitimate; sovereign states have sought to preserve

178

for themselves a monopoly of the legitimate use of violence. This came about in two stages: first, the forging of the distinction between public war, or war waged on the authority of a public body, and private war, or war waged without any such authority, and the curtailment of the latter; and second, the emergence of the idea that the state was the only public body competent to confer such authority. The development of the modern concept of war as organised violence among sovereign states was the outcome of a process of limitation or confinement of violence. We are accustomed, in the modern world, to contrast war between states with peace between states; but the historical alternative to war between states was more ubiquitous violence.

We need also to distinguish between war in the material sense, that is actual hostilities, and war in the legal or normative sense, a notional state of affairs brought into being by the satisfaction of certain legal or normative criteria, for example that it be recognised or declared by competent authorities. Wars in the material sense often take place that are not wars in the legal sense: most of the wars that have taken place since 1945 have been described, by those engaged in them, by some other name. On the other hand, war in the legal sense may be held to exist at times when no actual hostilities are taking place, for example in the interval between the cessation of hostilities at the end of a war and the conclusion of a peace treaty. If we are speaking of war in the legal sense, the distinction between war and peace is absolute: thus Grotius's doctrine *inter bellum et pacem nihil est medium*. War in the material sense, on the other hand, is sometimes hard to distinguish from peace. Between the two states of affairs there are gradations: when does a blockade become an act of violence? When does a rebel band take on the character of a political unit?

But while we may distinguish actual war from notional war, it would be mistaken to suppose that the former exists entirely apart from the latter. In any actual hostilities to which we can give the name 'war', norms or rules, whether legal or otherwise, invariably play a part. The persons conducting these hostilities are activated by the notion that they are engaged in an activity called 'war', that this is a different state of affairs from peace, that certain kinds of behaviour are appropriate to it, for example that they are acting as agents of a political group, and that certain other individuals must be viewed as the agents of an enemy group. Rules or norms, although they may be considered in abstraction, are also part of the material reality of war, the consideration of which requires attention to behaviour that is a response to accepted rules.

Finally, we should distinguish war as a rational, intelligent or purposive activity, from war which is blind, impulsive or habitual. Clausewitz's definition of war as 'an act intended to compel our opponent to fulfil our will' expresses the conception of war that was dominant in Europe under the sway of the doctrine of reason of state. Even when applied to the experience of modern Europe up till the post-Napoleonic period, out of which Clausewitz's analysis grew, it was a recommendation as to how wars should be conducted, not an accurate description of how wars were actually fought. War is very often not the servant of rational or intelligent purposes; it has been fought by primitive tribes as a form of ritual, by Christian and Saracen Knights in fulfilment of a chivalric code, by modern nations to test their cohesion and sense of identity, and throughout history from sheer lust for blood and conquest.

War in the Modern States System

The functions of war in the historical modern states system may be considered from three perspectives: that of the individual state, that of the system of states and that of the society of states.

From the point of view of the individual state, war has appeared as an instrument of policy, one of the means by which the state's objectives may be attained. It is true that when a state embarks upon a war, this does not always reflect a deliberate or calculated attempt to relate war as a means to some desired end; states have sometimes stumbled into war by accident or miscalculation, or have been swept into it by gusts of royal anger or public feeling. It is true also that when, as in August-September 1914, states do embark upon war as a deliberately chosen means of attaining some concrete and specific end, the war's own momentum sometimes so transforms the belligerent states and the objectives they set for themselves that the original ends for which the war was begun are lost to sight. Nevertheless, the idea that war can serve as an effective instrument of policy has been borne out throughout the history of the states system. Whether we look to Richelieu's embarking on war to curb the Habsburg power, to Frederick II's wars to make Prussia a great power, to England's wars to wrest empire from France, to Bismarck's wars to unify Germany and establish its hegemony in Europe, or the war fought by the United Nations to crush the Axis, there is no lack of examples showing that wars embarked upon may sometimes produce the intended results.

From the point of view of the international system, the single mechanism or field of forces which states constitute together by virtue of their interaction with one another, war appears as a basic determinant of the shape the system assumes at any one time. It is war and the threat of war that help to determine whether particular states survive or are eliminated, whether they rise or decline, whether their frontiers remain the same or are changed, whether their peoples are ruled by one government or another, whether disputes are settled or drag on, and which way they are settled, whether there is a balance of power in the international system or one state becomes preponderant. War and the threat of war are not the only determinants of the shape of the international system; but they are so basic that even the terms we use to describe the system – great powers and small powers, alliances and spheres of influence, balances of power and hegemony – are scarcely intelligible except in relation to war and the threat of war.

From the point of view of international society, that is from the point of view of the common values, rules and institutions accepted by the system of states as a whole, war has a dual aspect. On the one hand, war is a manifestation of disorder in international society, bringing with it the threat of breakdown of international society itself into a state of pure enmity or war of all against all. The society of states, accordingly, is concerned to limit and contain war, to keep it within the bounds of rules laid down by international society itself. On the other hand, war – as an instrument of state policy and a basic determinant of the shape of the international system – is a means which international society itself feels a need to exploit so as to achieve its own purposes. Specifically, in the perspective of international society, war is a means of enforcing international law, of preserving the balance of power, and, arguably, of promoting changes in the law generally regarded as just. The rules and institutions which international society has evolved reflect the tension between the perception of war as a threat to international society which must be contained, and the perception of it as an instrumentality which international society can exploit to achieve its purposes.

International society is impelled to restrict the right of states to go to war. To assert the right of a state to make war against other states for any reason whatever and without limitation of any kind, is to deny that states are bound by common rules and institutions. International society has sought to restrict the right to make war in four ways. First, as was noted above, it confines the right to wage war to sovereign states. Second, it seeks to impose restrictions on the way in which war is conducted – as, for example, through the traditional rules of war. Third, it has sought to restrict the geographical spread of wars that have broken out through laws of neutrality, laying down the rights and duties of neutrals and belligerents in relation to each other. Fourth, it has sought to restrict the reasons or causes for which a state can legitimately resort to war – from the beginnings of the states system through the influence of the doctrine that war should be begun only for a just cause, and in this century also through legal instruments such as the League Covenant, the Kellogg-Briand Pact and the United Nations Charter.

But while international society has been impelled to restrict and contain war, it has also sought to assign to some kinds of war a positive role in the maintenance of international order. First, it has seen war as a possible means of enforcement of international law. Given the absence of a central authority or world government, international law can be enforced only by particular states able and willing to take up arms on its behalf. At its minimum this conception of war as law enforcement relates only to the case of war waged in self-defence by a state whose rights of territorial sovereignty have been violated by an attacker. At its maximum the conception extends also to war waged on behalf of the victim by third states whose own rights have not been infringed, and to war waged in defence not simply of territorial integrity but of a wide range of legal rights.

Second, international society, at least from the beginning of the eighteenth century, has seen in war a means of preserving the balance of power, that is the situation in which no one state is preponderant and can lay down the law to others. The preservation of a general balance of power has been perceived as essential to the survival of the states system, and war directed to this end as carrying out a positive function.

Third, and more doubtfully, it is possible to argue that international society at large has sometimes regarded war as fulfilling a positive function when it is fought not on behalf of the international legal order or the balance of power, but in order to bring about just change. The international order is notoriously lacking in mechanisms of peaceful change, notoriously dependent on war as the agent of just change. The society of states, always divided about the rules and institutions necessary to sustain order, is more divided still about the requirements of justice. But there have sometimes been occasions when the acquiescence of international society in a change brought about by force reflects, among other things, a widespread feeling that the use or threat of force has been a just one.

War at the Present Time

The view that war no longer fulfils the functions outlined above rests principally on the idea that, given the existence of nuclear weapons, force has become politically unusable as between states. Thus it is commonly said that, from the point of view of individual states, war is no longer the continuation of policy by other means but represents the breakdown of policy. It is said that force and the threat of force are no longer basic determinants of the character or shape of the international system, or at all events that they will cease to be such when nuclear weapons have become available to all states. It is argued also that international society can no longer regard war as an instrument of purposes such as the enforcement of international law. 'In former times', Professor B. V. A. Röling has written, 'the threat and possibility of war were factors in the maintenance of law. War can no longer serve this purpose, however, for humanity can also be annihilated by a just war.'[1] It is true and obvious that war fought without restraint or limitation by states equipped with nuclear weapons and other advanced military technology cannot serve as an instrument of foreign policy, at least in the sense in which that phrase has been understood in modern European experience. Such a war must lead to the breakdown, if not the annihilation, not merely of the enemy society but also of the society initiating the war. But it does not follow from this that war and the threat of war are deprived of all political utility.

In the first place, most international conflicts do not directly involve the nuclear powers. While there are about 140 states only six of them have so far conducted nuclear explosions. In the case of conflicts between non-nuclear states, war and the threat of war continue to play a political role, as has been demonstrated in the wars between Israel and her neighbours in 1948, 1956, 1967 and 1973, in the Indo-Pakistani wars of 1947–8, 1965 and 1971, and many others.

In wars such as these the course of events is much affected by the background presence of nuclear weapons. Whenever armed conflict breaks out between sovereign states, there does register throughout the world a sense of alarm that derives from the fear of nuclear war and is expressed in attempts, for example through the United Nations or regional international organisations, to bring the fighting quickly to a halt. The effect of this background presence of nuclear weapons, however, is not to deprive states of the possibility of exploiting the military force at their command, only to alter the setting in which they do so – to pose for them such problems as how best to make or threaten war with these risks in mind, how to avoid or postpone intervention by the great powers, how to catch them unawares, present them with a *fait accompli,* ensure that they will be divided, or make do in the event that they cut off supplies of arms.

In the second place, where a nuclear power is directly involved in an international conflict, its opponent is sometimes non-nuclear. The use of nuclear weapons by the United States against Japan, and the threat of their use by the United States against the Soviet Union before August 1949 and China before October 1964, took place in these circumstances. In a conflict between a nuclear and a non-nuclear power the use of nuclear weapons will often be judged to involve a political and moral cost out of proportion to the end in view; it seems unlikely that any nuclear power could decide to use nuclear weapons in such a situation without facing great and adverse repercussions in world opinion which may out-weigh the military gains to be expected. To the extent that this is appreciated also in the country subject to nuclear threats, such threats will not carry conviction. In the Anglo-Indonesian conflict of 1963–5 over President Sukarno's 'confrontation' of Malaysia, for example, the British government could not conceivably have regarded the use of nuclear weapons as a politically viable option, nor does it seem likely that the Indonesian government would have found British threats credible, had they been made. But where a nuclear power's stake in employing the force at its disposal is large, such threats may appear credible. When the United States confronted a non-nuclear Soviet Union, what was at stake was, in the American view, the continued independence of Western Europe; the threat of the United States to use the force at its disposal, in a situation in which it was in no danger of suffering nuclear attack itself, must have seemed convincing. It is an historical accident that each of the five present nuclear powers views its nuclear forces as directed at one or more of the others. There are, however, a number of potential nuclear powers – including Israel, South Africa and Australia – in which it is sometimes argued that the chief role of nuclear forces would be to provide defence against, or deterrence of, an attack by non-nuclear powers superior in numbers.

In the third place, even where nuclear weapons are available to both parties in an international conflict and the prospect of mutual destruction is immediately present, the possibilities of the political exploitation of force are considerable. This is the crucial point, for it means that the persisting utility of force in the nuclear age is not merely a feature of the present imperfect distribution of nuclear weapons among the nations of the world, but could be expected to obtain also were these weapons to become generally available.

Nuclear powers that are engaged in a conflict with one another are not necessarily in a situation of mutual deterrence or stalemate. For this to obtain a number of conditions must be satisfied, among which the possession of nuclear weapons on both sides is only one. Each party must have a nuclear force that is capable of surviving a first blow by the opponent, and penetrating to its targets with sufficient destructive effect. Each side must believe that the other has both the capacity and the will to produce damage, and it must judge this damage to be unacceptable.

Nuclear powers have in the past confronted one another without being in any such situation of stalemate. Between 1949 and 1954 the Soviet Union did not possess a means of delivering nuclear weapons on the United States. China, from the time of her first nuclear test in 1964 until the time of writing, has been a nuclear power without the means of delivering nuclear weapons on the United States; and even after China acquires a force of Intercontinental Ballistic Missiles, experts are likely to debate whether this force would be capable of surviving a first blow from the United States and penetrating that country's anti-missile defences. The ability of British nuclear forces since 1952 and French since 1960 to provide a credible deterrent in relation to the Soviet Union has been the subject of constant disagreement among experts. It is in fact only in the case of relations between the United States and the Soviet Union in the period since the mid-1950s that there would be any general agreement among students of strategic matters about the existence of a nuclear stalemate. Moreover, where a nuclear stalemate exists, it is not necessarily stable, but is subject to being undermined by technological developments that would make possible an effective defence of cities and population, or a disarming strike against retaliatory forces. A nuclear stalemate can also be rendered unstable by changes of a political and psychological nature – in the will of one side to use its retaliatory forces, or the belief of one side in the other's will or capacity.

Where, as between the United States and the Soviet Union now, there is a relationship of mutual deterrence, and this is basically stable (despite complicating elements in the calculus of deterrence such as the Anti-Ballistic Missile and the multiple and individually targeted warhead), the exploitation of force for purposes of foreign policy will be closely circumscribed. But there exist in principle two outlets.

The first of these is the limited use of force. The prospect of suffering unacceptable damage at the hands of the opponent may deter the nuclear powers confronting one another from any use of force against each other at all, or it might deter them only from an unlimited or unrestrained conflict. In the late 1950s it was widely believed in the Western world that the very stability of mutual deterrence of unrestrained strategic nuclear warfare would create the conditions in which limited war between the super powers could be conducted with maximum confidence that the limitations would be preserved. The Soviet-American nuclear stalemate that grew up at that time provided the impetus for a whole range of studies of, and preparations for, possible limited wars and possible ways of keeping them limited: various forms of limited strategic nuclear exchange; nuclear war restricted to battlefield or military targets; conventional war; sub-conventional or guerrilla war.

The position so far has been that the United States and the Soviet Union have avoided becoming directly involved in battle at all; the fear of expansion of a conflict to the level of unrestrained nuclear war has in fact deterred them from putting the theory of limited war to the test of a direct encounter. Only if we treat the Korean War, the French Indochina War or the Vietnam War as wars fought 'by proxy' between the super powers could we say that they have had experience of fighting a limited war with each other, and such a treatment would be quite artificial. Nevertheless, we cannot assume on the basis of the Soviet-American stalemate so far that these or other nuclear powers will not be prepared to risk direct military conflict with each other, including limited nuclear war.

The other outlet available to contending nuclear powers locked in a position of stalemate, but seeking a means of the political exploitation of force, is the threat of its use. While each of the contestants may possess force sufficient to produce damage the other would regard as unacceptable, they may be unequal in demonstrating resolve to use the force at their disposal. Superior technique in 'brinkmanship' or 'crisis management' may establish the greater willingness of one side to go to war rather than back down, and so bring a diplomatic victory in its train, as demonstrated by the United States in the Cuban missile crisis of 1962.

Thus war is not robbed of its historic political functions merely because of the existence of nuclear weapons and other advanced military technology; nor could these political functions be expected to disappear as a consequence of the spread of nuclear weapons. What is the case, however, is that in international politics at the present time the role of war, at least in the strict sense of interstate or international war, appears more closely circumscribed than before the end of the Second World War. The range of political objects war can serve has become narrower, the costs of resorting to it greater.

From the vantage-point of the individual state, war remains an instrument of policy, but one that can be used only at greater cost and in relation to a narrower range of purposes than before 1945. Where nuclear weapons are involved, the costs may include the destruction of the society resorting to war, should limitations break down. Even without nuclear weapons war for an advanced state can involve such physical destruction, and such political, economic and social dislocation as to make war almost unthinkable as an instrument of policy unless it be a strictly limited war fought well beyond the territory of the state itself. It is in fact only wars of this latter sort that have been fought by the economically advanced states since the Second World War, and even these (one thinks, for example, of the impact of the Suez War on Britain, of the Indochinese and Algerian Wars on France, and of the Korean and Vietnam Wars on the United States) have in some cases brought severe domestic repercussions.

Apart from the destruction and dislocation caused by the war itself to the state which initiates it, there must be measured the cost to the state's standing in world politics. The legal obstacles placed by the United Nations Charter in the way of resort to war for any purpose other than individual or collective self-defence are not in themselves formidable, but they express a collective fear of war which if it is mobilised against the state resorting to war can provide a significant deterrent.

While the costs of resort to war have expanded, the range of foreign policy purposes which war can effectively promote appears to have contracted. Historically, states have gone to war for one or more of three kinds of objective. First, wars have been fought for economic gain, measured in terms of bullion, or trade monopolies or access to markets, raw materials and investment opportunities; the classic examples were perhaps the trading and colonial wars fought by the European powers in the age of mercantilism. Second, wars have been fought for reasons of security, to resist or remove some external threat to the state's integrity or independence; classical examples are the great preventive wars – such as the Peloponnesian War, the War of the Spanish Succession, and perhaps the First World War. If a great war between the United States and the Soviet Union had broken out in our time, its underlying motive would have been security in this sense. Third, wars have been fought to promote ideological objectives, to advance a religious or political faith; the wars of Islamic expansion, the Crusades, the wars of the French Revolution and Napoleon were for ideological objectives, at least in part.

It is now widely doubted whether war can effectively promote economic gain, at all events through the conquest of territory. Even as recently as the Second World War Germany in Eastern Europe and Japan in South-east Asia sought to conquer territory at least partly so as to control markets and sources of raw materials. In the post-1945 period it seems unlikely that any state has contemplated territorial conquest for such a reason. It has been demonstrated, not least by Germany and Japan, that economic growth does not require the political control of foreign territory, while the countries which at the end of the Second World War possessed colonial territories have now all concluded that the costs of attempting to control them outweigh the gains.

Wars are still fought to advance ideological objectives, and in the post-1945 period have been fought to advance communism and to liberate peoples from colonial rule. It is difficult, however, to find examples of a state going to war to spread a faith by the sword among a foreign people, except in circumstances where that people is already divided within itself by an ideological conflict. Resort to war to spread an ideology has typically taken the form of intervention in a civil conflict. The Soviet Union, China, Cuba, the United Arab Republic and Algeria, in promoting revolutionary doctrines abroad, have sought to aid and abet revolutionary movements with local roots in foreign nations, not to impose such doctrines through open invasion.

It would be rash to conclude that the military conquest of foreign territory can no longer bring economic gain or promote ideologies, or to predict that these functions of war will not reappear in any form. Indeed, there are signs that resource scarcity, or the belief in resource scarcity, may lead to a revival of interest in the use of force to gain or to preserve access to raw materials. But states now are reluctant to embark upon war except to achieve objectives of security. Security, of course, may include the making secure of economic assets enjoyed – such an objective, for example, has provided part of the rationale of Britain's willingness to use her forces in Malaysia and Singapore in the post-Second World War period. Security may also include the making safe of governments abroad with congenial ideologies – this objective has underlain the American use of force in Vietnam and Santo Domingo in 1965 and the Soviet use of force in Hungary in 1956 and Czechoslovakia in 1968. At present, however, it would seem that only considerations of security can cause the government of an advanced industrial state to conclude that war is worth the cost.

From the point of view of the international system, war remains a basic determinant of the shape of the system. But among the great nuclear powers it is the threat of war rather than war itself that determines the relationships. Mutual deterrence as between the great powers rules out unlimited war as a means of resolving disputes between them, and this affects the place of war in the system as a whole. Three changes from the pre-1945 international system, in particular, are notable.

First, where the armed forces of the United States and the Soviet Union directly confront one another, as for more than three decades they have done in Central Europe, actual war has not come into play to resolve the conflict. Unlimited war cannot serve as an instrument of policy for either side; limited war has been regarded by both sides as carrying too high a risk; the attempts to change the *status quo,* and to defend it, as in the Berlin crisis of 1958–61, have taken the form of elaborate threats. War itself not being available, and the main issues having so far proved unamenable to diplomatic solution, the result has been no change, what Raymond Aron once called 'the slowing down of history'.[2]

Second, while war outside the area of direct relations between the great nuclear powers plays much the same part in international history that it has done in the past, this is subject to the proviso that if the nuclear great powers are supporting opposite sides in a local conflict, they will try to control it in such a way that the ground rules of their own relationships are respected. The restraint imposed by the Soviet Union on China and the United States on Taiwan during the Far East conflicts of the 1950s, and that imposed by the United States on Israel and the Soviet Union on Egypt since 1967, illustrate this pattern. War could assume its 'normal' historical function of bringing these conflicts to an end in favour of one party or the other only if one or both of the super powers were to disengage.

Third, the obstacles standing in the way of resort to war between sovereign states have encouraged the tendencies making for war or violence within them. International war, as a determinant of the shape of the international system, has declined in relation to civil war. The principal territorial changes of the last quarter century –

the break-up of European empires – have been brought about by civil violence or the possibility of it, rather than by interstate violence. The territorial integrity of many states, new and old, is now more threatened by separatist violence within their frontiers than by violence from outside. The ideological struggles between communist and anti-communist, neo-colonialist and radical nationalist, can take a violent form more readily in a domestic than in an interstate context.

The civil violence now so prominent in many countries does not exist apart from the international system. Civil wars are internationalised by virtue of the intervention of outside states in them. There is a contagion of civil violence between one country and another – brought about by common inspiration, common organisation or emulation. Some revolutionary groups, committed to violence in a particular country, have become violent actors in world politics in their own right; in kidnapping diplomats or seizing civil aircraft of foreign countries, they are challenging the sovereign state's monopoly of international violence. The reasons underlying the expanding international role of civil war are many and complex, but among them is the now circumscribed political role of war in the strict sense, interstate war.

From the perspective of international society, war retains its dual aspect: on the one hand, a threat to be limited and contained; on the other hand, an instrumentality to be harnessed to international society's purposes. But it is the perception of war as a threat to international society that is now dominant; the perception of war as a means of enforcing the law, preserving the balance of power and effecting just change, is now qualified by a sense of the overriding need to contain war within tolerable bounds.

International society is now reluctant to view war as law enforcement except in cases where it is resorted to for reasons of self-defence. Grotius, in his celebrated account of the just causes of war, mentioned three: self-defence, the recovery of property and the infliction of punishment. Until recently, states have been able often enough to find support in international society for the view that in going to war to recover property or protect their nationals abroad, as European states frequently did in the last century, they have been enforcing the law. States have also in the past been able to gain international support, as the victors did in the two World Wars this century, for the view that war aims could legitimately include not only the restoration of rights but also punishment of the transgressor.

The balance of power remains a condition of the continued existence of the system of states, and limited wars that affect the distribution of power among the great powers contribute to it. But a central part of the general balance of power is now the relationship of mutual nuclear deterrence between the United States and the Soviet Union, now in process of becoming a triangular relationship including China. In this relationship of mutual deterrence, unlimited war can have no positive role but can only represent the collapse of the system.

At a time when two of the three main groups of states in the world contend that war may justly be fought to liberate colonial territories from metropolitan powers, or on behalf of the rights of black Africans in Southern Africa to self-determination, it cannot be said that international society has ceased to recognise in war a means of effecting just change. The acquiescence of international society in India's seizure of Goa in 1961, and Indonesia's infiltration of West Irian in 1962, and in 1971 India's war against Pakistan on behalf of Bangladesh, was facilitated in each case by a widespread though not universal feeling that resort to war to accomplish the change in question was just.

But the positive role still assigned by international society to wars that sustain its own purposes is now overridden by a sense of the need to limit the conduct of war. In the post-1945 period international society has had a certain success in confining interstate war within limits consistent with the survival of the states system – less through any respect paid to the laws of war than through tacit rules of the game improvised under the discipline of the fear of war. But as this has happened, war waged by political units other than states has expanded in scope. Civil factions have emerged as violent world actors, challenging the monopoly of international violence which sovereign states have long claimed for themselves, and escaping the restraints and rules by which sovereign states are bound. The freedom of the revolutionary group from international constraints, by contrast with the subjection of the sovereign state, was dramatised by the United Nations Security Council in 1968, when it condemned Israel for carrying out a retaliatory raid against Lebanon in response to acts of violence committed by Lebanon-based Palestinian guerrillas against El Al aircraft in Athens, but failed to do anything to constrain the Palestinian guerrillas themselves. International society will not be able to afford to allow these new forms of war to lie permanently beyond the compass of its rules.

9

The Great Powers and International Order

In this chapter I propose to consider the following:

(i) What are the great powers?

(ii) What role do great powers play in relation to international order?

(iii) What is the role of the great powers in relation to international order at the present time?

The Great Powers

When we speak of great powers (or today of super powers – a term we shall consider below) we imply three things. First, we imply that there are two or more powers that are comparable in status; we imply, one might say, the existence of a club with a rule of membership. Thus there could not be simply one great power. It strains the meaning of the term to speak of the Roman Empire or of Imperial China as having been a great power, for these were political entities whose position, in the wider international systems in which they operated, was unique. In the mid-1960s some writers began to argue that the United States had so far outstripped the Soviet Union as to have become the single dominant power in world politics.[1] They argued that the so-called 'bipolar' model of the post-1945 international system no longer applied, and they looked instead to the model of Rome. Since that time the position of the United States in relation to the Soviet Union has sharply declined; and indeed, the United States was far from being ready to assume the mantle of Rome even when its global influence was at its highest point. But if the United States were indeed the single dominant power, it could no longer rightly be called a great power or super power.

Second, we imply that the members of this club are all in the front rank in terms of military strength; that is to say, that countries which are great powers are comparable in military strength, and that there is no class of power that is superior to them. That great powers must be great military powers may seem a truism, but in 1970 it was denied by the Japanese Prime Minister Mr Sato, who asserted that Japan was about to become the first country in history to be a great power without having the military accoutrements which such powers in the past have always had.[2] Mr Sato, in sustaining this view, would be able to point to the great political influence that Japan had by then come to wield by virtue of her economic strength, and also to the inhibitions that now circumscribe resort to force as an instrument of foreign policy. There is, however, no reason to believe that Japan or any other country can reach the front rank politically without also taking the steps that are necessary to reach the front rank militarily, and today these include the development of strategic nuclear weapons.

Ranke, in his essay on *The Great Powers,* tries to define the military status of a great power in terms of self-sufficiency or independence of allies. He says that a country is a great power when it can maintain itself against all others, even when they are united against it.[3] This definition is too vague to be acceptable as it stands, but it helps us to understand what is special in the position of the United States and the Soviet Union now. These countries both have allies, and they could not dispense with them without dispensing also with many of their objectives in foreign policy; but, subject to certain qualifications, the United States and the Soviet Union can in the last resort maintain their security without allies and against all comers.

One qualification concerns the special circumstances of the nuclear age. The United States and the Soviet Union are physically vulnerable to nuclear attack by each other, and possibly by other nuclear powers. Each nuclear power can take steps to reduce the likelihood of such an attack, for example it can maintain a deterrent, seek to resolve political conflicts and reach understandings in the field of arms control; but in the last analysis it cannot prevent the other power from attacking. In this sense no state today can assure its own security unilaterally.

Another qualification concerns the large number of middle and small powers which today pursue successful policies of non-alignment or neutralism. These states are able to provide for their security for long periods while dispensing with allies. But their ability to do so is conditional upon the maintenance of a general balance of power in the international system by states other than themselves. By contrast, the ability of the great powers to dispense with allies is not conditional in this way.

Third, great powers are powers recognised by others to have, and conceived by their own leaders and peoples to have, certain special rights and duties.[4] Great powers, for example, assert the right, and are accorded the right, to play a part in determining issues that affect the peace and security of the international system as a whole. They accept the duty, and are thought by others to have the duty, of modifying their policies in the light of the managerial responsibilities they bear. States which, like Napoleonic France or Nazi Germany, are military powers of the front rank, but are not regarded by their own leaders or others as having these rights and responsibilities, are not properly speaking great powers.

The idea of a great power, in other words, presupposes and implies the idea of an international society as opposed to an international system, a body of independent political communities linked by common rules and institutions as well as by contact and interaction. Recognition of the special rights and duties of great powers by the accord to them of permanent membership of the Council of the League of Nations or the United Nations Security Council is not the source of these rights and duties, but has rather been made possible by the fact that such rights and duties are in any case recognised.

In the period since the Second World War the term 'great power' has given place to another, now of doubtful utility: 'super power'. This term was first used by Professor W. T. R. Fox in 1944, when he applied it to Britain as well as to the United States and the Soviet Union.[5] What was essentially recognised was the appearance of a new class of power, superior to the traditional European great powers, and alone capable of undertaking the central managerial role in international politics they had played in the past. The emergence of the United States and the Soviet Union in 1945 so dwarfed Britain, France and Germany that it has ever since seemed inappropriate to use the term 'great power' to describe a status that all of these countries have in common. It has seemed necessary either to reserve the term 'great power' for the United States and the Soviet Union and to treat the major European powers as having an inferior status (as 'middle powers' or 'secondary powers'), or to speak of the United States and the Soviet Union as 'super powers' possessing a higher status than that of merely great powers.

The new concept of a 'super power', however, adds nothing to the old one of a 'great power'. The role which the United States and the Soviet Union played in the quarter century after 1945 was one they inherited from the former European great powers. The import of the term 'super power', during its vogue, was simply that only states of the size of the United States and the Soviet Union could now be, in the full sense, great powers. With the decline of the United States and the Soviet Union in relation to China, Japan and the combination of Western European states, the term is ceasing to be helpful.

It may be noted that it is a mistake to define great powers or super powers in terms of possession of strategic nuclear weapons. Although military nuclear capability is today a necessary condition of super powerhood or great powerhood it is not a sufficient condition, as is shown by the cases of Britain and France. Moreover, the United States and the Soviet Union were recognisable as super powers before their strategic nuclear arms were fully developed, and in the case of the latter before it had acquired them at all.

Who, then, are the great powers now? At most, the United States, the Soviet Union and China are great powers: Japan is only a potential great power; and Western Europe, while it is not amalgamated in a single state, is not a power at all. We have also to recognise that China is less clearly a great power than the other two.

To take the first criterion, comparability of status, the United States, the Soviet Union and China do appear to be powers of roughly similar standing in world politics, accepted by one another and by international society at large as having a common pre-eminence, even though (as noted in Chapter 5) the sources of their diplomatic standing are somewhat different in each case. The status or standing of these three powers can be gauged by the degree of attention paid to them by other states in their foreign and military policies. It is by its stance in relation to the United States, the Soviet

Union and China that the general character of any country's foreign policy, at the present time, is defined – just as during the Cold War period the general character of any country's foreign policy was determined by its attitude to the first two.

In terms of the second criterion, being in the front rank in military strength, it is arguable that China should be excluded because of its relative backwardness in strategic nuclear technology (not only in relation to the United States and the Soviet Union but also in relation to Britain and France) and also because of the inferior mobility of its non-nuclear forces. The proper validation of China's credentials as a great power awaits the demonstration that it has a viable nuclear deterrent in relation to both the United States and the Soviet Union. Moreover, while China is lacking in the global strategic reach of the other two, it remains a great power only on a regional scale.

Do all three powers also conform to the third requirement of great powerhood? In the official rhetoric of the United States a prominent position is accorded to the idea of international society and of the special rights and duties in it of a great power; nor can there be any doubt that the bulk of international society regards the United States as a power with such special rights and duties.

In the case of the Soviet Union, however, the official rhetoric subordinates these ideas to the conception of the Soviet state as the centre of global revolution and of an expanding Socialist Commonwealth destined to engulf the rest of international society. But if we look at the evidence of practice rather than rhetoric there is reason enough to treat the Soviet Union as a power which displays a sense of the rights and duties of a great power; the role of the Soviet Union in the United Nations, in arms-control negotiations, and in contributing to the settlement of political issues beyond its immediate national concern – in Europe, Asia and the Middle East – display acceptance of the Soviet Union's rights and duties as a great power both by the Soviet leadership and by international society at large.

In China's case the official rhetoric goes so far actually as to deny explicitly that China is, or seeks to become, a great power; it instead presents China as the champion of the 'have-not' states of the Third World in their struggle against 'super power hegemonism'. As in the case of the Soviet Union, practice belies theory: China's status as a nuclear power, a member of the United Nations Security Council, a donor of foreign aid, and above all as a power willing to reach a political settlement with the United States on the basis of equality, and in disregard of the interests of its small power associates, all these indicate the behaviour of a member of the great power club, not of a spokesman of the international proletariat. Nevertheless, the gap between rhetoric and reality is greater in the case of China than of the Soviet Union, and the former power, unlike the latter, has no history of participation in the great power club dating from before the rise of its communist party to power.

If, then, the special rights and duties of a great power are accepted not only by the United States, but by the Soviet Union and China also, this acceptance is tentative only, and not acknowledged explicitly. The traditional idea of a great power has only a precarious foothold in international politics at the present time, like the wider idea of an international society which it presupposes.

The Role of the Great Powers

The contribution of the great powers to international order derives from the sheer facts of inequality of power as between the states that make up the international system. If states were equal in power as they are in law, and every state could assert its claims with the same degree of force as every other, then it is difficult to see how, apart from resort to alliances that may introduce a contrived element of inequality, international conflicts could ever be settled and laid to rest, or the claims of any one state definitely granted or denied.

Because states are grossly unequal in power, certain international issues are as a consequence settled, the demands of certain states (weak ones) can in practice be left out of account, the demands of certain other states (strong ones) recognised to be the only ones relevant to the issue in hand. Because the United States is not merely one of a number of equal powers within the Western alliance, but enjoys a position of leadership or primacy, certain conflicts within this alliance are kept within bounds or prevented from reaching the surface of conscious political activity. Because the Soviet Union enjoys a hegemonial position in Eastern Europe, which it has been willing to defend by force, certain conflicts of interest in that area are for this reason resolved or contained; the claims that Poland, Czechoslovakia, the German Democratic Republic, Hungary, Bulgaria and Rumania might make of the Soviet Union or of each other are known to have no prospect of being met and are for this reason not even raised. When the two alliances negotiate over European political questions or the arms balance in Central Europe, it is known that the views of the United States and the Soviet Union have a significance which, for example, the views of Belgium or of Bulgaria do not have, and for this reason a structure is imparted to the negotiations which otherwise would not be present.

The inequality of states in terms of power has the effect, in other words, of simplifying the pattern of international relations, of ensuring that the say of some states will prevail while that of others will go under, that certain conflicts will form the essential theme of international politics while others will be submerged. Thus it is possible for Ranke to tell the story of European international history (although with some distortion) as the history of relations among the great powers, and for the contemporary student or practitioner of international politics, contemplating the vast and amorphous world body politic, to distinguish the relations among the great powers as its essential skeleton.

But over and above this contribution, the great powers may be said to make, simply by virtue of their superior strength, to the simplification of international relations, they may play a role in the promotion of international order by pursuing policies that work for it rather than against it. Great powers contribute to international order in two main ways: by managing their relations with one another; and by exploiting their preponderance in such a way as to impart a degree of central direction to the affairs of international society as a whole. More particularly, great powers manage their relations with one another in the interests of international order by (i) preserving the general balance of power, (ii) seeking to avoid or control crises in their relations with one another, and (iii) seeking to limit or contain wars among one another. They exploit their preponderance in relation to the rest of international society by (iv) unilaterally exploiting their local preponderance, (v) agreeing to respect one another's spheres of influence, and (vi) joint action, as is implied by the idea of a great power concert or condominium.

This, of course, is not a description of what great powers actually do. It is rather a statement of the roles they can, and sometimes do, play that sustain international order. In fact great powers, like small powers, frequently behave in such a way as to promote disorder rather than order; they seek to upset the general balance, rather than to preserve it, to foment crises rather than to control them, to win wars rather than to limit them, and so on.

Nor, of course, is this statement of the roles or functions of great powers in relation to international order to be taken as a series of recommendations or prescriptions as to what they should do. To treat them in this way would be to beg the question of the value or importance of international order as a human objective, or of its place in the hierarchy of objectives.

The two main roles or functions are closely interconnected and difficult to separate in historical reality: the steps the great powers take to manage their relations with one another lead directly to the attempt to provide central direction or management of the affairs of international society as a whole; the steps they take to exploit their preponderance in relation to the rest of international society presuppose some effective management of their relations with one another.

(i) *Preservation of the General Balance*

The first and cardinal contribution of the great powers to international order is to manage their relations with one another. It is this function that they perform in relation to international order that is most widely recognised in international society at large, and which provides the basis of the willingness of other states to accept the notion of the special rights and duties of great powers.

The management by the great powers of their relations with one another involves, first and foremost, the actions they may take to preserve the general balance of power, and so provide the conditions under which the system of states can endure. The preservation of the general balance has already been discussed (see Chapter 5). Here we have only to note that this general balance is one in which the great powers are the principal ingredients, and that actions taken to preserve it depend principally on measures of contrivance, including measures of collaboration, among the great powers. At the present time these measures include the actions which the great powers may take to preserve the relationship of mutual nuclear deterrence.

(ii) *Avoidance and Control of Crises*

The preservation of the general balance of power, as we have noted, does not by any means ensure that there will be peaceful relations among the great powers; nor does the mere existence of a stable relationship of mutual nuclear deterrence by any means imply that the nuclear peace among the great powers is assured. Thus the management of great power relations in the interests of international order must be taken to embrace also the action they take to avoid crises carrying the danger of war with one another, or to control them when they occur. What I have in mind here is something different from what is called 'crisis management'. What underlay the use of that term, when it became fashionable in the United States in the aftermath of the 1962 Cuban missile crisis, was the feeling that President Kennedy had managed that crisis in such a way as to score a great diplomatic victory while at the same time avoiding a war, and that the precepts that underlay his management of it could be studied and generalised to provide guidance on future occasions. By contrast, I am concerned here with the measures the great powers may take, separately or jointly, to promote their common interests in avoiding crises involving the danger of war, and controlling them when they occur.

This is an area of international experience which has not yet been satisfactorily charted.[6] There are some misconceptions about it which it is necessary to avoid. It would be illusory to imagine that great powers are always concerned to avoid dangerous crises, or to dampen these down when they occur. Crises are sometimes deliberately manufactured by the great powers, or deliberately brought closer to the point of war, because the preoccupation of the great power concerned is with securing a diplomatic victory. In the era of nuclear weapons the consciousness of the great powers of their common interest in avoiding war may be greater than it was in earlier times, and it is no accident that it is in the present era that interest has come to focus on this subject. But even now it is by no means the case that the overriding element in the policies of the great powers towards crises is the desire to avoid or control them, any more than the governing element in their arms policies is the desire to co-operate with their adversaries in arms control. Furthermore, it would be mistaken to assume that crises, or the intensification of them, could never play a constructive role in relation to the purposes of international order. The maintenance of the balance of power in past periods against attempts to upset it, or, in the present era, the preservation of relationships of mutual nuclear deterrence, would scarcely have been possible without the resolve of particular great powers, or combinations of them, at particular times, to issue threats and so create or intensify crises.

Nevertheless, we can say not only that measures to avoid or control crises are an essential part of what has been called 'management of great power relations', but also that it clearly does play some part in the relations of the great powers. During the period of Soviet-American predominance in world affairs, now drawing to a close, the United States and the Soviet Union have acted both separately and jointly to avoid certain crises in their relationships, and also to prevent their intensification.

The unilateral actions they have taken are easier to recognise than the joint ones. The United States and the Soviet Union have sought to avoid crises in their relationships by refraining from intervening unilaterally within one another's spheres of influence – the Soviet sphere in Eastern Europe, the American spheres in Western Europe and the Caribbean; the 1962 Cuban missile crisis owed its seriousness to the fact that, in the American view, the Soviet Union was failing to respect an established sphere of American influence. They have sought to avoid direct confrontations between their armed forces, such as threatened to take place in the Cuban missile crisis and during the several Berlin crises.

In cases where they have been allied or closely associated with opposite sides in a local dispute, they have sought to restrain their respective allies or associates. This has been the pattern of American and Soviet policy towards their respective European allies throughout the period of the confrontation of NATO and the Warsaw Pact in Europe: it was also the pattern of their policies in East Asia in the 1950s, when the Soviet Union was allied to China, and the United States to Taiwan; and it has been the pattern in the Middle East, where especially since the 1967 war the United

States has sought to restrain Israel and the Soviet Union its Arab associates. They have also, in some cases, taken the further step of urging each other to restrain their respective associates; both great powers did this, for example, in the Taiwan Straits crisis of 1958 and in the Middle East crisis of 1967.

The United States and the Soviet Union have each refrained from directly intervening in a number of conflicts outside the established spheres of influence of both of them, in cases where it was clear that intervention by either one of them would be likely to lead to intervention by the other; examples are the Congo crisis of 1960, the Nigerian civil war of 1967–70, and the Indo-Pakistani war of 1971. It is also clear that the United States and the Soviet Union, in direct diplomatic confrontations with each other, have sometimes acted with studied caution and self-restraint – seeking to avoid provocative behaviour and to allow one another a means of retreating with minimum loss of face – the classic and best documented case being President Kennedy's handling of the Cuban missile crisis. The concept of joint action to avoid or control crises covers a spectrum of possibilities: Carsten Holbraad has distinguished actions that are parallel but unco-ordinated, actions where there is some element of co-ordination or concerting of parallel policies, and the extreme case of jointly planned and executed diplomatic or military action.[7] The record of the United States and the Soviet Union in dealing with crises in the period of their ascendancy in world politics contains many examples of the first kind of joint action – that which is parallel but unco-ordinated; some slight evidence of the second, parallel and co-ordinated actions, as in the concerted efforts of the two powers to urge restraint on Israel and Egypt during the 1967 Middle East crisis; and none at all of the third kind.

A question which is in need of further study is to what extent these measures of restraint, unilateral and joint, have been, or could usefully be, formulated as general principles or rules. It may be argued that the United States and the Soviet Union, in the course of their diplomatic confrontations with one another in the 1950s and 1960s, have evolved certain operational rules or rules of the game that assist them in the avoidance and control of crises that endanger peace between them. For example, they behave as if they recognise a rule that prohibits direct interference in one another's established spheres of influence: a rule that (since the U2 crisis of 1960) prohibits illegal overflying of one another's territory; a rule that prohibits certain kinds of unconventional military action within each other's territory, such as sabotage or the clandestine planting of nuclear weapons or arming of subversive groups; a rule (since the removal of Soviet missiles from Cuba and U.S. missiles from Turkey) prohibiting the deployment of offensive missiles in countries adjacent to one another; and so on.

The evidence that can be provided of the existence of these rules is simply the fact that the two global great powers have behaved in accordance with them. This, of course, does not establish that the leaderships of the two countries are aware of these rules; and even if each of the leaderships were guided by the precept or principle that the behaviour proscribed by the rules was to be avoided, this would not mean that they had come to any agreement about them.

If such operational rules do exist, there are difficulties in assessing precisely what their content is. In the case of rules – like the purported rule proscribing interference in one another's spheres of influence – to which powers signify their assent by their actions rather than their words, it is difficult to know whether an action that infringes an existing rule is a violation of the rule, an attempt to modify the rule, or a sign that the rule has changed.

It is possible that scholarly attempts to formulate explicitly some of the unwritten rules of crisis avoidance and control may not only assist the understanding of what has happened in the past but also provide some practical guidance in the future. It will be necessary, however, to study not only crisis avoidance and control, as it has been practised by the United States and the Soviet Union in the period of their predominance, but also to extend the inquiry to embrace the avoidance and control of crises in a system of several great powers. It has been the special dangers of the nuclear era that have made us conscious of the avoidance and control of crises as a central element in the management of great power relations, and it would be erroneous to assume that in earlier periods such crises were viewed with the same urgency and alarm with which they are viewed today, or that the actions and operational rules evolved to cope with them were similar. But the avoidance and control of crises involving the risk of great power war is a perennial function of the great powers in relation to international order, and not a special feature of the nuclear era.

(iii) *Limitation of War*

A third way in which the great powers may manage their relations with one another in such a way as to contribute to international order is through measures taken to avoid war, or limit it if it occurs. Once again, this may be regarded as a perennial role of the great powers in relation to international order, although it would be wrong to assume that in earlier periods this task was generally perceived to have the same degree of urgency or centrality that it is viewed as having in the nuclear era. A great deal has been written about this subject, and it is touched upon elsewhere in this study (see Chapter 8). Here I shall simply sketch a few of the most general features of this enterprise, so as to complete my account of the management of great power relations.

The attempt to avoid war among the great powers includes the measures to preserve the balance of power and to avert or control dangerous crises (which have just been discussed), but it embraces much else as well. In the present context it includes attempts to avert war by accident or miscalculation; to reduce misunderstanding or misinterpretation by the great powers of one another's words and actions (what in Chapter 6 is called 'friction'); to settle or contain political disputes between the great powers by negotiation (in terms of recent history, to move from confrontation to *détente* among the great powers); to control competition in armaments, through tacit and formal arms-control agreements; to prevent wars among lesser powers which may expand to embrace the great powers, or, if they occur, to limit them geographically and end them quickly; and, more generally, to manage and direct the relationships of the lesser powers with one another and with the great powers, with this end in view. The efforts made by the great powers to avoid war among themselves are not separable from the role they play in seeking to direct the affairs of international society as a whole.

The attempt to limit wars that have broken out among the great powers embraces, in the present context, efforts to preserve the distinction between conventional and nuclear war, or to preserve limitations in a war that has become a nuclear one; to preserve effective channels of communication among the great powers in the course of a war so as to facilitate preservation of limitations in the war, and termination of it; and to preserve effective command and control of forces so as to reduce the danger of unintended expansion of a war. It may take the form of unilateral policies – such as the enunciation of strategic doctrines that recognise the desirability of preserving limitations in war, and the development of weapons systems and war plans that make such limitations feasible. But it may also take the form of the attempt to evolve operational rules or tacit understandings to co-operate in the preservation of these limitations, and to make use of formal legal limitations on the manner in which war is conducted.

(iv) *The Unilateral Exercise of Local Preponderance*

Great powers also contribute to international order through the unilateral exercise of their preponderance in particular areas of the world or among particular groups of states. This unilateral exploitation of preponderance takes three forms, which I shall call 'dominance', 'primacy' and 'hegemony'.

Dominance is characterised by the habitual use of force by a great power against the lesser states comprising its hinterland, and by habitual disregard of the universal norms of interstate behaviour that confer rights of sovereignty, equality and independence upon these states. A good example of dominance was the position of Britain in relation to Egypt (and later in relation to Iraq and Jordan) from the bombardment of Alexandria in 1882 to the withdrawal from the Suez Canal in 1956. Another example is the position of the United States in relation to the states of Central America and the Caribbean from late in the last century until the introduction of Franklin Roosevelt's 'good-neighbour policy' in 1933. In both these cases the preponderance of the great power was expressed in habitual and uninhibited military intervention in the internal affairs and external relations of the local states, including prolonged military occupation, and in failure to pay more than lip-service to notions of the sovereignty, equality and independence of these states.

Dominance is a relationship in which a great power, while stopping short of the establishment of imperial sovereignty over the areas in question, treats the small states or quasi-states within its hinterland as second-class members of international society. It belongs essentially to the phase of Europe's ascendancy in world politics, in which the idea persisted that relations between European states (and states of European or Christian civilisation) and non-

European ones were on a different footing from relations among European states themselves. It is difficult to find any clear example of dominance, in the sense in which I have defined it here, in contemporary international politics, and indeed dominance has ceased to represent a viable form of great power preponderance.

At the opposite extreme to dominance there exists what may be called *primacy*. A great power's preponderance in relation to a group of lesser states takes the form of primacy when it is achieved without any resort to force or the threat of force, and with no more than the ordinary degree of disregard for norms of sovereignty, equality and independence (some degree of disregard of these norms is characteristic of all international relationships). The position of primacy or leadership which the great power enjoys is freely conceded by the lesser states within the group concerned, and often expresses the recognition by the latter of the disproportionately large contribution which the great power is able to make to the achievement of common purposes. The great power may command powerful bargaining levers in disputes with the lesser states, but the bargaining takes place without coercion and within the confines of a normal degree of acceptance of basic norms of international behaviour.

A good example of primacy was the position of Britain in relation to the Old Dominions from the time of the first emergence of the international personality and diplomatic independence of the latter states until the end of the Second World War. The British Commonwealth formed, in this period, a close-knit diplomatic *entente*, in which Britain enjoyed a position of leadership that did not owe anything to coercion or to the systematic disregard of sovereign rights. Another example of primacy is the position of the United States today within NATO. The United States enjoys the leadership of NATO because this is felt by the other members of the alliance to be its due, given that Western Europe and Canada are dependent on the United States for their defence, whereas the United States is not similarly dependent on them. It is a characteristic of primacy that it takes place among a group of states whose peoples together display some of the signs of a single political community. The British Commonwealth in the period mentioned displayed a lingering ambiguity as to whether it was constitutionally one state or many, the former idea being represented in the doctrine of the indivisibility of the Crown.

Occupying an intermediate position between dominance and primacy there is *hegemony*. Where a great power exercises hegemony over the lesser powers in a particular area or constellation, there is resort to force and the threat of force, but this is not habitual and uninhibited but occasional and reluctant. The great power prefers to rely upon instruments other than the direct use or threat of force, and will employ the latter only in situations of extremity and with a sense that in doing so it is incurring a political cost. The great power is ready to violate the rights of sovereignty, equality and independence enjoyed by the lesser states, but it does not disregard them; it recognises that these rights exist, and justifies violation of them by appeal to some specific overriding principle. As Georg Schwarzenberger has written, hegemony is 'imperialism with good manners'.[8]

Hegemony characterises the relationship in which the Soviet Union stands with regard to the countries of Eastern Europe. The Soviet Union has used force in East Germany in 1953 to suppress a challenge to the government of the German Democratic Republic, to overthrow the government of Hungary in 1956 and to overthrow the Czechoslovak government in 1968. Except in Yugoslavia its military occupation of Eastern European countries facilitated the establishment of communist governments in the area in the period 1944–8. However, in bringing about the conformity of Eastern European states to Soviet policy, it has preferred to rely upon the influence it commands as the centre of the international communist movement, and as the chief defensive bulwark against a threat to the Warsaw Pact countries from the West. It has allowed breaches to be made in the solidarity of the Soviet/East European bloc of states, rather than incur the cost of preventing them by force: most notably, it did not seek forcibly to prevent the defection of Yugoslavia from the bloc in 1948, and later the defection of Albania, and the development of a degree of independence in foreign policy by Rumania.

The Soviet Union recognises that the states of Eastern Europe have the ordinary rights of sovereignty, equality and independence. But in the so-called 'Brezhnev Doctrine' of 1968, as also in earlier formulations of the principles of 'socialist internationalism', it limits or qualifies these rights by stipulating that an internal or external threat to any socialist country, involving the danger of a return to capitalism, is a threat not only to that country but to the Socialist

Commonwealth as a whole. Thus Czechoslovakia's rights of sovereignty could not, on the Soviet view, be invoked to protect her against the military intervention in 1968 of the Soviet Union, Poland, East Germany, Hungary and Bulgaria to prevent an internal change. The extent to which the ordinary rights of socialist states in international law are limited by 'socialist internationalism' is not clear. Who is to judge the existence of a danger of the return of capitalism – the socialist states collectively, or the Soviet Union alone? What are the limits of the Socialist Commonwealth – does it, for example, include Yugoslavia or Cuba? Does not the appeal to 'socialist legality', as against the 'bourgeois legality' of the principle of non-intervention, imply the possibility of qualifying all international law? The 'Brezhnev Doctrine', however, while it qualifies the sovereign rights of socialist states, does not deny that they exist. Moreover, it does not formally treat the Soviet Union as having rights and duties that are in any way different from those of other socialist states; while in practice the 'Doctrine' is an instrument of Soviet preponderance, in principle it limits the rights of the Soviet Union in just the same way as those of other members of the Socialist Commonwealth.[9]

The relationship of the United States to the countries of Central America and the Caribbean (although not to those of South America) may also be described as one of hegemony. The United States used force indirectly against Guatemala in 1954; it attempted an indirect use of force against Cuba in the Bay of Pigs invasion of 1961; it explicitly threatened an invasion of Cuba during the missile crisis of 1962; and it invaded Santo Domingo in 1965. It is clear that the United States prefers to rely upon economic forms of pressure upon states in the area, and on diplomatic pressure mobilised through the Organisation of American States (O.A.S.); it is conscious enough of the political cost of a resort to force to be willing to choose the latter instrument only in cases of extremity. The United States, at least since the 1962 missile crisis, has permitted Cuba to breach the system rather than resort to force, although in this case its reluctance to use force is the consequence of the risk this would entail of heightened conflict with the Soviet Union.

The United States recognises the international law rights of states in the area. The Charter of the O.A.S., drawn up at Bogota in 1948, contains one of the strongest of all recent statements of the principle of non-intervention in the domestic affairs of foreign countries, condemning such intervention against a member state, whether it is direct or indirect, whether it is carried out by an individual state or by the O.A.S. collectively. The United States has sought to qualify its duty of non-interference by reference to the argument that the O.A.S. has an overriding responsibility to take action against aggression. It has sometimes added to this the argument that communism within a Latin American country is *ipso facto* aggressive intervention, requiring American counter-intervention to uphold the principle of non-intervention.

There are, of course, differences as well as resemblances as between the Soviet position in Eastern Europe and the American position in the Caribbean. While anti-communist ideology has provided an instrument of American policy there is no equivalent in Latin America of the international links between governing communist parties. The geopolitical or geo-strategic configurations of the two areas are quite different: the one a group of adjacent land powers blocking the western approaches of the Soviet Union, the other a group of peninsular and island states. In some respects the analogy is between the Caribbean and the area of East Germany, Poland, Czechoslovakia and Hungary, these being the countries over which the Soviet Union exerts the closest control, with Rumania, Yugoslavia, Bulgaria representing an area of lesser control, comparable with continental South America within the American sphere.

Both the Soviet position in Eastern Europe and the American position in the Caribbean are, however, examples of hegemony. Moreover, there is a close similarity in the ways in which the two great powers have sought to legitimise their military intervention within the areas concerned. Both have been at pains to ensure that their intervention has not been unilateral, but has been part of a collective action: the Soviet Union was accompanied by its Warsaw Pact allies in the Czechoslovak intervention of 1968, while the United States has always been able to secure O.A.S. approval of its interventions in the Caribbean (although, in the case of the intervention in Santo Domingo, this approval only came after the event). Moreover, while both have sometimes made use of ideological justifications of intervention, both have appealed chiefly to norms of peace and security rather than doctrinal rectitude or human justice in justifying their interventions to the world at large.

In doing so they reflect the primacy of norms of order over norms of justice in the positive law and practice of international society.

The Soviet and American hegemonies both produce a kind of order. The lesser states in each area cannot resort to force against each other, nor can their governments be overthrown, except by leave of the hegemonial power. Territorial disputes – like those between Poland and Russia, Poland and East Germany, Hungary and Rumania, of which the world has heard nothing in the post-1945 era – are not only held in check but prevented from reaching the surface of conscious political activity. Such a state of affairs, in which a great power unilaterally imposes conformity to rules to which it is not itself subject, is bound to be widely regarded as unjust, but it is nevertheless a form of order.

(v) *Spheres of Influence, Interest or Responsibility*

Great powers contribute to international order not only by unilaterally exploiting their preponderance in particular areas of the world or among particular groups of states, but also by agreeing to establish spheres of influence, interest or responsibility. The simplest and most common function of these agreements is to confirm the great powers concerned in their positions of local preponderance, and avoid collision or friction between them.

The idea of spheres-of-influence agreements among the powers presumably goes back to the papal bulls assigning exclusive rights of conquest in particular areas to Castile and Portugal and the early agreements between these two powers directed towards the same end, such as the treaty of 1479 assigning the West Coast of Africa to Portugal and the Canary islands to Castile. The term 'sphere of influence', however, arose only in the second half of the last century: Curzon in his Romanes Lecture on *Frontiers* says that the first significant use of it was by Gortchakoff in a letter to Clarendon in 1869, declaring that Afghanistan lay outside the Russian sphere of influence.[10]

The classic period of spheres-of-influence agreements was the late nineteenth century, especially after 1885. M. F. Lindley has distinguished three main kinds of such agreements.[11] The first was an agreement between colonial powers to recognise each other's exclusive rights in areas which were either *territorium nullius* or inhabited by groups not recognisable as sovereign states. This was the characteristic spheres-of-influence agreement that accompanied the expansion of the European powers in Africa and Oceania. The second was an agreement between colonial powers about the territory of some third state, all or part of which was assigned to the exclusive sphere of one colonial power, usually with a view to economic exploitation. This sort of agreement belongs chiefly to European expansion in Asia, and has sometimes been called an agreement to establish a sphere of interest as opposed to a sphere of influence. Examples are the agreements between Britain and France dividing Siam into spheres of interest, between Britain and Russia dividing Persia in the same way, or between Japan and various powers recognising its paramount interests in Korea. The third kind of agreement was between a colonial power and a local state, in which the latter agreed not to dispose of territory or concessions to any third state. Examples are the agreements reached between China and various colonial powers, assigning them spheres of exclusive economic interest, and the agreement of 1904 between Britain and Tibet.

In thinking about spheres-of-influence understandings, there are a number of important distinctions that need to be made. First, we should distinguish an agreement or understanding between two powers to recognise the fact of one another's preponderance in some area, from an agreement to recognise each other's *rights* in that area. It is one thing for the United States and the Soviet Union to recognise the fact that certain parts of the world are within each other's spheres of influence; it is another to treat such spheres of influence as legitimate. A sphere of influence, moreover, which in one country's view exists as a matter of right, may in another country's view exist only as a matter of fact. The United States asserted in the Monroe Doctrine a right to exclude European intervention in the Americas; but to European powers the Doctrine did not confer any rights upon the United States to exclude them, it merely stated an American policy or objective providing them with a warning of which they needed to take account. The spheres-of-influence agreements reached by European powers in the partition of Africa involved merely a mutual recognition of rights between the contracting parties; they did not confer upon the parties any general rights in international law. The Fashoda crisis of 1898, for example, arose out of the fact that the rights which Britain was recognised to have in the Upper Nile in agreements reached with Germany and with Italy were not recognised by France. The distinction between an agreement about facts and an agreement about rights cannot always be clearly drawn. When two great powers recognise the fact of each other's preponderance in a particular area, there does not follow from this any mutual recognition of legal or moral rights. But the great powers may come to think of each other as enjoying rights conferred by operational rules or rules of the game. It may be understood on both sides that, given the fact of a great power's preponderance in a particular area, interference by other powers in this area is a dangerous or hazardous enterprise. Beyond this, there may be developed a code of behaviour for avoiding dangerous collisions, a code that may not be formalised in any agreement, but which is understood on both sides and confirmed by unilateral declarations of policy and by behaviour consistent with the code. Such rules of the game, respected over a period, give rise to settled expectations on each side as to what the other side's behaviour will be, and in a sense involve mutual recognition of rights. President Kennedy's reaction to what he took to be the Soviet Union's violation of the 'rules of the game' in deploying offensive missiles in Cuba included an element of moral indignation, real or feigned.

Second, we may distinguish an agreement in which the parties confer limited and specific rights on each other from one in which there is conceded what in diplomatic parlance has been called 'a free hand'. The formal treaties of the classic period of spheres-of-influence agreements conferred only specific rights; in the Anglo-German treaty of 1890 regarding Africa, for example, each party agrees that it 'will not in the sphere of the other make acquisitions, conclude treaties, accept sovereign rights or protectorates nor hinder the extension of the influence of the other'.[12] The phrase 'a free hand', as when it was said that Britain gave France a free hand in Morocco while France gave Britain a free hand in Egypt, implies the willingness on the part of each power to disinterest itself entirely in what the other power does within its sphere, so long as this *désintéressement* is reciprocal – it may be doubted whether reference to 'a free hand' was ever intended to be taken literally; there was rather recognition that each party had a free hand within certain limits taken for granted, for example within the limiting condition that local individuals, groups and political entitles had certain rights, even if they did not enjoy the rights of sovereign states. Nevertheless, the practical political effect of agreements exchanging recognition of limited and specific rights was sometimes to bring about a situation in which both parties were left with 'a free hand'. Curzon, in 1907, noted the tendency of spheres of interest to become spheres of influence, of spheres of influence to be transformed into protectorates, and of protectorates to give place to outright annexation.

Third, we should distinguish spheres-of-influence agreements which are negative from those which are positive. The spheres-of-influence treaties of the phase of European expansion were negative, in the sense that by means of them each power sought to exclude other powers from its sphere of operations, to have them acknowledge their *désintéressement* in what the power concerned was seeking to achieve in a particular area. By contrast, a spheres-of-influence agreement which is positive sets up a division of labour among the parties to it in the execution of a common task. It establishes spheres of responsibility.

An example of a positive spheres-of-influence agreement was that reached by the United States, the Soviet Union, Britain and France in the closing stages of the Second World War concerning the post-war occupation of Germany (of course, it had a negative purpose also). It was assumed that the powers concerned had a common task in occupying the territory of the defeated enemy, exacting reparations, bringing war criminals to trial, preventing the resurgence of the Nazis, and so on. In occupying the particular zone of Germany which it was allotted, each power was assuming its share of responsibility in implementing a common policy.

At this time also there was discussion of a positive spheres-of-influence agreement of more far-reaching importance: the idea, at one time favoured by Churchill, and spelt out by Walter Lippmann in his *U.S. War Aims* (1944), was that international order in the post-war era should be based on a division of the world into three or four spheres of responsibility, within each of which a great power or combination of great powers would keep the peace. Lippmann envisaged four regional systems: the Atlantic system, policed by the United States and Britain; the Russian system; the Chinese system; and, eventually, an Indian system. Within each of these systems, the preponderance of a great power was to be recognised; each small power was to accept the protection of the great power in whose region it found itself, and was to forgo the right to form alliances with any extra-regional power. To the question whether this did not imply that the lesser powers within each region would be at the mercy of the regional great power, Lippmann responded that the interests of the small powers would be guaranteed by the pursuit of 'good-neighbour policies' by each of the great powers.[13] Lippmann's scheme was in fact one for the generalisation throughout all regions of the world of the relationship in which the United States stood to the Western hemisphere, more particularly the relationship that existed at the time of Roosevelt's 'good-neighbour policy'.

In what sense are there spheres-of-influence understandings between the United States and the Soviet Union at present? It is clear that there are no formal spheres-of-influence agreements of any kind; indeed, as I shall argue, the formalisation of such agreements in present circumstances would be likely to undermine their effectiveness. We are concerned with understandings which are not embodied in a treaty, and which may arise from reciprocal declarations of policy, or simply from behaviour of the parties which is *as if* in conformity with a rule, even though that rule is not agreed, not enunciated nor even fully understood.

The two super powers recognise the facts of each other's predominance in certain areas, but they recognise one another's rights to a sphere of influence only in the sense of rights that are conferred by rules of the game. If the United States had intervened in Hungary in 1956 or in Czechoslovakia in 1968, the Soviet Union would not have felt that there had been any infringement of special legal or moral rights arising out of an understanding with the United States, but it would have felt that there had been violation of rights conferred upon it by an implicit rule that had up to that time been accepted, that the great powers should not intervene militarily in international or domestic conflicts within the opposing alliance. The fact that the United States did not intervene helped to confirm Soviet confidence in the existence of such an implied rule. At the time of the Cuban missile crisis President Kennedy felt, or at all events said, that the Soviet Union had violated an understanding that nuclear weapons should not be deployed clandestinely, and that the two super powers should not deliberately mislead each other about the deployment of such weapons. Whether or not any such understandings existed before the crisis, the fact that the United States held that there was such a rule, and reacted strongly against Soviet behaviour that contradicted it, may have had the effect of establishing such a rule after the crisis.

It is clear that such spheres-of-influence understandings as exist between the United States and the Soviet Union confer only limited and specific rights, not 'a free hand'. The United States accepts that intervention within the Warsaw Pact area would represent violation of an operational rule of great power coexistence. But it is far from disinteresting itself in the affairs of the area. It seeks to uphold universal legal norms conferring rights on Eastern European states *vis-à-vis* the Soviet Union by diplomatically supporting them, and by developing links with these countries of the sort dramatised by President Nixon's visit to Rumania in 1969. The Soviet Union similarly shows no sign of washing its hands of the affairs of countries within the American sphere of influence. These links, which are preserved between each great power and the lesser states within the other's sphere of influence, are an important condition of the retention by the latter of some element of freedom of manoeuvre.

It is clear also that Soviet-American spheres-of-influence understandings have so far been negative in content rather than positive. In these understandings each power seeks to secure for itself the exclusion of the other from its own sphere, and the function of the agreement is to confirm each power in its position of local preponderance and to avoid collisions or minimise their consequences. The United States and the Soviet Union co-operate positively in a number of areas, but it is difficult to find evidence of any understanding about spheres of responsibility assigning to each power its duties or roles in carrying out a common task, unless we are to take agreements, like the agreement on post-war occupation of Germany mentioned above, that quickly become defunct.

Curzon has pointed out that 'some of the most anxious moments in history' have arisen as the consequence of vagueness in interpretation of a spheres-of-influence understanding.[14] Vagueness and imprecision in Soviet-American spheres-of-influence understandings are the necessary consequence of their tacit and informal character. The obligations of NATO and the Warsaw Pact, which commit the two super powers to the defence of specified areas, provide the basis for these understandings. The function of the two alliances in advertising the will of each super power to exclude military intervention by the other against or within it may be thought a more central one in international politics at present than the function they have of combining the military strength of the lesser parties in each alliance with its super power leader. But even here the precise nature of the ground rules is uncertain.

These spheres-of-influence understandings are established, and their terms are altered, not by discussion and negotiation, but through struggle and competition: one power establishes itself in an area, as the Soviet Union has done in the Arab world, especially since 1967, and an operational rule conferring rights upon it in that area tends to arise if its position is not challenged by the other party. The Soviet Union, in the Cuban missile crisis, challenged the American sphere of influence in the Caribbean, and succeeded in changing the ground rules for that area, to the extent that the United States has since been bound, in the Soviet view (and the United States knows that this is the Soviet view), to desist from invading Cuba, even though the Soviet Union is bound (as it was before the crisis) to desist from deploying offensive missiles there. If (as seemed possible during the mini-crisis of October 1970, arising over the presence of Soviet nuclear submarines at Cienfuegos) the Soviet Union were to resume the deployment of offensive missiles, this would be treated by the United States as a violation of an understanding, but if it succeeded it would constitute an alteration in the terms of the understanding.

(vi) *A Great Power Concert or Condominium*

Great powers may be thought to contribute to international order by agreeing, not upon a division of the world into spheres of influence, interest or responsibility, but to join forces in promoting common policies throughout the international system as a whole. This is what is involved in the idea of a great power condominium, co-imperium or concert.[15] The term 'condominium' implies joint government (as in the Anglo-French condominium in the New Hebrides), and thus does not aptly describe what is better seen as management by the great powers than as government. 'Co-imperium' has overtones of a formal hierarchy of states, and is again misleading. 'Concert' is perhaps the best term, reminding us as it does of the principal historical model of joint management by the great powers, the Concert of Europe.

The establishment of a Soviet-American condominium or concert was often advocated in the early 1960s, for example by John Strachey, who favoured a Soviet-American combination for the purposes of controlling the 'central' strategic balance and resisting the spread of nuclear weapons.[16] Today it is sometimes said, chiefly by those alarmed about the growth of Soviet-American co-operation (that is to say China, some Third World countries and remnants of Gaullist sentiment in Europe) that such a condominium already exists, the implication being that it is prejudicial to the interests of other states.

In fact, however, the structure of understandings that at present exists between the United States and the Soviet Union cannot usefully be described as a concert or condominium. The United States and the Soviet Union, it is true, recognise common interests not only in combating abstract dangers like nuclear war, but also in thwarting particular other powers. They have co-operated against potential nuclear powers within the framework of the Non-Proliferation Treaty, which came into force in 1970, of which they are the principal sponsors. During the 1960s they recognised common interests in the containment of China, and so operated tacitly to this end, most notably in the Indian subcontinent – even though each, at the same time, valued the power and independence of China as a check on the other. Ever since 1945 they have implicitly co-operated to contain the power of Germany, and especially to oppose any move by West Germany to acquire control of nuclear weapons or to alter the territorial *status quo* by force. While the Warsaw Pact has been directed, among other things, against West German expansion to the east, NATO has fulfilled the role of providing a multilateral framework within which the inevitable recovery of West German power could take place while causing the minimum alarm to others.

However, there has been no attempt to formalise a Soviet-American concert. There is no regular attempt to concert, in the sense of the holding of regular discussions concerned to define common and unique objectives, to map out a common strategy for attaining them and for distributing the burdens of such a strategy (of the sort that have taken place, for example, within NATO). Nor has there been enunciated any theory or ideology of world order, such as underlay the Holy Alliance or the later European Concert, that would give direction and purpose to a Soviet-American

concert. Such a theory of order imposed by great power collaboration lies at hand in the provisions of the United Nations Charter
relating to the Security Council, but there has been no attempt to
reactivate it.

If there ever was a moment when the establishment of a Soviet-
American concert or condominium was a possibility, this moment
passed with the emergence of China, after the Cultural Revolution
of 1966–9, as an active great power, and the attempt of the United
States to co-opt China into the great power club, while at the same
time seeking to preserve and strengthen the *détente* between the
United States and the Soviet Union. The policy of the United States
in the 1970s shifted away from the attempt to fashion international
order on the basis of an 'adversary partnership' with the Soviet
Union alone, towards the attempt to call into being a system of
three or possibly more great powers. There has not been any
comparable shift in the policy of the Soviet Union, but if at the time
of writing there is any question of the establishment of a great
power concert, this concerns a concert of at least three powers.

The Great Powers at Present

The United States and the Soviet Union today do in fact, at least in
some measure, carry out the six roles that have been mentioned, and
thereby help to sustain an order of sorts. But in the view of China,
of some Third World states and of some elements of opinion within
the powers of secondary rank, this is an unjust order; the great
powers manage their relations with one another and provide central
direction in such a way as to secure special privileges for themselves,
and if an order exists it is one in which they have a special stake.

It is obvious that the international order sustained by the great
powers does not provide equal justice for all states. The measures
they take to provide central direction of international affairs – by
exploiting their local preponderance, by concluding spheres-of-
influence agreements and by co-ordinating their policies in relation
to other states – involve them directly in the defence of the existing
distribution of power. The measures they take to manage their
relations with one another – by preserving the balance, controlling
crises and limiting wars – while they promote objectives that are
widely accepted in international society as a whole (the preservation

of the states system, the avoidance of nuclear war), they also tend to confirm the existing pattern of power.

If, however, the international order of the great powers does not afford equal justice, it does not necessarily follow from this that it should or will be regarded as intolerable. The question which needs to be asked is whether an international order that embodies perfect justice is possible at all, whether it is not the case that any international order must have its custodians and guarantors, whose stake in the order will be greater than that of other states. The alternative to an international order in which the United States and the Soviet Union, or these two powers plus China, have a special stake may not be an order in which the rights of all states are equally provided for, but simply one in which these custodians and guarantors are replaced by others.

In fact the international order sustained by the great powers enjoys a wide measure of support throughout international society. The great powers do, however, have a permanent problem of securing and preserving the consent of other states to the special role they play in the system. Great powers can fulfil their managerial functions in international society only if these functions are accepted clearly enough by a large enough proportion of the society of states to command legitimacy. It is worth considering what some of the conditions are under which the super powers may seek to legitimise their special role.

First, the great powers cannot formalise and make explicit the full extent of their special position. International society is based on the rejection of a hierarchical ordering of states in favour of equality in the sense of the like application of basic rights and duties of sovereignty to like entities. To make explicit the full extent of the special rights and duties of the great powers (for example, by writing hegemonial rights, or rights to a sphere of influence, or rights jointly to enforce the global peace into positive international law) would be to engender more antagonism than the international order could support.

Second, the great powers have to try to avoid being responsible for conspicuously disorderly acts themselves. International society may accept an order that does not embody perfect justice, because all states treat order as ultimately prior to justice, and a system which is able to provide order will engender support, even though it leaves powerful demands for just change unsatisfied. But when the great powers appear to be undermining order as well as denying justice, the legitimacy of their position is eroded.

Third, the great powers have to seek to satisfy some of the demands for just change being expressed in the world. Demands from the poor countries for economic justice, demands from non-nuclear states for 'nuclear justice', the demands of black African states for 'racial justice' in Southern Africa, all have to be accommodated within the great powers' scheme of policy; where the demands cannot be met, at least the motions have to be gone through of seeking to meet them, so as to avoid alienating important segments of international society. A great power hoping to be accepted as a legitimate managerial power cannot ignore these demands or adopt a contrary position, in a way that lesser powers can do; its freedom of manoeuvre is circumscribed by 'responsibility'.

Fourth, in parts of the world where the political position of the great powers is limited by secondary powers of major importance, the great powers may seek to accommodate these powers as partners in the management of the regional balance concerned. At the present time Britain, France and West Germany are leading middle powers in Europe and the Mediterranean (the former two in Africa also), while Japan is a 'great indispensable' in any attempt to manage the balance of Asia and the Pacific. While these middle powers have very different attitudes towards each of the great powers and towards co-operation between them, and do not have any concerted policy of checking or limiting tendencies towards a great power concert, nevertheless the possibility of such a combination serves as a check against great power arrogance. One of the means by which the great powers can seek to legitimise their role is by co-opting the major secondary powers, which are by definition their major potential rivals, as junior partners in their system of global management.

Part 3

Alternative Paths to World Order

10

Alternatives to the Contemporary States System

We must begin our inquiry into alternative paths to world order with the question: what forms of universal political organisation, alternative to the present states system, are there? The number of alternatives that can be conceived is, of course, boundless. Here I confine my attention to a few that may be judged significant.

Before we can answer the question with which this chapter is concerned we must remind ourselves what the essential attributes of the states system are – or we shall be in danger of mistaking for an alternative to the states system what would be merely a change from one particular phase or form of the states system to another. The essential attributes of the states system, as they have been defined here, are first a plurality of sovereign states; second, a degree of interaction among them, in respect of which they form a system; and third, a degree of acceptance of common rules and institutions, in respect of which they form a society.

Alternative Forms of States System

A number of changes in the present political structure of the world may be conceived that would be quite basic, yet nevertheless would represent simply a transition from one phase of the states system to another, not the supersession of the states system itself.

225

A Disarmed World

One such change would be the advent of a 'disarmed world', the realisation of the vision of 'general and complete disarmament' contained in the American and Soviet disarmament plans and ritually endorsed by successive disarmament conferences.[1] In both plans it is envisaged that in the final stage of a process of phased disarmament, sovereign states would cease to possess armaments and armed forces, except for purposes of internal security. In the American plan it is envisaged also that as states are progressively deprived of armed force, there will be a simultaneous process of the strengthening of a world authority, in whose hands armed force might ultimately be concentrated.

The realisation of the idea of 'general and complete disarmament' would imply so radical a transformation of the present structure of international politics as to require us to think out the whole basis of relations among states afresh if we were to render it intelligible. It would not, however, represent the demise of the states system, for it does not in itself involve an end to the existence of sovereign states, to systematic interaction among them or to their forming together an international society. If – as the American plan allows – the achievement of this state of affairs was accompanied by the development of a world authority commanding force and political loyalty sufficient to undermine the supremacy of states in their own dominions and over their own populations, this would imply the demise of the first of the three essential attributes. But this is not a logically necessary consequence of a disarmed world. It is possible to visualise such a world as one in which – as in the final stage of the Soviet plan – the central authority that exists does not command armed force in its own right, and is still subject to the veto of the great powers.

The argument in favour of a world in which disarmament is general, in the sense that it involves all powers, and complete, in the sense that it embraces all categories of armaments and armed forces, sometimes takes what may be called the 'strong' form – that total disarmament would make war physically impossible, because states would not be able to make war even when they wanted to; and it sometimes takes the 'weak' form, that the maximum possible disarmament would make war less likely.[2]

When Litvinov first advanced the idea of total disarmament in the context of the League of Nations disarmament discussions, it was the strong form of the argument that he put forward.[3] His contention was that total disarmament was qualitatively different from any lesser form of disarmament. On the one hand, it promised more than any lesser kind of disarmament; for if arms and armed forces were completely abolished, war would be simply unavailable as an instrument of policy even to those states which sought to resort to it. On the other hand, it was easier to achieve than any lesser form of disarmament, such as 'the reduction of national armaments to the lowest point consistent with national safety and the enforcement by common action of international obligations' (the formula propounded in Article VIII of the Covenant of the League of Nations, to the realisation of which the disarmament discussions of that time were directed). This was because, Litvinov contended, if nations agreed to disarm totally they could bypass 'the thorny questions' that inhibited attempts to agree on what arms and armed forces would be retained.

The objection to 'total disarmament' in Litvinov's sense is that there can be, in principle, nothing of the kind; the physical capacity for organised violence is inherent in human society, and cannot be abolished by treaty. It is not merely that all actual proposals for so-called 'total disarmament' envisage the retention of internal security forces, and sometimes also of forces that could be made available to a world authority for the maintenance of order. Even a disarmament system which made no provision for the retention of any such forces would leave states with the capacity to wage war on a primitive level; and, moreover, with the capacity to raise this level – to re-establish what has been disestablished, to remember or to re-invent what has been put aside. All that a disarmament treaty can do is prohibit certain kinds of arms and armed forces that are specified, and the effect of this is to augment the strategic significance of whatever is left outside the scope of the treaty. What is called 'total disarmament' is not in fact qualitatively different from lesser forms of disarmament.

Thus there is no force in Litvinov's contention that 'total disarmament' would make war physically impossible in some sense in which lesser forms of disarmament would not. Moreover, even the most drastic disarmament system must leave some states with greater capacity for war than others; a nation's war potential does not reside simply in its 'armaments', but in the whole complex of its economic, technological and demographic resources, strategic position, political leadership, military experience and ingenuity, morale, and so on. Thus it will be a consequence of 'total disarmament', just as much as of any lesser form of disarmament, that it leads to a ratio of military power within the 'disarmed world'. It follows from this that there is equally no force in Litvinov's other argument, that the simplicity of 'total disarmament' enables it to bypass the difficulties of negotiation.

The weak form of the argument for general and complete disarmament is not open to objections of this kind. It is not logically impossible or contrary to the nature of human society that armaments and armed forces should be few in number and primitive in quality; nor is it impossible that there should exist habits, institutions, codes or taboos which might help preserve this state of affairs. There is a strong *prima facie* case for holding that a world in which sophisticated armaments and advanced forms of military organisation and technique had been abolished would provide more security against war than a world in which states are armed as they are now. In particular, it may be argued that, other things being equal, in such a world wars would be less likely to break out, because large military establishments would not exist as a factor making for war, because there would be less strategic mobility and thus fewer other states within military striking distance of any one state, and because there would not exist weapons-systems capable of generating the fear of surprise attack. It might also be argued that, other things being equal, such a world war, if it did break out, would be less catastrophic, because it would be more slow-moving, less costly and would involve less physical destruction and economic dislocation.[4]

Whether or not the realisation of the vision of a disarmed world is in any sense practically attainable, the common instinct is soundly based that leads us to see in this vision a superior kind of world order to that which is provided in the contemporary form of the states system. We have also to recognise, however, that merely to have imagined a world in which states have disarmed to low quantitative and qualitative levels is not to have given an account of how order in such a world would be maintained. The vision of a disarmed world is at best an incomplete one, if it is not accompanied by an explanation (in terms of the argument of Chapter 3) of the rules and institutions by which the elementary goals of social life can be attained.

There is first of all the question of how the states of the world, having disarmed to low levels, are to be kept disarmed. This must lead us to a consideration of a system of verification that will detect violations of the disarmament agreement, and of a system of sanctions or reprisals that will deter such violations, or provide for the security of innocent parties in the event that they occur. There are strong reasons for holding that in a system of drastic disarmament that included the complete abolition of nuclear weapons and other weapons of mass destruction, successful violation of the system would place the violator in a position of military preponderance in relation to other states. In order to deter violations of this kind, or to assure the security of innocent parties in the event that they take place, it would seem essential to presuppose a world authority with a preponderance of military power, including nuclear weapons.

More serious, however, than the question of how the system of drastic disarmament is to be preserved, is the question of how order in general is to be provided for. A disarmed world, as we have seen, is still a world in which the capacity for organised violence exists and must play its part in human affairs. It is still a world divided into sovereign states and subject to the political conflicts by which such a world has always been characterised. Internal or domestic order would still have, as one of its requirements, the existence of preponderant armed force in the hands of governments. International order would still depend on the operation of rules and institutions to control or contain the use of military power – whether by preserving a balance of power, allowing for its use in law enforcement, limiting the means by which it is conducted, facilitating the settlement of political conflicts that might involve the use of force, or exploiting the preponderance of the great powers in concert.

The idea of a disarmed world, in addition to raising these familiar questions concerning the maintenance of order, also raises questions about the achievement of just change. If a disarmed world were to prove more peaceful and secure than a heavily armed world such as exists now, this might also mean that it was a world less amenable to just change brought about by force, and more dependent on the availability of institutions of peaceful change. Whether a lightly armed world is less capable of providing for just change, or more capable, the point is that merely to have imagined drastic disarmament is not to have shown how this function can be fulfilled.

In other words, the same range of issues that arise concerning the maintenance of order in the present, heavily armed world could also be expected to arise in a lightly armed world. This does not mean that the former is preferable to the latter, but it does mean that the vision of a disarmed world does not by itself indicate an alternative path to world order.

The Solidarity of States

Another possible political structure of the world would be one in which the United Nations, or some comparable body founded upon the co-operation of sovereign states on a global basis, had become the predominant force in world politics. Such a state of affairs we might describe as one in which the United Nations Charter is observed by member states in the way in which it was hoped that they would do so by the more visionary founders of the organisation. It would represent the fulfilment of the Grotian or solidarist doctrine of international order, which envisages that states, while setting themselves against the establishment of a world government, nevertheless seek, by close collaboration among themselves and by close adherence to constitutional principles of international order to which they have given their assent, to provide a substitute for world government.[5] Its central assumption is that of the solidarity, or potential solidarity, of most states in the world in upholding the collective will of the society of states against challenges to it. Again, such a condition of world politics would be radically different from what exists now, but would represent a new phase of the states system, not its replacement by something different.

The Grotian or solidarist doctrine seeks to achieve a more orderly world by restricting or abolishing resort to war by individual states for political ends, and promoting the idea that force can legitimately be used only to promote the purposes of the international community. It thus seeks to reproduce in international society one of the central features of domestic society. The system of rules which Grotius devised was intended to assist the triumph in any war of the party or parties whose cause was just, and who therefore were acting on behalf of the community as a whole.

In the twentieth century, as we noted in Chapter 2, neo-Grotian ideas have been reflected in the Covenant of the League of Nations, which prohibited member states from going to war in disregard of certain procedures which it laid down – the Paris Pact of 1928, which prohibits resort to war as an instrument of national policy, and the United Nations Charter, which prohibits the use or threat of force against the territorial integrity or political independence of any state – or in any other manner inconsistent with the purposes of the United Nations. The Covenant and the Charter, while imposing these restrictions on resort to force by states, at the same time provide for the use and threat of force by states acting in the name of the international organisation to uphold a system of collective security. The principle of collective security implies that international order should rest not on a balance of power, but on a preponderance of power wielded by a combination of states acting as the agents of international society as a whole that will deter challenges to the system or deal with them if they occur.

The solidarist formula promises a superior form of maintaining order because it seeks to make force solely or chiefly the instrument of international society as a whole. It is, however, crucially dependent on the actual existence among states of a sufficient degree of solidarity in recognising common objectives and acting to promote them. In the actual circumstances of the twentieth century this solidarity has not been present. The attempt to apply the Grotian or solidarist formula has had the consequence not merely that the attempt to construct a superior world order is unsuccessful, but also that, as we noted in Chapter 6, classical devices for the maintenance of order are weakened or undermined. The action taken by the League of Nations against Italy in 1935 over the invasion of Abyssinia, and against the Soviet Union in 1939 over the invasion of Finland, not only failed to vindicate the principle of collective security, but also endangered the objective of preventing Germany's overthrow of the balance of power. The action taken by the United Nations General Assembly in 1950 to endorse the role of the United States and its allies in Korea as a collective-security operation not only served to weaken rather than enhance the role of the organisation in world politics, but, by presenting the issue as one in which the law-enforcing powers confronted the delinquents, impeded the processes of great power diplomacy.

If in the twentieth century the attempt to apply the solidarist formula has proved premature, this does not mean that the conditions will never obtain in which it could be made to work. The whole history of relations among states could be adduced in support of the view that sovereign states are inherently incapable of achieving solidarity in subordinating the use of force to common purposes. But to conclude that this is so would be to go beyond the evidence.

A World of Many Nuclear Powers

Another basic change in the character of the contemporary states system, which would still fall short of the replacement of the states system by something different, would be the emergence of a world of many nuclear powers. This alternative to the contemporary form of the states system attracts attention more because it is widely held that the process of nuclear proliferation may eventually bring it about than because it is thought that it embodies a more effective means of achieving world order, although advocates of nuclear proliferation sometimes take that view.

A world of many nuclear powers would be most dramatically different from the present one if the conditions were present for what Morton Kaplan has called 'the unit veto system' and Arthur Burns 'the deterrent system'.[6] This would require that nuclear weapons were available not merely to many but to all states, or to all groups or blocs of states. (It is in fact easier to visualise a world in which every state enjoyed the protection of some group or bloc 'nuclear umbrella', than to imagine that all of the 140 or so states in the world possessed nuclear forces of their own.) It would also require that there existed relationships of mutual nuclear deterrence among all of these states or blocs. We have to assume, in other words, not merely that every state or bloc possesses nuclear weapons, but also that it can inflict 'unacceptable damage' upon every other state or bloc, but cannot prevent their inflicting such damage upon itself.

The central characteristic of the 'unit veto' system is thus the ability of each state or bloc to veto the deliberate and 'rational' resort to unlimited nuclear war by each of the others, in the same way that the United States and the Soviet Union possess a veto of this kind in relation to each other at the present time. It is important to note that this is in itself a very incomplete description of what the behaviour of states in a 'unit veto system' would be, from which only limited inferences can be drawn. It is only by making assumptions extraneous to his model that Kaplan can argue that 'the unit veto system' would be a Hobbesian state of nature in which the interests of all are opposed; that actors within the system can exist only at one level; that coalitions and the shifting or balancing of alignments in such a system would be eliminated; that no role in it could be played by universal actors such as the United Nations; that the system would perpetuate the existing state of affairs; and that it would be non-integrated and non-solidary to a high degree, and would be characterised by extreme tension.[7]

If we were to make the assumption that strategic nuclear weapons are the only instruments available to actors in the 'unit veto system' for promoting their objectives, then the possession by every actor of a veto over the use of this instrument by every other actor would lead to consequences of this kind. This, however, would be a very odd assumption to make. If 'the unit veto system' were to embody on a universal scale the characteristics of what may be called the present, Soviet-American mutual veto system, then each actor, while being able to neutralise the use of strategic nuclear weapons by the others, would also be able to bring into play other instruments of power and influence – military, political and economic – through which diplomatic conflict and collaboration would continue. It should not be assumed, therefore, that gradations of power and influence among the various actors would not continue to exist, that coalitions and the shifting of alignments would not continue to play a role, or that changes could not be effected in the *status quo;* nor does it follow that the system must be a Hobbesian state of nature, or that it must be marked by extreme tension or that universal actors such as the United Nations could play no role in it. It is not inconceivable that the actors in such a system, while neutralising their strategic nuclear instruments, at the same time might contain if not resolve their political disputes. It might even be imagined that an international system existing for generations under the discipline of fear might eventually discover that the order it had achieved could exist independently of that discipline, that the apparatus of universal nuclear deterrence had become superfluous and could be discarded like an empty shell. These are, of course, mere speculations; my point is that behaviour of this kind is just as consistent with the assumption of a 'unit veto system' as are the deductions made by Kaplan.

Are there any grounds for considering that a world of many nuclear powers is a form of the states system more conducive than the present one to world order? There is a familiar argument that the more states that possess nuclear weapons, the more able the international system will be to achieve the objectives of peace and security, since this will generalise the factor of mutual nuclear deterrence that has helped to preserve peace in the relationship between the United States and the Soviet Union. This argument exaggerates the stability of the Soviet-American relationship of mutual nuclear deterrence, which can be overthrown by political or technical change, and which even while it lasts does not make nuclear war impossible but simply renders it 'irrational' (see Chapter 5). Moreover, it wrongly assumes that the spread of nuclear weapons will necessarily result in the duplication in other relationships of international conflict of the relationship of mutual nuclear deterrence that exists between the super powers; it assumes, in other words, that the spread of nuclear weapons is bound to lead to a 'unit veto system', which of course it is not.

There is a stronger argument, which is that whether or not the spread of nuclear weapons would lead to increased security, it would, if it made these weapons available to all states or blocs, advance the cause of international justice. International justice in the sense of equality with regard to the possession of nuclear weapons can be met fully only by complete nuclear disarmament, or by a system in which these weapons are available to all states or blocs. Any regime which draws a distinction between nuclear-weapon states and non-nuclear-weapon states is open to objection on this score. It is important to note that in the argument between those powers which support and those which oppose the 1968 Nuclear Non-Proliferation Treaty, or more generally between nuclear 'have' and 'have-not' powers, the issue is not whether or not a line should be drawn between nuclear-weapon states and non-nuclear-weapon states, but rather where this line should be drawn, which states should be within the club and which left outside. The principal 'recalcitrant' states – China, France and India – while they have sometimes justified proliferation with arguments that apply to others as well as themselves, have at no stage argued in favour of general and complete nuclear proliferation, and have been principally concerned to remove obstacles to their own inclusion in the nuclear-weapon club. This is one area in which goals of international order and of international justice or equal treatment are in conflict with one another.

Whether a world of many nuclear powers is taken to represent a desirable alternative to the present form of the international system or not, it must be reckoned an alternative that has a fair prospect of being realised. Like the vision of a disarmed world, the vision of a world of many nuclear powers is by itself incomplete. The prospects of order and of justice in an alternative form of states system characterised by many nuclear powers would depend on other factors besides the prevailing military technology and the number of states with access to it.

Ideological Homogeneity

Another alternative form of states system is one marked by ideological homogeneity, as distinct from the ideological heterogeneity that prevails in the states system at present. The exponents of political ideologies frequently maintain that the triumph of their doctrines throughout the states system as a whole would, in addition to conferring other benefits, eliminate or reduce the sources of war and conflict, and lead to a more orderly world. Theorists of the Reformation and the Counter-Reformation, of the Revolution and the Counter-Revolution, and in our own times the apologists of Communism and of Anti-Communism, alike maintain, even as they are calling for war, that their own cause is the cause of peace.

These ideological revolutionaries and counter-revolutionaries, as has been noted, sometimes embrace the goal of a universal society that would replace the states system (see Chapter 2). But they also sometimes adhere to the vision of a world that is still organised as a system of states, but in which all states embrace the true ideology and can in consequence maintain harmonious relations with one another. It is this vision that concerns us here.

Kant's espousal of the ideology of the French Revolution led him to the idea that peace should be founded upon a world republic or *civitas gentium*, but in *Perpetual Peace* he despairs of this and turns to the 'negative surrogate' of a league of 'republican' or constitu-tionalist states, which averts war and seeks to spread itself over the globe.[8] The Legitimist ideologists of the post-Napoleonic era saw the prospects of international peace and domestic tranquillity as lying in a Holy Alliance of sovereign states held together by bonds of piety and dynastic right. Mazzini saw the prospects of peace as lying in the universal triumph of nationalism, which would be assisted by a Holy Alliance of the Peoples among whom no conflicts of interest existed. In their different ways President Wilson in the United States, the members of the Union for Democratic Control in Britain and the Bolsheviks in Russia all held that control of foreign policy by democratic or popular forces was a source of peace and concord among states.

Marx saw the prospects of peace as bound up with the abolition of capitalism and class struggle. He held that the state was simply an instrument of class struggle, and also (although the point is less clear) appears to have thought of the nation as a transitory phenomenon; hence his theory may be taken to imply that with universal proletarian revolution the state, and hence the states system, will disappear. On the other hand, Marx and Engels sometimes spoke as if separate units would still exist after the revolution. Marxists-Leninists since 1917 have had to settle for the negative surrogate of a league of socialist states or Socialist Commonwealth. They live in a world in which proletarian revolution has taken place only in a limited number of countries, and in which even in these countries the state survives as an instrument of the dictatorship of the proletariat. In the thinking of Marxist-Leninists today the vision I have in mind is exemplified by the doctrine that relations among socialist states, while they are governed by the principles of 'socialist internationalism', are to be distinguished on the one hand from the relations among capitalist states, which are governed by the principles of 'imperialism', and on the other hand from the relations between socialist and capitalist states, which are subject to the principles of 'peaceful coexistence'.

The vision of a states system that achieves order or harmony through the triumph in all countries of the true ideology is different from the Grotian or solidarist vision, for the latter assumes that conflicts of interest will continue to exist among states, and seeks to curb them through the overwhelming power of the collectivity, whereas the former maintains that when the true ideology is universally enthroned, conflicts of interest will not exist or will only be of slight importance. The two visions, however, are sometimes uneasily combined in the thinking of the same person or persons; President Wilson, for example, placed his hopes on the solidarist idea of the League of Nations, but he was also drawn to the idea that this should be a league of democracies; and the architects of the United Nations, who were also primarily committed to a solidarist vision, nevertheless made a bow to the notion that true ideology is the source of peace in their requirement that the member states of the organisation should be 'peace-loving'.

We should distinguish the idea that an ideologically homogeneous states system would be more orderly because it would rest on a single ideology, and would not give rise to conflicts of ideology, from the idea that it would be more orderly because the particular ideology it would rest upon would reduce or eliminate conflicts of interest among states. The latter idea is open to some powerful objections, whatever the ideology in question.

In the era when foreign policy was shaped by monarchs and their ministers, and wars were occasioned by dynastic conflicts and fought by standing armies led by landed aristocrats, liberal or bourgeois ideologists were able to make plausible the thesis that international conflicts were artificially manufactured by the prevailing political groups, and that domestic political change on a universal scale would reveal a natural harmony of interests among peoples. This was the perspective that led Paine to the view that the cause of war lay in monarchical sovereignty, Cobden to hold that commerce was the grand panacea, and Comte to proclaim a general incompatibility between war and industrial society.

But as domestic changes took place that led to a decline in monarchical and aristocratic control of foreign policy and increased the role of the middle classes, this thesis became less plausible; German and French burghers and Manchester manufacturers were less moved by dynastic quarrels and rivalries, but this did not mean that they were without motives of their own for international conflict. Reasons of state came to be given content in terms of national interest, rather than dynastic interest, and royal pride or passion, as a cause of conflict and war, was replaced by the public pride or passion of nationalism. Early in the twentieth century Lenin, with some help from Hobson, was able to make plausible the thesis that it was precisely the struggle of finance capitalists and industrialists that led to international tension and war, and that the prospects of peace lay in another domestic political change that would bring the proletariat to power.

But just as bourgeois governments, while free of some of the motives that led the feudal classes to war, had motives of their own that led to war, so governments which reflect the interests of the proletariat, as defined by the Communist Party, have motives of their own that lead to international conflict, even if they are free of some of the motives that bourgeois or capitalist governments have had. The experience of the Soviet Union, the Peoples Republic of China, and the other socialist countries in their relations with one another, does not lend any support to the idea of a natural harmony of interests among the peoples or the working classes. Socialist or proletarian states in their dealings with each other have displayed the same conflicts of perceived interest that states of all kinds have manifested in earlier periods.

The view that a certain section of society is naturally internationalist is plausible only when it is asserted before that section of society has achieved power. It is the elements of society which do have power that most closely identify themselves with the maintenance or extension of the state's power abroad. Those elements in society which do not enjoy power at home are less concerned with the state's external honour and interests, and are natural dissenters from its foreign policy, and sometimes sympathisers with its opponents. But once they rise to power at home, they inherit the concern for the state's power abroad. The doctrine that peace will be established by the universal triumph of the true ideology does not take account of the argument Hegel made in his critique of Kant that it is the state *qua* state that is the source of tension and war, not the state *qua* this or that kind of state.[9]

However, a states system which rested upon a single ideology, whichever this might be, and was free of the conflict of ideologies, we might expect to be more orderly than that which exists at present. The states system in the past, as Raymond Aron has noted, has undergone phases at least of relative ideological homogeneity, in the intervals between the wars of religion, the wars of the French Revolution and Napoleon, and the World Wars and Cold War of the twentieth century, which have been the phases of maximum ideological conflict.[10] It is possible to agree with Aron that the coincidence of major wars and maximum heterogeneity of the states system is not accidental – not only because the successive ideological conflicts have been a cause of these major wars, but also because the wars themselves tend to accentuate ideological conflict, as each warring state allies itself with domestic factions within the enemy state.

These periods of relative ideological homogeneity, however, have been characterised by the toleration of ideological differences rather than by ideological uniformity. The wars of religion and the wars of the French Revolution and Napoleon, while superficially ending with the victory of one side, led, through a process of exhaustion, to compromises that made possible ideological coexistence, as the ideological conflicts of the twentieth century may also do. What we have in mind by a states system that is ideologically homogeneous is one in which states are united not by a formula that allows different political, social and economic systems to coexist, but by determination to uphold a single kind of political, social and economic system. We have in mind, in other words, a universal Holy Alliance that is able to make a single ideology prevail throughout the states system as a whole, as such an ideology now prevails within the limited spheres of the American alliance system and the Socialist Commonwealth.

Such a system promises a high degree of domestic order because any challenger to the prevailing political, social or economic system would have to face not merely the state immediately concerned but the society of states at large: interventions of the sort whereby the Soviet Union has upheld challenges to the socialist system in Eastern Europe, or of the sort whereby the United States has sought to exclude the same system from Central America, could take place in support of the existing regime, with the difference that they would not be met with the condemnation or criticism of other states. The system also promises a high degree of international order; while conflicts might occur between one state and another, arising from clashing material interests or anxieties about security, ideological tension would not divide them. Indeed, the common interests of all states in defending the entrenched political, social and economic system would provide them with a strong incentive to moderate their conflicts of interest.

It may be doubted, however, whether world politics is likely ever to display the kind of ideological uniformity that would be necessary to establish or to maintain an alternative form of the states system such as this. If we assume that in the future as in the past there will be constant change and variety in the ideologies that are espoused in different parts of the world, then the attempt to remould a states system on principles of ideological fixity and uniformity is likely to be a source of disorder, and we are driven back to the principle that order is best founded upon agreement to tolerate ideological difference, namely the principle upon which the present states system is founded.

Beyond the States System

If an alternative form of universal political order were to emerge that did not merely constitute a change from one phase or condition of the states system to another, but led beyond the states system, it would have to involve the demise of one or another of the latter's essential attributes: sovereign states, interaction among them, such that they form a system; and a degree of acceptance of common rules and institutions, in respect of which they form a society.

A System But Not a Society

It is conceivable that a form of universal political organisation might arise which would possess the first and the second of these attributes but not the third. We may imagine, that is to say, that there might exist a plurality of sovereign states, forming a system, which did not, however, constitute an international society. Such a state of affairs would represent the demise of *the* states system, which, it has been argued here, is an international society as well as an international system. There would be states, and interaction among them on a global basis, but the element of acceptance of common interests or values, and, on the basis of them, of common rules and institutions, would have disappeared. There would be communications and negotiations among these states, but no commitment to a network of diplomatic institutions; agreements, but no acceptance of a structure of international legal obligation; violent encounters among them that were limited by the capacity of the belligerents to make war, but not by their will to observe restraints as to when, how and by whom it was conducted; balances of power that arose fortuitously, but not balances that were the product of conscious attempts to preserve them; powers that were greater than others, but no agreed conception of a great power in the sense of a power with special rights and duties.

Whether or not the states system, at some point in the future, has ceased to be an international society, it might well be difficult to determine. There may be acceptance of common rules and institutions by some states, but not by others: how many states have to have contracted out of international society before we can say that it has ceased to exist? Some rules and institutions may continue to find acceptance, but others not: which rules and institutions are essential? Acceptance of rules and institutions may be difficult to determine: does it lie in verbal assent to these rules, in behaviour that conforms strictly to them, or in willingness to defer to them even while evading them? Granted these difficulties, it has already been shown that there is ample historical precedent for an international system that is not an international society (see Chapters 1 and 2).

An international system that is not an international society might nevertheless contain some elements of order. Particular states might be able to achieve a degree of domestic order, despite the absence of rules and institutions in their relations with one another. Some degree of international order might also be sustained by fortuitous balances of power or relationships of mutual nuclear deterrence, by great power spheres of preponderance unilaterally imposed, by limitations in war that were the consequence of self-restraint or limitations of capacity. But an international system of this kind would be disorderly in the extreme, and would in fact exemplify the Hobbesian state of nature.

States But Not a System

It is also conceivable that a form of universal political organisation might emerge which possessed the first of the essential attributes that have been mentioned but not the second. We may imagine that there are still sovereign states, but that they are not in contact or interaction with each other, or at all events do not interact sufficiently to cause them to behave as component parts of a system. States might be linked with each other so as to form systems of states in particular regions, but there would not be any global system of states. Throughout the world as a whole there might be mutual awareness among states, and even contact and interaction on a limited scale, but it would no longer be the case that states in all parts of the world were a vital factor in one another's calculations.

It might be difficult to determine how much decline in the global interaction of states would have to have taken place before we could say that they had ceased to form a system. If there is a high degree of interaction throughout the world at the economic and social levels, but not at the strategic level, can we say that there is a global system? Does a global states system cease to exist merely because there are some societies that are excluded from it? Even today in the jungles of Brazil or in the highlands of Papua/New Guinea there are societies scarcely touched by what we nevertheless call the global states system.

Once again, there is ample historical precedent for an alternative to the states system of this kind; as we have noted, it was not before the nineteenth century that there arose any states system that was global in dimension. Does such an alternative represent a superior path to world order?

It has often been maintained that it does. A series of isolated or semi-isolated states or other kinds of community might each achieve a tolerable form of social order within its own confines, and a form of world order would exist that was simply the sum of the order that derived from each of these communities. At the same time the classic sources of disorder that arise in a situation of interaction between states would be avoided because interaction itself would be avoided or kept to a minimum.

This was the substance of Rousseau's vision of a world of small self-sufficient states, each achieving order within its own confines through the operation of the general will of its community, and achieving order in their relations with one another by minimising contact.[11] It also entered into the prescription that Washington laid down for the United States in his Farewell Address: 'The great rule of conduct for us in regard to foreign relations is, in extending our commercial relations, to have with them as little *political* connection as possible.'[12] This for Washington was a maxim only for the United States, which was in a position of actual physical isolation from the powers that might threaten her. Cobden later transformed it into a general prescription for all states in his dictum: 'As little intercourse as possible betwixt the governments, as much connection as possible between the nations of the world.'[13]

Cobden believed in non-intervention in the most rigid and absolute sense. He opposed intervention in international conflicts as well as civil ones; for ideological causes (such as liberalism and nationalism on the European continent) of which he approved, as well as for causes of which he disapproved (such as the interventionism of the Holy Alliance); and for reasons of national interest such as the preservation of the balance of power or the protection of commerce. He rejected the distinctions John Stuart Mill drew between intervention in the affairs of civilised countries and intervention in a barbarian country, and between intervention as such and intervention to uphold the principle of non-intervention against a power that had violated it.[14] He even opposed the attempt to influence the affairs of another country by moral suasion, and declined to sanction the formation of any organisation in England for the purpose of interfering in another country, such as the organisations formed to agitate against slavery in the United States. However, in Cobden's vision the promotion of the maximum systematic interaction at the economic and social levels was just as important as the promotion of minimum interaction at the strategic and political levels. Assuming as he did the desirability of universal pursuit by governments of *laissez-faire* policies in relation to the economy, he was able to imagine that the strategic and political isolation of states from one another might coexist with their economic interdependence.[15]

A form of universal political organisation based on the absolute or relative isolation of communities from one another, supposing it to be a possible development, would have certain drawbacks. If systematic interaction among states has in the past involved certain costs (international disorder, the subjection of the weak to the strong, the exploitation by the rich of the poor), so also has it brought certain gains (assistance to the weak and the poor by the strong and the rich, the international division of labour, the intellectual enrichment of countries by each other). The prescription of universal isolationism, even in the limited form Cobden gave it of political and strategic non-interventionism, implies that the opportunities arising from human interaction on a global scale will be lost, as well as that the dangers to which it gives rise will be avoided.

World Government

It is conceivable also that a form of universal political organisation might arise lacking the first of the above essential attributes, namely sovereign states. One way in which this might occur is through the emergence of a world government.

We may imagine that a world government would come about by conquest, as the result of what John Strachey has called a 'knock-out tournament' among the great powers, and in this case it would be a universal empire based upon the domination of the conquering power;[16] or we may imagine that it would arise as the consequence of a social contract among states, and thus that it would be a universal republic or cosmopolis founded upon some form of consent or consensus. In the latter case it may be imagined that a world government would arise suddenly, perhaps as the result of a crash programme induced by some catastrophe such as global war or ecological breakdown (as envisaged by a succession of futurologists from Kant to Herman Kahn), or it may be thought of as arising gradually, perhaps through accretion of the powers of the United Nations. It may be seen as coming about as the result of a direct, frontal assault on the political task of bringing states to agree to relinquish their sovereignty, or, as on some 'functionalist' theories, it may be seen as the indirect result of inroads made on the sovereignty of states in non-political areas.

There has never been a government of the world, but there has often been a government supreme over much of what for those subjected to it was the known world. Throughout the history of the modern states system there has been an undercurrent of awareness of the alternative of a universal government, and of argument on behalf of it: either in the form of the backward-looking doctrine calling for a return to Roman unity, or in the form of a forward-looking doctrine that sees a world state as the consequence of inevitable progress. In the twentieth century there has been a revival of world government doctrine in response to the two World Wars.

The classical argument for world government is that order among states is best established by the same means whereby it is established among individual men within the state, that is by a supreme authority. This argument most commonly relates to the goal of minimum order, and especially the avoidance of war, which is said to be an inevitable consequence of the states system. But it is also sometimes advanced in relation to goals of optimum order; it is often argued today, for example, that a world government could best achieve the goal of economic justice for all individual men, or the goal of sound management of the human environment.

The classical argument against world government has been that, while it may achieve order, it is destructive of liberty or freedom: it infringes the liberties of states and nations (as argued by the ideologists of the successful grand alliances that fought against universal monarchy); and also checks the liberties of individuals who, if the world government is tyrannical, cannot seek political asylum under an alternative government.

The case for world government may thus appear to rest on an assumed priority of order over international or human justice or liberty. It may be argued, however, that the states system affords a better prospect than world government of achieving the goal of order also (this is argued in Chapter 12 below) .

A New Mediaevalism

It is also conceivable that sovereign states might disappear and be replaced not by a world government but by a modern and secular equivalent of the kind of universal political organisation that existed in Western Christendom in the Middle Ages. In that system no ruler or state was sovereign in the sense of being supreme over a given territory and a given segment of the Christian population; each had to share authority with vassals beneath, and with the Pope and (in Germany and Italy) the Holy Roman Emperor above. The universal political order of Western Christendom represents an alternative to the system of states which does not yet embody universal government.

All authority in mediaeval Christendom was thought to derive ultimately from God and the political system was basically Theocratic. It might therefore seem fanciful to contemplate a return to the mediaeval model, but it is not fanciful to imagine that there might develop a modern and secular counterpart of it that embodies its central characteristic: a system of overlapping authority and multiple loyalty.

It is familiar that sovereign states today share the stage of world politics with 'other actors' just as in mediaeval times the state had to share the stage with 'other associations' (to use the mediaevalists' phrase). If modern states were to come to share their authority over their citizens, and their ability to command their loyalties, on the one hand with regional and world authorities, and on the other hand with sub-state or sub-national authorities, to such an extent that the concept of sovereignty ceased to be applicable, then a neo-mediaeval form of universal political order might be said to have emerged.

We might imagine, for example, that the government of the United Kingdom had to share its authority on the one hand with authorities in Scotland, Wales, Wessex and elsewhere, and on the other hand with a European authority in Brussels and world authorities in New York and Geneva, to such an extent that the notion of its supremacy over the territory and people of the United Kingdom had no force. We might imagine that the authorities in Scotland and Wales, as well as those in Brussels, New York and Geneva enjoyed standing as actors in world politics, recognised as having rights and duties in world law, conducting negotiations and perhaps able to command armed forces. We might imagine that the political loyalties of the inhabitants of, say, Glasgow, were so uncertain as between the authorities in Edinburgh, London, Brussels and New York that the government of the United Kingdom could not be assumed to enjoy any kind of primacy over the others, such as it possesses now. If such a state of affairs prevailed all over the globe, this is what we may call, for want of a better term, a neo-mediaeval order.

The case for regarding this form of universal political organisation as representing a superior path to world order to that embodied in the states system would be that it promises to avoid the classic dangers of the system of sovereign states by a structure of overlapping authorities and crisscrossing loyalties that hold all peoples together in a universal society, while at the same time avoiding the concentration of power inherent in a world government. The case for doubting whether the neo-mediaeval model is superior is that there is no assurance that it would prove more orderly than the states system, rather than less. It is conceivable that a universal society of this kind might be constructed that would provide a firm basis for the realisation of elementary goals of social life. But if it were anything like the precedent of Western Christendom, it would contain more ubiquitous and continuous violence and insecurity than does the modern states system.

Non-Historical Alternatives

We must finally note the possibility that an alternative will develop to the states system which, unlike the four that have just been considered, does not conform to any previous pattern of universal political organisation.

Of course, any future form of universal political organisation will be different from previous historical experience, in the sense that it will have certain features that are unique and will not exactly resemble any previous system. My point is not this trivial one but the more serious one that a universal political system may develop which does not resemble any of the four historically derived alternatives even in broad comparison. The basic terms in which we now consider the question of universal political organisation could be altered decisively by the progress of technology, or equally by its decay or retrogression, by revolutions in moral and political, or in scientific and philosophical ideas, or by military or economic or ecological catastrophes, foreseeable and unforeseeable.

I do not propose to speculate as to what these non-historical alternatives might be. It is clearly not possible to confine the varieties of possible future forms within any finite list of possible political systems, and for this reason one cannot take seriously attempts to spell out the laws of transformation of one kind of universal political system to another. It is not possible, by definition, to foresee political forms that are not foreseeable, and attempts to define non-historical political forms are found in fact to depend upon appeals to historical experience. But our view of possible alternatives to the states system should take into account the limitations of our own imagination and our own inability to transcend past experience.

11

The Decline of the States System?

It is often argued today that the states system is in decline, that it is giving place, or will give place, to some fundamentally different form of universal political organisation. What evidence is there that between now and the end of the century the states system is likely to be replaced by one or another of the alternatives discussed in the last chapter?

A System But Not a Society

It is not difficult to imagine that the states system, while continuing to be an international system, might cease to be an international society. It has already been argued that while there is an element of society in the contemporary states system, it enjoys only a precarious foothold (see Chapter 2). Since the outbreak of the First World War, despite the illusion of the strengthening of international society created by the growth of the scope of international law and the multiplication of international organisations, it is likely that there has been a decline in the consensus about common interests and values within the states system. The ideological divisions following upon the Bolshevik Revolution, the revolt of non-European peoples and states against Western dominance, and the expansion of the states system beyond its originally European or Western confines, have produced an international system in which the area of consensus has shrunk by comparison with what it was in 1914. It may readily be imagined that in the next few decades such

248

stresses will be placed on this remaining area of consensus that it will decline drastically or even disappear altogether.

It is hardly necessary to enumerate the sources of a possible collapse and disappearance of international society. The ideological tensions between communist and anti-communist states that dominated the 1950s and 1960s have lessened, but are still substantial. The tensions between rich, industrialised states and poor agricultural states show no sign of abating, and may have yet to reach their apogee. Conflicts of interest now arising over the heightened perception of resource scarcity provide a new source of tension. It has also to be recognised that the degree of strain on common rules and institutions that emerges in the late twentieth century may be determined in large measure by factors that are 'accidental' in the sense that they are the consequence simply of breakdowns in the diplomatic management of a particular conflict; a single, large-scale nuclear war, even if it were confined to the two belligerents as regards actual employment of nuclear weapons, might suddenly transform the world political scene and bring about a rapid and general disintegration of respect for the rules and institutions of international society. Indeed, the international history of this century so far may be regarded as a prolonged attempt to cope with the drastic decline of the element of society in international relations brought about by the single, catastrophic 'accident' of the First World War.

However, while we must recognise that the disappearance of international society is 'on the cards', we may also take note of some factors making for its endurance. Given the stresses to which international society has been subjected in this century, what is most remarkable is perhaps that it has survived at all. While the area of consensus among the 140 or so states that now exist, radically divergent in ideology, culture or civilisation, wealth and power, is much less than that which prevailed among the small number of states that existed in 1914 – relatively homogeneous in ideology and predominantly European – a framework of rules and institutions has survived within which the great schisms of this century have been contained.

Thus the system of international law that derives principally from European experience has been challenged by non-European states, especially the new states of Asia and Africa, as having been built upon the special interests of European powers, and designed to serve as an instrument of their domination. But while changes have been sought, and in some measure achieved, in relation to establishing the illegitimacy of colonial sovereignty, asserting the right of new states to sovereignty over their natural resources, the desirability of transferring wealth from rich to poor states, the limits within which new states succeed to the obligations of their predecessors, all this has taken place against the background of acceptance by the new states of the basic structure and tenets of the system.[1]

The mechanism of diplomatic relations among states has been shaken by the ideological struggle of communist and anti-communist states, leading during the Cold War period to the virtual disappearance of consular representation between the two blocs, and to a reduction of diplomatic representation. But even at the height of this struggle, some diplomatic relations between states in the two blocs persisted, and diplomatic forms and procedures were observed. Likewise the sudden ingress into the diplomatic society of states of the non-European members of it who are now its majority, while it has had its impact on the prevailing style and method of diplomacy, is remarkable less for this than for the evidence it provides of the willingness of the new states to conform to an established institution of the society of states.

There is no general consensus in international society, at least in explicit terms, as to the need for a balance of power or how it should be maintained, but one can say that there does exist a general balance of power, whose basis is the Soviet-American relationship of mutual nuclear deterrence, and that this balance is not wholly fortuitous but is brought about partly by Soviet and American contrivance, in which a Soviet-American sense of common interests plays some part.

The United Nations, like the League of Nations before it, has failed to provide an alternative path to world order by way of the solidarity of states in enforcing collective security. But it has succeeded in surviving as a single, universal international organisation, and thus as a symbol of a sense of common interests and values that underlies the discord of the present international system. The contraction and disappearance of the element of international society in international relations is a future development which we must regard as entirely possible and as a natural projection of some present trends, but we have no reason to assume that it is bound to occur.

States But Not a System

A second conceivable alternative mentioned in the last chapter was that states might continue to exist but cease to form a global system of states, because they had become completely isolated from one another, or because, although there was contact among them, there was insufficient interaction to cause them to behave as a set of parts. Such a state of affairs would represent a return to the situation that existed before the nineteenth century when, while there were states, and indeed systems of states, and regional political conglomerations of other kinds, in various parts of the world, there was no single, global states system of which all were part.

The disappearance of the element of a system from the present pattern of universal politics could come about only as the consequence of the collapse of our present scientific, industrial and technological civilisation. Clearly, the progress of industry and technology in the last two centuries has brought with it an increase in the amount of economic, social and strategic interaction among the various parts of the globe. It is not inconceivable that these trends will be reversed: energy scarcity, the pursuit of resource self-sufficiency, the questioning of economic development as a goal of policy, the rising influence of anti-scientific philosophies, all are trends making in this direction. Such trends, however, are scarcely of the order that might cause states to cease to form a system and constitute the congeries of isolated communities of Rousseau's imagining.

It is of course possible to see a trend in contemporary world politics towards greater regionalism, both in the organisation of peace and security, and in the management of international economic affairs. It is not inconceivable that the preference for global over regional international organisations that was displayed by the victorious powers towards the close of the Second World War, when they rejected the regionalist schemes favoured by Churchill and others in favour of the United Nations and its specialised agencies, might come to be reversed. It is possible that *Peace in Parts* (to quote the title of a recent book) might come to dominate thinking about the role of international organisations in matters of peace and security; that trade, money and development assistance affairs might also be handled chiefly by regional rather than global bodies; and that the United Nations and other global bodies might go into decline or even disappear altogether.² One vision of the near future that embodies this possibility is that of the division of the world into spheres of great power responsibility: the United States, the complex of West European states, the Soviet Union, China and Japan would each be responsible for managing the affairs of a particular region of the world, with only a loose form of co-operation among them.

This and other visions of a more regionalised world system, however, fall a long way short of a state of affairs in which there is no global states system. The essential feature of this system is not the existence of global international organisations but global interaction between states. The latter seems likely to persist whether the former do or not; no vision of the future is realistic which does not take account of the existence of social, economic, diplomatic and strategic interaction on a global scale. Catastrophic changes induced by global nuclear war that reduced all life to a low economic and technological level, the exhaustion of sources of energy and a consequent breakdown in global transport and communication, or a revolution in human values that brought about a universal return to a simpler and more localised style of life, represent the sort of conditions which alone could bring about a return to a pattern of states that does not form a states system.

World Government

There is not the slightest evidence that sovereign states in this century will agree to subordinate themselves to a world government founded upon consent. The idea of a world government brought about by social contract among states has always rested on the argument that the need for it will create the conditions that make it possible; that what must be, if order is to be brought about in world politics, will be. However, the fact of modern international politics has always been that states do not recognise any such need. Governments that are not capable of agreeing with each other, even to the extent of accepting one another's right to exist and desisting from the use or threat of force in resolving their disputes, can scarcely be thought capable of agreeing to entrust their security and other vital interests to a world authority. If this has been true in the past, how much more so is it true of the present and the foreseeable future, when the area of consensus among the chief groups of states is evidently small in comparison with some past periods, and many states are revelling in the independence they have won from colonial authorities? The idea that world government may come about as the result of some catastrophe such as a global nuclear war or a world economic or ecological breakdown – Kant's idea that states will be led by adversity to the course that they would have adopted in the first place, had they been willing to act rationally – presumes that in such a post-catastrophic situation international behaviour will be more 'rational', but we have no means of knowing whether it would be more so or less.

The idea of world government by contract involves a dilemma. The case for world government, as it is made out by Kant and others, begins with the proposition that sovereign states are in a Hobbesian state of nature, from which they need to escape by subordinating themselves to a common government. But if states are indeed in a Hobbesian state of nature, the contract by means of which they are to emerge from it cannot take place. For if covenants without the sword are but words, this will be true of covenants directed towards the establishment of universal government, just as it will hold true of agreements on other subjects. The difficulty with the Kantian prescription is that the description it contains of the actual condition of international relations, and the prescription it provides for its improvement, are inconsistent with one another. Action within the context of continuing international anarchy is held to be of no avail; but at the same time it is in the international anarchy that the grand solution of the international social contract is held to take place. The advocate of world government can show his scheme to be feasible as well as desirable only by admitting that international relations do not resemble a Hobbesian state of nature; that in it covenants without the sword are more than words, and the materials may be found with which to bring about collaboration between sovereign governments. But to make this admission is to weaken the case for bringing the international state of nature to an end.

World government by conquest has in the past seemed a much more likely possibility than world government by agreement. It was, after all, by conquest – as the outcome of a 'knock-out tournament solution' – that particular princes first made themselves supreme in the oldest of modern nation-states. It was conquest that led to the establishment of previous universal empires. The modern states system has several times come close to being transformed by conquest into a universal empire with a single supreme government.

In the late twentieth century, however, the prospects that world government will be established by conquest appear slight. Three factors militate against it. The first is the nuclear stalemate, which greatly augments the stability of the central or Soviet-American balance, and is coming to affect other great power balances in the same way. Any power with a secure nuclear retaliatory force has a trump card with which to deter attempts to overthrow it, no matter what the state of the military balance in relation to its adversaries may be, when measured by other indices. The second is the growth in the 1970s of a complex or multilateral balance of power, which also increases the stability of the general balance of power; given the military self-sufficiency which the United States, the Soviet Union, China and perhaps Japan and a combination of Western European states may have later in the century, it does not seem likely that any one great power will be able to achieve a position so preponderant as to make the others acquiesce in the establishment of an imperial system. The third factor is the political activisation of the peoples of the world, especially, although not exclusively, as it is expressed in nationalism. Opposition to the ascendancy of a single nation or race can so readily be mobilised that it is difficult to conceive that an imperial or hierarchical system could be established, or if established, could be other than short-lived, as was Hitler's New Order in Europe. Ours is an age of the disintegration of empires, and the prospects for universal monarchy have never seemed more bleak.

A New Mediaevalism

Is there any evidence that the states system may be giving place to a secular reincarnation of the system of overlapping or segmented authority that characterised mediaeval Christendom?

It is obvious that sovereign states are not the only important actors or agents in world politics. The mere existence in world politics of actors other than the state, however, does not provide any indication of a trend towards a new mediaevalism. The crucial question is whether the inroads being made by these 'other associations' (to use the mediaevalists' expression) on the sovereignty or supremacy of the state over its territory and citizens is such as to make that supremacy unreal, and to deprive the concept of sovereignty of its utility and viability. There are five features of contemporary world politics which provide *prima facie* evidence of such a trend.

(i) *The Regional Integration of States*

The first is the tendency of some states to seek to integrate themselves in larger units. The member states of the European Economic Community have not ceased to claim or to possess territorial sovereignty, but they have gone some distance in a process of integration which is seen, at least by some, as leading eventually to the loss of their sovereignty. No other regional association can match the record of the E.E.C. in measures of economic integration actually accomplished, but associations such as Comecon, the Organisation of African Unity, the Organisation of American States, the Central American Common Market and the Association of South East Asian Nations have been affected by its example.

The rhetoric of the 'European' movement has always included the claim that European integration would have novel and beneficial effects on international order, both because it would lead to a 'security-community' or zone of peace within Europe itself, and because it would demonstrate to the world at large the ability of a group of states voluntarily to submerge their sovereignty.[3]

The difficulty in this view is that if the process of integration of European states were to lead to the creation of a single European state (and if similar processes, sparked off by this example, were to have the same result in other regions), the upshot would be to reduce the number of sovereign states but to leave the institution of the sovereign state precisely where it was before.

It may be argued that a European state that arose in this way, while it would still be a sovereign state, would at least not be a nation-state, and that being free of the nationalist drives and ambitions that have brought nation-states into conflict with each other in the past, it could be expected at least to be more restrained and law-abiding than the states which had surrendered their sovereignty to it; it would be a sovereign state whose tendency to engage in 'power politics' (in the sense of the pursuit of power as an end and not merely as a means) had been emasculated.

Such a view ignores the fact that the movement for European integration reflects not only the ambition of some Europeans to 'transcend power politics', but also the ambition of others to create a unit that, in a world dominated by states of continental dimensions such as the United States, the Soviet Union and China, Europeans can engage in 'power politics' more effectively. It neglects the connection to which European federalists rightly draw attention, between the development of a European federal state, and the development, as a prior condition of it, of a sense of European personality or identity asserted in relation to other peoples, a 'new fatherland' which Frenchmen, Germans and others can discover as their own nation becomes a less exclusive focus of their loyalties. At a deeper level, the view that a state which is not a nation-state can be expected to abstain from 'power politics' overlooks the fact that the period of nation-states is itself only a particular historical phase of the states system, and that the place that can be occupied by 'power-politics' in the relations of states that are not nation-states is amply illustrated by the history of the states system in its dynastic or absolutist phase.

If we are looking for evidence that European integration is bringing a qualitative change in the states system, it is more profitable to look not to the imagined end-product of this process, a European super-state which is simply a nation-state writ large, but at the process in an intermediate stage. It is possible that the process of integration might arrive at the stage where, while one could not speak of a European state, there was real doubt both in theory and in reality as to whether sovereignty lay with the national governments or with the organs of the 'community'. A crucial test might be the question whether national governments within the 'community' had the right, and, in terms of the force and the human loyalties at their command, the capacity, to secede. From a situation of protracted uncertainty about the locus of sovereignty, it might be a small step to the situation of a 'new mediaevalism', in which the concept of sovereignty is recognised to be irrelevant. But such a state of affairs, if it existed in Europe, would not mean that the global states system had been eclipsed, only that in this particular area (as, in the early centuries of the states system, in Germany), there was a hybrid entity which did not conform to the prevailing norms.

(ii) *The Disintegration of States*

Alongside the efforts of some states to integrate in regional units, we may set another tendency, which in the 1960s and 1970s has been more impressive, the tendency of existing states to show signs of disintegration. It is not merely that 'new' states, whose governments are engaged in promoting a sense of national identity and cohesion where previously this has not existed or has existed only in a precarious form, have been shaken and in one case (Pakistan) broken by secessionist movements; disintegrative tendencies have also marked the recent history of an older 'new' state, Yugoslavia, and of such long-established nation-states as Britain, France, Spain, Belgium and Canada.

It is possible to imagine that out of the demands of the Welsh, the Basques, the Quebecois, the Flemish and others, there may arise qualitative changes in the states system. It is true that within the ranks of these dissident groups there are some who hope only for local autonomy and do not wish to challenge the sovereignty of the state in which they find themselves. Moreover, there are others who wish to bring about the break-up of the state which they believe oppresses them, but only in order to set up another sovereign state of their own. If the upshot of these disintegrative tendencies were simply that Nagaland, Biafra, Eritrea, Wales, Quebec and Croatia were to take their places as sovereign states (as Bangladesh has done), then the number of sovereign states in the world would have increased, but the institution of the sovereign state would be no more affected than by the creation of a United States of Europe.

As in the case of the integration of states, the disintegration of states would be theoretically important only if it were to remain transfixed in an intermediate state. If these new units were to advance far enough towards sovereign statehood both in terms of accepted doctrine and in terms of their command of force and human loyalties, to cast doubt upon the sovereignty of existing states, and yet at the same time were to stop short of claiming that same sovereignty for themselves, the situation might arise in which the institution of sovereignty itself might go into decline.

We cannot ignore this possibility, any more than we can dismiss the possibility that sovereignty will be undermined by regional supranational institutions. The political realist who dismisses such possibilities impatiently is too facile. One reason why European integrationists and such groups as the Quebecois and the Basques (let us call them 'disintegrationists') are drawn towards solutions which would result simply in the creation of new sovereign states is the tyranny of existing concepts and practices. The momentum of the states system sets up a circle (vicious or virtuous according to the point of view) within which movements for the creation of new political communities tend to be confined. Perhaps the time is ripe for the enunciation of new concepts of universal political organisation which would show how Wales, the United Kingdom and the European Community could each have some world political status while none laid claim to exclusive sovereignty. But, meanwhile, secessionist movements, like those that have given rise to the break-up of European empires, only confirm the institution of the sovereign state and do not bring it into question.

(iii) *The Restoration of Private International Violence*

Another development which may be interpreted as a sign of the decline of the states system and its transformation into a secular reincarnation of the mediaeval order is the resort to violence on an international scale by groups other than the state, and the assertion by them of a right to commit such violence.

We have already noted that one of the basic features of the modern states system has been that in it sovereign states have sought to monopolise the right to use force in international politics (see Chapter 8). In the modern states system, by contrast with the experience of mediaeval Christendom, it has been held that legitimate violence can be committed only by a public authority, and that the only public authority entitled to use it is a sovereign state.

The state's monopoly of legitimate international violence, it could be argued, has been infringed by international organisations such as the United Nations, for example during the Korean War and the Congo crisis, which has claimed the right to exercise force on an international scale; but in these cases the international organisation concerned can be regarded simply as the agent of a group of states co-operating in the exercise of their established right to resort to force. A more important infringement of the state's traditional monopoly is the practice of resort to violence by political groups which are not sovereign states, and which are only doubtfully public authorities at all, yet which – like the Palestinian guerrillas based in Arab countries – attack the territory of a foreign state, and its personnel and property in third countries, or seize the citizens of third countries as hostages; or which – like the Tupamaros in Uruguay and comparable revolutionary organisations in many countries – use violence not only against the government they are seeking to overthrow, but kidnap the diplomats or private citizens of third countries in order to bring pressure to bear on the government with which they are in conflict.

What is more impressive than the fact that international violence is resorted to by these non-state groups is the fact that their claim of the right to do so is accepted as legitimate by a substantial proportion of international society. The society of states has not been able to muster, against this challenge to its monopoly of legitimate violence by groups that are politically motivated, the kind of solidarity it has displayed against the privately motivated international violence of classical piracy. Attempts to curb the hijacking of aircraft and the kidnapping of diplomats by international action have foundered on this lack of solidarity. In 1972 the United Nations General Assembly was not able to endorse a U.S.-sponsored convention against 'international terrorism'.[4] Most Socialist and Third World states, so far from seeking to condemn resort to international violence by non-state groups, have sought to extend to them the protection of the laws of war, at all events in cases where these groups are engaged in armed struggle for self-determination, against colonial rule, alien occupation or 'racist' governments.[5]

If these trends were to be taken further, it would be possible to see in the growth of private international violence evidence that the state is losing its monopoly of the legitimate use of violence, and that a restoration is taking place of the mediaeval situation in which violence can legitimately be exercised by public authorities of many kinds if not also by private persons. However, private international violence of this kind is not new or unprecedented; all that is clearly new is the global scale on which it takes place. The violence of anti-governmental groups has often spilled across frontiers. The seizure of foreign aircraft and their passengers by revolutionary organisations had its precedents in the seizure of ships by such groups; in 1877, for example, the iron-clad *Huascar* was seized by Peruvian insurgents, who put to sea and stopped two British ships, from which they abducted Peruvian officials. The kidnapping by rebel groups of citizens of a third country has an important precedent in the kidnapping of two American citizens in Tangier in 1904 by the Moroccan brigand El Raisuli, who was able to bring pressure to bear on his local enemy, the Sultan of Morocco, by having the United States and other governments bring pressure to bear on him.[6] The idea that only states are entitled to use force in world politics has been the prevailing legal doctrine, but it has never been an exact reflection of reality.

We have also to take into account that the non-state groups which at present assert the right to engage in international violence appear in every case to aim to establish new states, or to gain control of existing ones – and that the sympathy that exists for them, within a large section of the society of states, is sympathy for these aims, not any desire to undermine the privileged position of states in relation to other groups within the world political system.

(iv) *Transnational Organisations*

The non-governmental group engaging in violence across boundaries in pursuit of its aims may be seen as a special case of a larger phenomenon threatening the survival of the states system: the transnational organisation. This is the organisation which operates across international boundaries, sometimes on a global scale, which seeks as far as possible to disregard these boundaries, and which serves to establish links between different national societies, or sections of these societies. It includes multinational corporations such as General Motors or Unilever; political movements such as the Communist Party or the Tricontinental Solidarity Organisation; international non-governmental associations, such as scientific or professional bodies; religious associations such as the Roman Catholic Church; and inter-governmental agencies that operate across frontiers, such as the World Bank.[7]

It is helpful to take account of Huntingdon's distinction between the control of these organisations, the national composition of the personnel operating them, and the geographical scope of their operations. Thus, as he says, most of the largest multinational corporations are under national control (they mainly have head-quarters in the United States with American top management); they are multinational in their staff; and they are transnational in their scope of operations – that is, they carry on 'significant centrally-directed operations in the territory of two or more states'.[8] On Huntingdon's definition, organisations are transnational if the scope of their operations is transnational. Thus the U.S. Air Force, which is national in control and in personnel, qualifies as a transnational organisation, as does the World Bank, which is international in control and multinational in personnel.

It is often argued that these transnational organisations, or some of them, because they bypass the states system and contribute directly to the knitting together of the global society or the global economy, are bringing about the states system's demise. It is said, more particularly of the role of multinational corporations, that their proliferation, their increasing size and their increasing share of the world's gross product represents the inevitable triumph of 'geocentric technology' over 'ethnocentric politics'.

The multinational corporation is not a new phenomenon in world politics, and no present-day corporation has yet had an impact comparable with that of the English East India Company, which employed its own armed forces and controlled territory. Multinational corporations have impressed themselves on the world recently because of the huge scale of their operations (they frequently have more capital than the state on whose territory they operate), the global nature of their enterprise, which seeks to ignore boundaries, and their ability within limits to evade control by sovereign states. Their growth in the 1950s and 1960s has led to claims by George Ball and others that they are a great, new constructive force in world politics, symbols of the geocentric technology that will and should prevail over ethnocentric politics, but also to denunciation of them by nationalists (especially by Latin Americans and Canadians, but also by J.-J. Servan-Schreiber in *Le Défi Américain*) who see them as instruments of American imperialism, or in some cases as instruments of a wider imperialism of the advanced capitalist countries.[9]

It is not clear, however, that transnational organisations are undermining the states system. In the first place, sovereign states have displayed a considerable ability to stand up to multinational corporations: to deny them access altogether for their operations (as, until recently, all communist countries have virtually excluded multinational corporations); or to impose restrictions on their activities (as is increasingly the tendency both in Third World countries and in advanced capitalist countries such as Australia, Canada and the countries of Western Europe). Suggestions that the sovereign states of Western Europe and the Third World are impotent in face of the demands or the attractions of multinational corporations are the product of the first decade of the inroads made by these organisations. As awareness of the economic impact of the multinational corporation has grown, and international debate about it has proceeded, a reaction has set in that is demonstrating the capacity of sovereign states, able as they are in most cases to command the predominant loyalties of their citizens, to lay down their own terms as to whether or not or on what basis multinational corporations will be given access to national territory. As Robert Gilpin has pointed out, in a conflict between 'geocentric' or any other technology, and 'ethnocentric' or any other politics, there is no reason to assume that it is politics that has to give way.[10]

In the second place, in cases where transnational organisations do achieve access to national territory, it is not clear that this necessarily results in a diminution of the power or a setback to the objectives of the state concerned. Huntingdon argues that predictions of the demise of the nation-state are

based on a zero-sum assumption about power and sovereignty: that a growth in the power of transnational organisations must be accompanied by a decrease in the power of nation-states. This, however, need not be the case . . . an increase in the number, functions and scope of transnational organisations will increase the demand for access to national territories and hence also increase the value of the one resource almost exclusively under the control of national governments.[11]

Certainly, the agreements into which states enter with multinational corporations may be viewed as an exercise of their sovereignty and not as an impairment of it. If many countries prefer to provide multinational corporations with access to their territory because of the advantages they believe it brings them in providing capital, employment or an infusion of technology, this is because they choose to do so and not because they are impotent in the face of 'geocentric technology'.

Third, multinational corporations are able to operate only in conditions in which a modicum of peace and security has been provided by the action of states. It is sovereign states which command most of the armed force in the world, which are the objects of the most powerful human loyalties, and whose conflict and co-operation determine the political structure of the world. The multinational corporation does not even remotely provide a challenge to the state in the exercise of these functions. Its scope of operations and even its survival is in this sense conditional upon the decisions taken by states.

(v) *The Technological Unification of the World*

It is sometimes contended that the demise of the states system is taking place as a consequence of the technological unification of the world – of which the multinational corporations and the non-state groups which conduct international violence are only particular expressions, and which is bound to lead to the politics of 'spaceship earth' or of the 'global village' in which the states system is only part.

But it is also clear that 'the shrinking of the globe', while it has brought societies to a degree of mutual awareness and interaction that they have not had before, does not in itself create a unity of outlook and has not in fact done so. The point is well put by Brzezinski:

> The paradox of our time is that humanity is becoming simultaneously more unified and more fragmented. . . . Humanity is becoming more integral and intimate even as the differences in the conditions of separate societies are widening. Under these circumstances proximity, instead of promoting unity, gives rise to tensions prompted by a new sense of global congestion.[12]

Brzezinski goes on to argue that McLuhan's idea of the 'global village' overlooks the personal stability, interpersonal intimacy and shared values and traditions that are ingredients in the life of the primitive village, and that a more helpful image is von Laue's one of the 'global city' – 'a nervous, agitated, tense and fragmented web of interdependent relations better characterised by interaction than by intimacy'.[13]

Not only does 'the shrinking of the globe' create new sources of tension between societies that are of different ideological persuasions, different sizes, different cultures or civilisations, and different stages of economic development; it is doubtful whether the growth of communications as such does anything to promote global rather than regional or national perspectives and institutions. Technological advances in the means of moving goods, persons and ideas around the earth's surface facilitate global integration, but they facilitate regional, national and local integration also. It is well known, for example, that in this century the value of foreign trade of the industrial powers has declined as a proportion of their gross domestic products.[14] The growth of communications has increased their range of options for international trade, but it has increased their options for domestic trade as well, and it is the latter they have exploited the more. If trade, migration, travel and exchange of ideas are growing possibilities for the world as a whole, so are they within the narrower focus of the Western world, or of Europe, or Latin America or the Andean Group. Australia is often considered to be the classic victim of 'the tyranny of distance', and it may be thought to have benefited uniquely from 'the technological unification of the globe', but it is not clear whether the more important effect of the growth of communications in the last hundred years has been the integration of Australia with the rest of the world, or the integration of the different parts of Australia with each other.[15] What determines whether it is the global, the regional, the national or the sub-national options created by the progress of technology that are taken up is not technology itself but political and economic criteria of various kinds.

The regional integration of states, their tendency to disintegration, the growth of private international violence, the role of transnational organisations, and the opportunities for regional and global integration provided by the technological unification of the world, are awkward facts for the classical theory of world politics as simply the relations between states. That theory, however, has always had to contend with the existence of anomalies and irregularities: the German Empire up to 1871 – a group of states whose sovereignty was theoretically limited; the Vatican till 1929 – a state without territory; pirates – men without the protection of a state, whom all states were committed to treat as *hostes humani generis;* the British Commonwealth between 1919 and 1939 – a group of states which denied that the principles of sovereignty operated *inter se;* transnational bonds of religion or secular religion, ethnicity or nationality, class or political allegiance – which cut across the conventional division between municipal and international affairs; the East India Companies – corporations exercising rights of war and conquest; the Barbary Corsairs – as awkward for the theory as are the Palestinian guerrillas today.

The classical theory has held sway not because it can account by itself for all the complexity of universal politics, but because it has provided a truer guide to it than alternative visions such as that of an imperial system or a cosmopolitan society. A time may come when the anomalies and irregularities are so glaring that an alternative theory, better able to take account of these realities, will come to dominate the field. If some of the trends towards a 'new mediaevalism' that have been reviewed here were to go much further, such a situation might come about, but it would be going beyond the evidence to conclude that 'groups other than the state' have made such inroads on the sovereignty of states that the states system is now giving way to this alternative.

The question with which this chapter began we must answer by saying that there is no clear evidence that in the next few decades the states system is likely to give place to any of the alternatives to it that have been nominated. It may be objected that this conclusion, stated thus baldly, has a self-fulfilling quality, and derives from the drawing of too sharp a distinction between description of existing trends and prescription. We have recognised, after all, that there are certain trends – particularly in relation to the possible emergence of a 'new mediaeval' form of universal order – which do make against the survival of the states system, and which, if they went a great deal further, might threaten its survival. Might it not assist the further development of these trends to proclaim their potential for creating an alternative to the states system? We have noted that one reason for the continuing vitality of the states system is the tyranny of the concepts and normative principles associated with it: regional integrationists in search of new supranational forms, 'disintegrationist' separatists in search of new forms of autonomy for minority communities, revolutionary movements engaged in international violence – are alike intellectually imprisoned by the theory of the states system, and are in most cases as committed to it as the agents of sovereign states. Is there not a need to liberate thought and action from these confines by proclaiming new concepts and normative principles that would give shape and direction to the trends making against the existing system, as Grotius and others gave intellectual coherence and purpose to the trends making against an earlier political order? This is the perspective that underlies Richard A. Falk's view that the form of universal political organisation that has prevailed since the Peace of West-phalia is undergoing drastic modification in the direction of 'increased central guidance' and 'increased roles for non-territorial actors', re-establishing some of the features of the mediaeval period. An essential part of Professor Falk's view is that students of the subject can play an active role in accelerating this modification, which he takes to be beneficial.[16] It appears to me, on the contrary, that there is greater danger in the confusion of description and prescription in the study of world order than in drawing too sharp a distinction between them. Trends making against the states system may be strengthened by being recognised and dramatised, but only so far; there are certain realities which will persist whatever attitude we take up towards them. We have also to avoid begging the questions whether a trend towards 'increased central guidance' actually exists; and whether, if it did, this would make for a viable world order rather than against it.

The World Political System

If our analysis has led us to reject the view that the states system is in decline, it should also lead us to notice one of the cardinal features of its present phase. This is that there is now a wider world political system of which the states system is only part.

By the world political system we understand the world-wide network of interaction that embraces not only states but also other political actors, both 'above' the state and 'below' it. A view of world politics which took account only of the states system might recognise that each state had relations with international organisa-tions to which it belonged, and with political groups within its jurisdiction which helped to shape its own policy. International organisations, on this view, are an expression of the policies of states, and groups within the state are part of the causation of each state's policy.

But the reality is more complex than this. Political groups within a state do not simply affect world politics through the influence they may have on their own state's foreign policy. First, they may enter into relations (whether of combination or of opposition) with political groups in other states; business enterprises, trade unions, political parties, professional associations, churches, all have their being partly within the transnational nexus that bypasses the level of state-to-state relations. Second, they may enter into relations with foreign states, as when a multinational corporation enters into an agreement with a host government, political groups engage in a protest outside a foreign embassy, or revolutionary groups in one country assist their co-ideologists in another to overthrow the government. Third, they may enter into direct relations with an international organisation, as when non-state groups achieve representation at a United Nations specialised agency, or become the spokesmen or antagonists in their own country of the United Nations, the E.E.C. or the Organisation of African Unity.

Joseph Nye and Robert Keohane take relationships of this kind to exemplify 'transnational interactions', which they define as 'the movement of tangible or intangible items across state boundaries when at least one actor is not an agent of a government or an inter-governmental organisation'.[17] They contend that the orthodox study of international relations has been in the grip of a 'states-centric' paradigm in which the existence of transnational phenomena has been admitted but treated simply as part of the background of the subject, but that this should now be replaced by a 'world politics' paradigm that would bring these phenomena into the foreground, along with the relations of states. In so far as what they are arguing is that transnational relationships have in the past escaped systematic study and that this should now be corrected, there is much to be said for their point of view. The study of world politics should be concerned with the global political process as a whole, and this cannot be understood simply in terms of interstate politics in the strict sense. The 'world politics' perspective also has the advantage that it transcends the distinction between the study of international relations and the study of domestic politics by focusing upon the global political system of which the states system and national political systems are both part.

But if we should embrace the 'world politics' paradigm, we need also to disavow certain views with which it is sometimes associated.[18] First, it would be absurd to maintain that the existence of a political system involving other actors as well as states is in any sense a new or recent development. The states system has always been part of a wider system of interaction in which groups other than the state are related to each other, to foreign states and to international or supranational bodies, as well as to the state in which they are located. In the sixteenth and early seventeenth centuries, indeed, the relations of Catholic and Protestant groups across state boundaries to one another, to foreign powers and to supranational organisations such as the Papacy and the Empire was so prominent in relation to that of the relations of the Christian powers that the theory of European politics as the politics of the states system was still struggling to be born. All that is in any sense new or recent in the world political system of the nineteenth and twentieth centuries is its global or world-wide character; and, of course, it is only in this recent period that the states system itself has been world-wide.

Second, it is doubtful whether it can be shown that transnational relationships (using this term in the sense defined by Nye and Keohane) at present play a more important role, relatively to the relationships of states, than in earlier phases of the wider political system in which they both figure.

Raymond Aron has written in the following way of the 'transnational society' that existed in 1914, and which came to be 'totally ruptured' in the Cold War period 1946–53:

> Before 1914 economic exchanges throughout Europe enjoyed a freedom that the gold standard and monetary convertibility safeguarded even better than legislation. Labour parties were grouped into an International. The Greek tradition of the Olympic Games had been revived. Despite the plurality of the Christian Churches, religious, moral and even political beliefs were fundamentally analogous on either side of the frontiers. Without many obstacles a Frenchman could choose Germany as his place of residence, just as a German could decide to live in France. This example, like the similar one of Hellenic society in the fifth century, illustrates the relative autonomy of the inter-state order – in peace and in war – in relation to the context of

transnational society. It is not enough for individuals to visit and know each other, to exchange merchandise and ideas, for peace to reign among the sovereign units.[19]

Nye and Keohane argue that interstate relations today do not possess the autonomy which Aron attributes to them, and that they are more affected by 'transnational society' than they were in 1914. It is true that since that time state intervention has grown in economic and social life and in the sphere of private political or religious belief, and that, as a consequence of this, state-to-state relations have a much larger economic, social and ideological content than they had in 1914. But is this a sign of the increased importance in world politics of actors other than the state, or is it rather an indication that the states system has extended its tentacles over world politics to deprive business corporations and bankers, labour organisations, sporting teams, churches and intending migrants of the standing as autonomous actors that they once enjoyed?

Whether we judge the role of non-state actors in world politics today to be greater or less than in 1914, it is very unlikely that their role is as great as it was in the sixteenth and seventeenth centuries, when residual mediaeval transnational relations played a central role. As Nye and Keohane contend, the role of transnational relations has not yet been systematically studied. The studies that are now under way, however, are concerned with the contemporary world, and this may lead us to lose sight of the fact that it is the place of transnational relations in earlier phases of the states system that has been more seriously neglected by students.

Third, the factors consolidating the world political system do not in themselves assure the emergence of an integrated world society. By a world society we understand not merely a degree of interaction linking all parts of the human community to one another, but a sense of common interest and common values, on the basis of which common rules and institutions may be built. The concept of a world society, in this sense, stands to the totality of global social interaction as our concept of international society stands to the concept of the international system.

There is no doubt of the existence of one important and novel factor affecting transnational relations today: the development of global communications creating an unprecedented degree of mutual awareness among different parts of the human community, both through the relaying of messages and pictures and through opportunities created for travel and direct contact. However, it has to be noted that this has not by any means led to a situation of 'perfect' mutual awareness of all societies by one another. Many governments use their authority to exclude foreign radio or television contacts, and to deny freedom of travel to their citizens. All governments have opportunities to control and distort mutual awareness and contact, and even where the conditions for awareness of other societies are most favourable, what one society knows about another is always selective and partial. Moreover, awareness of other societies, even where it is 'perfect', does not merely help to remove imagined conflicts of interest or ideology that do not exist; it also reveals conflicts of interest or ideology that do exist.

There is also no doubt that there exists among all societies today a high degree of interdependence or mutual sensitivity in the pursuit of basic human goals. However, we have also to recognise that the term 'interdependence' has become a cant word that serves to rationalise relations between a dominant power and its dependencies, in which the sensitivity is more one-sided than it is mutual. Appeals to interdependence (among allies in NATO, among rich countries in the O.E.C.D., between producers and consumers of resources) have a strong political content, and frequently reflect fears that the interdependence of one society's decisions and another's will not be recognised, or demands that they should be recognised, rather than the belief that decisions are in fact interdependent.

Moreover, the interdependence of one society's decisions and another's, even where it genuinely exists and there is awareness of it, does not in itself generate a sense of common interest, let alone of common values. The fact of the mutual sensitivity of states and other actors to one another's strategic, economic or ecological decisions can be exploited by each actor for its own purposes and does not in itself determine whether there will be co-operation or conflict.

Fourth, we have to note that where in the contemporary world political system transnational relationships appear to have made significant inroads upon the states system, this has occurred in an uneven fashion. There are cases where transnational relationships assume an important place in the politics of a particular region, as in the E.E.C. through the role of the Community's institutions, in the Socialist Commonwealth through the part played by Comecon and the Communist Parties, or in the Arab states because of the factor of a common Arab nationalism. But if links of this kind have led or promise to lead to transnational social integration, this is of a purely regional kind, and does not necessarily assist global social integration.

On the other hand, some transnational relationships are of global and not merely regional importance, but their effect is to promote not the integration of world society as a whole, but rather the integration of a dominant culture, which as it draws closer together at the same time draws farther apart from those social elements that are left outside. It is familiar that the effect of the multinational corporations, the great foundations and the scientific and professional associations, whose centres lie in the advanced capitalist countries, and especially in the United States, is to promote a kind of integration that links together the societies of those advanced countries and elite groups within the poor countries, but whose effect is also to widen the social or cultural distance between advanced societies and poor societies, and between modernised elite groups and the ordinary people within the latter.[20] It is difficult to find evidence of transnational relationships whose effect is to promote an evenly distributed social integration throughout the world as a whole.

Fifth, the world political system of whose existence we have taken note in no way implies the demise of the states system. The states system has always operated within a wider system of political interaction, and within the world-wide political system of today the primacy of the states system is for the time being assured.

12

The Obsolescence of the States System?

It is sometimes argued that whether or not the states system is in decline, it is obsolete in the sense of being dysfunctional – that is to say, that it has ceased or is ceasing to be capable of fulfilling the basic ends or goals of man on earth. On this view the states system, whether or not it is judged to have provided a satisfactory means of attaining it in the past, does not now or will not in the future provide a viable path to world order. It follows from this that even if we accept the argument of the last chapter that there is no conclusive evidence that the states system is giving place to an alternative form of universal political organisation, we should nevertheless recognise that the goal of world order requires some alternative, and dedicate ourselves to work for it. This, for example, is the perspective of the editors of a recent series of volumes on *The Future of the International Legal Order*, Cyril E. Black and Richard A. Falk. It is stated also, with more passion, in Falk's *This Endangered Planet*.[1]

Those who take this view are inclined to advance one or more of the following propositions.

(i) That the states system can no longer provide, if it ever did provide, peace and security – or, more generally, minimum world order. This is the classic argument against 'the international anarchy', now reinforced by the special dangers of nuclear war.

(ii) That the states system, even though it might prove compatible with the continuation of a minimum of peace and security, cannot provide for the more ambitious goal of economic and social justice, among the nations of the world and within them, for which a politically awakened world is now in search.

(iii) That the states system is an obstacle to the attainment of man's ecological objective of living in harmony with his environment: that the connected issues of population control, food production and distribution, resource management and conservation can be effectively advanced only through a global approach and a sense of human solidarity that are vitiated by the division of mankind into states.

Peace and Security

Those who hold that the states system is dysfunctional begin with the traditional argument that, given the existence of a system of states, war is inevitable. This, they contend, is a situation which may have been tolerable in the past, but is so no longer. The recurrence of war throughout the history of the states system has been the cause of endless misery and tragedy, but at least the record shows that it has so far proved compatible with the survival of the human species, and indeed with the maintenance of civilised social life and with economic, scientific and artistic advance of various kinds. But, given the availability of nuclear weapons and other means of instant mass destruction, so the argument goes, the recurrence of war will lead sooner or later to the end of civilised social life, or perhaps to the end of human life itself. The remedy, therefore, must be to replace the system of states with some form of universal political organisation of which war is not an endemic feature.

It can hardly be denied that war is endemic in the system of states. Of course war is not made logically inevitable by the existence of the states system. There are examples of pairs and groups of states – the pairs and groups which Karl Deutsch calls 'pluralistic security-communities' – among which there have been not only long periods of peace, but also long periods in which neither party has seriously expected that disputes would be resolved by resort to force.[2] The relations of Canada and the United States and Britain and the United States, the relations among the Scandinavian countries, and the relations among the older states of the Commonwealth, provide principal examples. We can, indeed, imagine a system of states which is a universal 'pluralistic security-community' – in which the kind of interstate relationship that has developed among the English-speaking and Scandinavian groups of states has become general. Such a variety of states systems is not a logical impossibility, and indeed may be thought to provide a vision which offers hope. But we have no present reason to expect that in the system of states that seems likely to persist for the rest of this century, such a vision will be realised.

Within the states system no particular war is inevitable; it is frequently the case that a war which threatens to arise out of an international conflict is averted by skilful diplomacy or good fortune; but war in general is inevitable in the sense that its outbreak somewhere in the states system over a period is statistically probable. Given the existence of states that are sovereign, armed and politically divided, it has always been unreasonable in the past, and it would be unreasonable now, to expect universal and permanent peace in the foreseeable future.

Nor can it be denied that human society is less able than it was in the past to tolerate a form of universal political organisation in which war is endemic. Wars in the past have sometimes resulted in the crippling or even in the extinction of whole societies, but there has been no equivalent of the possibility of instant and global destruction and dislocation that is the consequence of modern military technology. Nor has there been any equivalent before this century of the economic and ecological interdependence of human communities over the whole of the world that increases their vulnerability to dislocation and destruction produced by war on a global scale.

But it does not follow from this that the states system is dysfunctional in relation to minimum world order. In the first place, the drawbacks of the states system have to be compared with those of such alternative forms of universal political organisation as might conceivably be available. It is superficial to contend that violent conflict among men is caused by the existence of a system of states without considering whether it does not have deeper causes that would also be operative in any alternative political structure: the availability of violence as a physical option for men in resolving their disputes, and their will to resort to it rather than accept defeat on matters that are vital to them.

The idea that under world government war would be impossible rests simply on the verbal confusion between war in the broad sense of organised violence between political units, and war in the narrow sense of international war or organised violence between states (see

Chapter 8). Wars that accompany the breakdown of a world government, like civil wars that take place within a state, are not less violent or destructive because they are not wars in the narrower sense.

Of course we can imagine a world government which would not lend itself to civil or internal violence, at least on a large scale, because in it there were institutionalised procedures for the peaceful resolution of conflicts that allowed for change and were generally accepted as legitimate. Under such a world government, as within some modern Western states that have a high degree of political stability and a relative absence of violent internal conflict, large-scale violence might be avoided for long periods. But if we are free to attribute to our imagined alternative form of universal political organisation these utopian features, we are also free to think of the states system in these utopian terms, as a system in which the conditions of a 'pluralistic security-community' are generalised.

Similarly, a 'new mediaeval' order would be one in which war in the sense of organised violence between sovereign states would not exist, because sovereign states would not exist; but this would afford no guarantee that there would be more peace and security than in the modern states system. We have already noted that the universal political order of Western Christendom contained more ubiquitous violence and insecurity than that which succeeded it (see Chapter 10). Again, we may imagine a 'new mediaeval' political order that contained institutionalised procedures for the peaceful resolution of conflicts that were more effective than those now contained in the modern states system, and that led to a degree of world order that was unprecedented. But if we are free to imagine a 'new mediaeval' order with utopian characteristics such as these, we must also be allowed to think of the states system not as it is, but as it may develop into a means of sustaining peace and security that is more effective.

The comparison of alternative utopias is an arbitrary and sterile exercise. A more fruitful question is whether, in the world political system which we can foresee in the remainder of this century, in which the means of violence are available and the will to use them only too evident, and in which therefore we should not attribute utopian characteristics to any conceivable form of universal political organisation, the attempt to make a world government or some other alternative viable gives more or less promise that the goals of minimum world order will be met, than the attempt to make the states system viable.

In the second place, to conclude that the states system is dysfunctional is to overlook the positive role it can play in the achievement of order in a human community that is deeply divided. The origin of the states system lay in the realisation that where religion and the authority of the Papacy and the Empire were matters of deep division rather than of consensus, order could be better achieved through acceptance of the division of Europe into states and of coexistence among them than through the attempt to work an alternative system that presupposed a wider consensus.

Government, involving as it does a legal monopoly of the use of force, provides a means of maintaining order; but it is also a source of dissension among conflicting groups in society which compete for its control. If governmental authority, once it is captured, may be wielded so as to deny the resort to force by private individuals or groups, it is also the case that the existence of the governmental mechanism constitutes a prize in political conflict which raises the stake in such conflict to a level above that it would otherwise be. In the typical modern nation-state, order is best preserved when conflict takes the form of a competition between the contending forces for the control of a single government, rather than that of competition among governments. Yet the political community is also familiar in which the reverse is the case; in which the dangers to order arising from the coexistence of sovereign governments are less than those involved in the attempt to hold hostile communities in the framework of a single polity. The partition of India in 1947 had this rationale, as did the further partition of Pakistan in 1971.

It is possible to view the problem of order in the world community in this way. The system of a plurality of sovereign states gives rise to classic dangers, but these have to be reckoned against the dangers inherent in the attempt to contain disparate communities within the framework of a single government. It may be argued that world order at the present time is best served by living with the former dangers rather than by attempting to face the latter.[3]

In the third place, before we conclude that the states system cannot provide for minimum world order, we need to take account of the possibility that states will maintain and develop the prudence and restraint they have so far displayed in relation to nuclear weapons and other weapons of mass destruction.

With the single exception of the American nuclear bombing of Japan, nuclear weapons have not yet been used in war. Powers possessed of nuclear weapons have not only refrained from using these weapons against each other, but have avoided becoming involved in direct military conflict with each other, apart from the border clashes between the Soviet Union and China in 1969. The United States and the Soviet Union have recognised the common interests they have in avoiding a nuclear conflict and have worked out guidelines or operational rules that help them to avoid crises or control them if they occur. They have also built up a structure of agreements on arms control, beginning with the Partial Nuclear Test Ban Treaty of 1963, that impose some significant restraints on their arms competition and symbolise their perception of common dangers.

We have no reason to assume that these elements of restraint in the policies of the two leading nuclear weapon states are bound to endure, or to be generalised so as to embrace other nuclear weapon states, actual and potential. It is all too easy to envisage the breakdown of Soviet and American restraints; the non-participation of China and other nuclear powers in the system of restraints; the emergence of new nuclear powers, less interested in restraint and co-operation than the older ones; the acquisition of nuclear weapons by groups other than the state; or the failure of the nuclear powers to consolidate and extend the present system.

It has certainly to be recognised that if this system of restraint is not maintained and extended, a minimum of peace and security, or of minimum world order, cannot be achieved through the states system. However, it is reasonable to hope that this system of restraint will be preserved and extended, and it is vitally important for world order to work for this goal. If, as was argued in the last chapter, the states system, functional or not, is likely to remain with us in the foreseeable future, it is only by promoting the restraints that will make it functional that the goal of minimum world order can be attained at all.

Economic and Social Justice

To the traditional claim that the states system cannot provide adequately for peace and security, there is sometimes added the argument that it cannot bring about economic and social justice in the world society or community.

Clearly, human society at present is characterised by massive economic and social injustice – both among states or nations, and among individuals and groups within them. We have already noted that the states system which exists at present is inhospitable to notions of world or cosmopolitan justice, that it gives only a selective and ambiguous welcome to ideas of individual or human justice, and that while it is not basically hostile to notions of international or interstate justice, it maintains itself in ways that systematically affront these latter notions (see Chapter 4).

Of course the existence of such injustice, and of forms of universal political organisation that tolerate or encourage it, is in no sense new or unusual. Throughout history such facts have been so much taken for granted as hardly to have seemed worthy of comment.[4] Before the nineteenth century no truly world-wide political system existed within which ideas of economic and social justice might be realised, and the pursuit of these latter goals, where it occurred at all, took place in a local or municipal context. But the world-wide political system of the nineteenth and twentieth centuries has produced the conditions of global interdependence and global consciousness or awareness, in which ideas of economic and social justice have been given a global application, most notably by Marx, whose doctrine of international proletarian revolution asserted the primacy or immediacy of economic and social goals, and applied them not in a local or municipal context but in the context of a nascent world society or community.

A world society or community, characterised by a sense of the common interests and values of all mankind – as distinct from a world political system characterised merely by global interdependence and global awareness – may not exist except in embryo, but it is widely held that it should exist (these terms are discussed in Chapter 11). Moreover, it is surely the duty of all intelligent and sensitive persons, however conscious they may be of the obstacles standing in the way of the emergence of such a world society or community, to recognise its desirability and dedicate themselves to work for it. If the states system is indeed an obstacle to the realisation of these goals of economic and social justice, this must today give cause for concern, even if in previous eras this would not have seemed one of the criteria by which the functionality or usefulness of this form of universal political organisation had to be assessed.

The states system, it may be argued, obstructs realisation of the goals of economic and social justice in two main ways. Because it imposes barriers to the free movement of men, money and goods about the earth's surface – and also to their movement according to a putative global plan of economic development – it inhibits world economic growth; and at the same time, because each state is responsible for the interests of only a limited segment of the human population, the states system obstructs the just distribution of economic and social benefits among states and nations, among individuals or according to some conception of the world common good.

The goal of economic and social justice at the international or interstate level is recognised by the commitment of states to the transfer of resources from rich to poor nations, which is sometimes said to be aimed at 'closing the gap' between the former and the latter, and sometimes said to be aimed at enabling all countries to achieve a minimum standard of welfare. However, not only is it the case that the gap has not been closed, but that there is no prospect that in the foreseeable future it will be.[5] It may be argued also that economic justice or equality among states and nations will not be achieved while the states system continues. Given the primary orientation of the rich states towards providing for the economic and social interests of their own peoples, it may be argued, they are unlikely to so re-orient their policies in relation to official aid, private foreign investment, trade or migration in the quite fundamental ways that would be necessary to 'close the gap', or perhaps even to achieve a global minimum standard of living or welfare.

Still less is it likely, it may be argued, that while the states system continues, goals of economic and social justice at the individual or human level can be realised. What is more important than economic justice among nations, is economic and social justice among individuals, whether this is conceived in terms of equality of benefits among all human beings, or in terms of a minimum level of such benefits, that is the global elimination of poverty and social deprivation. Achievement of this goal depends not merely on the transfer of resources to poor countries, but also on the just distribution of these resources or the benefits accruing from them among the citizens of these countries. Rich states, and the international agencies through which some of their 'development assistance' is channelled, may and do lay down conditions for the transfer of resources to poor countries; but because they are concerned with their own interests more than they are with the goal of human justice, the conditions they lay down may not be such as to secure a just distribution of benefits by the receiving governments. Moreover, their ability to impose conditions is limited by the sovereignty of the receiving governments; it is beyond the ability of donor states or agencies, even supposing that they were concerned primarily to promote human justice, to determine the over-all economic and social policies of the recipient governments in such a way that this goal will be realised.

The goal of economic and social justice at the world or cosmopolitan level, it may be argued, is completely beyond the reach of a world organised as a system of states. If all economic and social policy were shaped in accordance with a conception of the world common good, this would imply that states surrendered their control over economic and social affairs and acted simply as the agents or trustees of a world authority. It is difficult to conceive that they could act in this way unless they had actually subordinated themselves politically to such a world authority and thus ceased to constitute a states system.

These arguments in relation to the goal of economic and social justice involve difficulties of the same kind that we noted above in relation to the goal of peace and security. In the first place, economic and social injustice in human society have deeper causes than the existence of the states system, and these causes would be operative also in any alternative universal political order. If the world government or new mediaeval order with which we contrast the states system is one which we assume to provide not only peace and security but also economic and social justice on a global scale, then of course the states system is dysfunctional by contrast. But what reason do we have to assume this, rather than that the world government or other alternative universal order would be tyrannical and unjust, while being subject to collapse into global civil strife also?

The advocate of world government makes the tacit assumption that it is his own moral and political preferences that will be embodied in it; he conceives the world authority as a projection of his own ideas, that is powerful enough to sweep aside the obstacles which now exist to the realisation of them. But this is an evasion of the issue; the world government with which the states system has to be compared is one that would be subject to the factors making for injustice in the present world, not one arbitrarily decreed to be immune from them. The realisation of goals of economic and social justice, whether at the international, the human or the world level, requires a much greater sense of human solidarity in relation to these goals than now exists; but the task of creating and maintaining such a sense of solidarity would lie on the agenda of world politics under any alternative form of universal political organisation, just as it lies on the agenda of the states system.

In the second place, the argument we have expounded overlooks the positive role which the states system plays in providing a bulwark against greater social and economic injustice than might otherwise exist. It is no accident that it is from the richest and most powerful countries that the advocates of world government or of the strengthening of global institutions come, while it is the countries of the Socialist Commonwealth and of the Third World that are most insistent on the preservation of state sovereignty (this point is further developed in the next chapter).

The poorer and weaker countries perceive that a move now towards a world government would be likely to result not in a redistribution of economic resources in their favour, but rather in the consolidation of the existing distribution of resources, if not in a redistribution unfavourable to themselves. They regard the institution of state sovereignty as one which provides a safeguard against the attempt of more powerful states to wrest from them control of the economic resources they now enjoy. It has been by creating sovereign states in defiance of the colonial powers, and by defending these sovereign states against the intrusion or penetration of them by so-called 'neo-colonial' powers, that the poorer and weaker nations have been able to achieve some measure of international justice for themselves and, in some cases, of human justice for their inhabitants.

Nor does this positive role of the states system operate only in favour of the poorer and weaker countries. Such economic and social justice as is now enjoyed in the world by nations and individuals is largely the consequence of the activity of states or governments in regulating economic life and distributing and underwriting economic and social benefits. The institution of state sovereignty imposes obstacles not only to those kinds of external interference that might promote greater economic and social justice than now exists, but also to external interference that would threaten or undermine economic and social gains that have already been achieved.

In the third place, the argument we are considering overlooks the possibility that the states system may come to be infused with a stronger consensus about goals of economic and social justice; that while the division into sovereign states persists, these states in defining their objectives will be increasingly disciplined by a sense of human solidarity or of a nascent world society. We have no reason to assume that this will happen, and, as noted above, we may well witness a contraction rather than an expansion of the area of consensus among states (see Chapter 11). But it is not inconceivable that the sense of a world common good, this now so delicate plant, will survive and grow.

Man and the Environment

The states system is today often said to be dysfunctional not only in relation to objectives of peace and security and of economic and social justice, but also in relation to the objective which all men must pursue of living in harmony with their environment.

Thus it is argued that mankind today faces threats arising from the growth of population, the pursuit by this population of economic growth, the pressures imposed by demographic and economic growth on scarce resources such as land, energy, food and raw materials, and resultant stress or overload imposed upon the physical environment. These threats, it is said, are all connected with one another, and they must be met together. Meeting them, it is said, will require global unity and global planning, to which the division of mankind into sovereign states is a standing obstacle. Writing of 'the four dimensions of planetary danger' which he identifies as 'the war system', 'population pressure', 'the insufficiency of resources' and 'environmental overload', Richard Falk asserts that these issues cannot be treated as separate and separable: 'In essence', he writes, 'the threats are all outgrowths of a mismanaged environment that is an inevitable result of a defective set of political institutions.'[6]

It is obvious that if all men were as willing to co-operate in the pursuit of common goals as the crew of a spaceship, these threats to the human environment would be easier to meet than they are. The actual context in which these threats arise, however, is one in which the population policies pursued by states are different and conflicting; there are sharply divergent attitudes towards the goal of economic growth; food, energy and other raw materials are used as weapons in international conflict; some countries pollute the air and water used by others; and a traditional convention that the high seas and its resources are held in common is being eroded. In this context, it is by no means clear that transcending the states system is necessary or sufficient for effective action to deal with these interconnected threats to the environment.

First, what inhibits a common global plan for action in relation to the environment is not the existence of the system of states but the fact of human disagreement and conflict in the ecological realm itself. In relation to the human environment, as in relation to the goals of peace and of economic justice, it has to be recognised that human conflict has sources that are deeper than any particular form of universal political order. To avert a universal 'tragedy of the commons', all men in the long run may have to learn to accept limitations on their freedom to determine the size of their families, to consume energy and other resources and to pollute their environment, and a states system that cannot provide these limitations may be dysfunctional.[7] But so also will be a world state, a 'new mediaeval' order, or any other alternative form of universal political order that does not result in the curbing of these freedoms.

Second, the argument we are considering overlooks the contribution that the states system may make to dealing with environmental or ecological threats. As we have noted, the states system provides a means by which a human community in which disagreement and conflict are endemic can achieve a minimum of order. Acceptance by independent political communities of one another's right to independent existence, subject to observance of certain rules of coexistence, is a device for providing some element of order where otherwise none may be possible. Without such a basis of minimum order it is scarcely possible that common issues of the environment can be faced at all.

It is undoubtedly the case that effective action in the short run to limit population growth, to control economic development (both in the sense of curbing 'over-development' and eradicating 'under-development'), or to limit and justly apportion the consumption of resources, depends primarily on the action of states. If, as Falk and others maintain, action in relation to environmental dangers is urgently necessary immediately, it is not helpful to maintain at the same time that effective action can only be taken by political institutions fundamentally different from those which obtain in the present world. As Shields and Ott point out in a perceptive article, in the short run it is only national governments that have the information, the experience and the resources to act effectively in relation to these matters.[8]

Third, the argument that the states system is dysfunctional overlooks the possibility that through it a greater sense of human solidarity in relation to environmental threats may emerge. In the long run it is unlikely that action at the purely state level will be sufficient to cope with environmental dangers, and the functionality of the states system, or of any other form of universal political order, will depend upon the emergence of a greater sense of human cohesion than now exists. However, the idea that the states system should be regarded as an obstacle to the development of this greater sense of cohesion, rather than as the means through which it may come to take shape, is an unhelpful one. The states system provides the present structure of the political organisation of mankind, and the sense of common interests and values that underlies it – meagre though it is and inadequate as it is likely to prove in relation to long-term challenges to world order – is the principal expression of human unity or solidarity that exists at the present time, and such hopes as we may entertain for the emergence of a more cohesive world society are bound up with its preservation and development.

The States System and World Order

The states system will indeed prove dysfunctional if states are not able to preserve and extend the sense of common interests, common rules and common institutions that have moderated their conflicts in the past. An international system that had degenerated into a Hobbesian state of war no one could today defend as being adequate or viable in relation to goals of world order. Moreover, if the states system is to remain in any sense a viable structure, the area of consensus underlying it must be not only preserved but extended. But nor will any form of universal political organisation be viable in which a consensus cannot be reached upon certain minimum requirements of peace, justice and environmental management. The transcending of the states system is not sufficient, and may not be necessary, to bring this consensus about.

The story is sometimes told of the man who was lost somewhere in Scotland, and asked a farmer if he could tell him which was the way to Edinburgh. 'Oh sir,' the farmer replied, 'if I were you, I shouldn't start from here!' The doctrine that the states system does not provide the best starting-point for the pursuit of world order has something of this quality. The fact is that the form of universal political organisation which actually prevails in the world is that of the states system, and it is within this system that the search for consensus has to begin.

13

The Reform of the States System?

If the states system seems likely to persist in the foreseeable future, and at the same time is not necessarily destined to become obsolete or dysfunctional, how can it best be reformed or reshaped so as to more effectively promote world order? In this chapter we shall consider some of the possible answers to this question.

A Great Power Concert: 'The Kissinger Model'

One answer is that which points to the model of a concert of great powers. It has been called 'the Kissinger model', and it is certainly the case that it enjoys more backing from the United States than from any other great power. The Soviet Union, while in practice it collaborates with the United States for certain purposes, still in its rhetoric proclaims the vision of struggle between capitalism and socialism, and is hostile not only in theory but also in practice to a system of great power collaboration that includes China. China disavows entirely the role of a great power, and views itself as the champion of the Third World nations in their struggle against 'super power hegemonism'. The United States, however, is naturally drawn towards the conception of a great power concert; on the one hand, it is committed to upholding the existing international order, but, on the other hand, it senses the decline of its own power and the need to call new great powers into being as collaborators. Such a concert of great powers would be directed towards the creation of a 'structure of peace', although the peace which is upheld in the structure is that among the great powers, rather than

286

the peace of the world at large. It pays attention to the goal of international economic justice, although this is to be pursued, through measures of 'international development assistance', within the existing framework of power, and scarcely touches the goals of economic justice at the human or the cosmopolitan levels. The attention it pays to issues of the human environment is mainly rhetorical.

We have noted above that there does in fact exist a balance among three great powers, and other near or potential great powers, but that this balance differs from the European great power balance of the last century in important respects; in particular, we noted that there does not exist, as there did at that time, a concert or system of general collaboration among the great powers for the maintenance of the balance (see Chapter 5). We have also noted that great powers, when they do enter into a system of collaboration with one another, are able to promote international order by managing their relations with one another to that end, and by exploiting their preponderance in relation to the rest of international society (see Chapter 9). In the relationship that has evolved between the United States and the Soviet Union, some elements of such a system of collaboration are already present. The project of creating a concert of great powers in our time is one that looks to the strengthening of the system of Soviet-American collaboration, and its extension to include China; it is implicitly open also to Japan, the European Economic Community and others, if and when they demonstrate that they are great powers.

There can be no escape from the recognition that some element at least of co-operation among the great powers is one of the essential foundations of world order within the states system. Great powers exist and cannot be wished away: whether there is peace or war, security or insecurity in the world political system as a whole, is determined more by the leading groups within these powers than it is by any others. While the great powers continue to be in this position, world order is better served by harmony among them than by discord; the steps that have been taken, however faltering and incomplete, towards moving them from a posture of confrontation to one of negotiation are constructive from this point of view.

It is not the case, as is sometimes made out by critics of 'super power hegemonism', that the tentative moves that have taken place towards great power co-operation serve only the interests of the great powers themselves, and do not also promote the interests of international society as a whole. A nuclear war involving the United States, the Soviet Union and China, or any two of them, might be as much a catastrophe for any middle or small power as it would for the belligerents themselves, and, in taking action to reduce the risks of it, the great powers act as trustees for mankind as a whole.

It is true that in the motivation of the great powers that has led them to a modicum of collaboration, the part played by a sense of universal trusteeship may have been a negligible or even non-existent one; we do not have to look beyond the interests of the great powers, narrowly conceived, to account for the fact that *detente* has come about.

It is true that when the great powers do collaborate, it is not only to promote interests in avoiding unlimited nuclear war, which are interests shared with all mankind, but also to promote special interests of their own: in preserving the political *status quo,* in collaborating against potential challengers to their leading position, in preserving their ascendancy within their respective spheres of influence. It may even be that without these other, special interests of the great powers, collaboration would not have come about at all and would have no prospect of being taken further.

It is true that even where great power co-operation is directed exclusively towards the promotion of the universal interest in avoidance of unlimited nuclear war, this can still have the consequence of advancing the interests of the great powers at the expense of the interests of others. The United States, the Soviet Union and China may make war less likely among themselves by agreeing not to interfere in each others' spheres of influence, by abandoning allies and clients which might embroil them with one another, or by uniting to impose their will upon powers able to complicate or disturb their relationship.

For all these reasons the middle and small powers of the world, while they stand to gain from co-operation among the great powers, also stand to lose by it; and, from the point of view of their own interests, it is natural and proper that they should maintain a vigilant watch on signs of an emerging great power concert. But this in no way detracts from the fact that the avoidance of general nuclear war is as much an interest of all the lesser states as it is an interest of the powers by whose decision such a war would be initiated.

However, if great power co-operation to preserve the nuclear peace is necessary if the states system is to provide world order, it is not sufficient. The model of a great power concert ignores, where it does not actually seek to repress, the demands of weaker countries and peoples, for change. The states system, as we have argued, can remain a viable means to world order only if it proves possible to preserve and extend the consensus within it about common interests and values. No consensus is possible today that does not take account of the demands of Asian, African and Latin American countries and peoples for just change in respect of the elimination of colonialism and white supremacist governments, the redistribution of wealth and resources, and the ending of the relationship of dependence or subordination in which most of them stand to the rich countries.

It is true that a concert of great powers, especially if it came to include China, would not necessarily be wholly unresponsive to these demands, which the great powers even now seek to palliate by token measures. It is true that a concert of great powers might be successful in legitimising its role and mobilising a wide degree of support in international society; we have noted that this might be done by a great power concert which refrained from making its role explicit, which avoided conspicuously disorderly or rapacious acts, which sought to assuage demands for change and to co-opt the support of leading secondary powers for particular purposes (see Chapter 9). It is true also that the mere existence of a group of malcontent or dissatisfied states is not necessarily fatal to the survival of an international regime; all political systems contain at least some malcontent or dissatisfied elements, which feel that the benefits available have not been sufficiently shared, but it does not necessarily follow from this that the foundations of these systems are insecure.

It is difficult to believe, however, that the dissatisfaction of the 'have-not' countries can be assuaged by token gestures, or that it will not undermine any international regime that is not able to give effect to a radical redistribution of wealth, resources and power. It is true that, apart from China, the 'have-not' or proletarian powers are not yet impressive in military strength, and that even with China they are in no position to provide a military challenge to the world power structure whose basis is provided by the United States and the Soviet Union. The conflict of 'have' and 'have-not' power today is in this respect different from that which took place in the 1930s, when Britain and France, as the champions of the League and international legality, confronted revisionist Germany, Italy and Japan. At that time the 'have-not' powers represented one of the two main concentrations of military force in the world, and the alternative to a form of peaceful change that would appease their demands was war.

But the 'have-nots' of today represent a majority of the states in international society. Moreover, they represent a majority of the world's population, and are the predominant element in that world society, which, as we have noted, can scarcely yet be said to exist as a going concern, but of which there is a widespread consciousness. They are deeply divided among themselves and unlikely to be organised into any kind of axis or bloc; but some of them have united effectively for certain purposes, as over racism in Southern Africa, or questions of trade, aid and development, or in the exploitation of oil for economic and political purposes.

The military power of the 'have-not' countries, their capacity to combine effectively with one another, and their readiness to adopt tactics of confrontation with the great powers, may grow. But even if it does not, an international regime that cannot respond to their demands will be lacking in moral authority even within the 'have' countries and will be incapable of achieving the kind of consensus that world order will require.

Global Centralism: The Radical Salvationist Model

Another answer to our question points to the model of centralised direction of global affairs, based not upon the co-operation of the great powers but rather upon a sense of common will or unity of purpose among the human community as a whole, engendered by a developing sense of the global emergency of 'spaceship earth'. Like the model of a concert of great powers, the global centralist model derives from the Western world, but whereas the former is propounded chiefly in official or 'establishment' circles, the latter is urged by radical or dissenting intellectuals.

These radical intellectuals are drawn towards forms of centralised direction that would transcend the states system, but, recognising that the latter seems bound to persist in the foreseeable future, they seek to promote, as a first step, the maximum centralised direction that can be achieved, given that the states system continues. In this they are not unlike the advocates of a concert of great powers. But the radical intellectuals seek a form of centralised direction that reflects not simply the common interests of the great powers, but a sense of the overriding common interests of all mankind – which they recognise does not exist, but hope to create.

Let us take as a principal example the proposals of Richard Falk, as they are developed in *This Endangered Planet*. In a chapter entitled 'Designing a New World Order System', Falk sets out the goals towards which the system he favours would be directed. It is notable that they include not merely traditional goals of minimum order, such as the minimisation of violence on both the domestic and the international level, but a comprehensive vision of an optimum order: the unity of mankind and the unity of life on earth; the maintenance of environmental quality, including fixed ceilings on population increase, resource use and waste disposal; minimum standards of welfare, to be recognised as a right of all societies and individuals; the primacy of human dignity, including personal rights of conscience and autonomy and group rights of assembly and cultural assertion; the retention of diversity and pluralism with respect to languages, myths and political ideologies, on the ground that 'variety is itself part of the splendour of Life'; and the need for universal participation, both of all national governments and of non-state actors, so as to ensure that the system will be sensitive to all parts of the world and to avoid creating feelings of alienation.

To promote these goals Falk advocates a political structure whose elements are a strengthening of existing central institutions, such as the United Nations and the International Court of Justice; the development of the United Nations specialised agencies and other 'functional' bodies, whose role he believes will be greatly expanded to meet the demands of environmental management; informal patterns of co-operation among 'principal world actors', consisting of the five most populous states, together with representatives of regional, cultural and ethnic groupings; transnational and multinational actors, to be transformed into 'pressure groups lobbying for a new system of world order'; regional and sub-regional organisations, to move international relations beyond the nation-state and to create a stepping-stone towards the central

292 Alternative Paths to World Order

organisation of world affairs; changes of outlook within national societies towards a more cosmopolitan way of perceiving the world; and sub-national ethnic and religious movements, seeking to break off from an established state or seek autonomy within it, which help to weaken the power of existing states.

To establish this political structure Falk outlines a programme of 'world order activism' or 'consciousness-raising' by way of 'declarations of ecological emergency', 'survival universities', 'peacekeepers' academies', a world political party, and (to guard against the possibility that these efforts will fail and some modern equivalent of the Flood will ensue) an 'ark of renewal' that will enable a surviving nucleus of the enlightened to rebuild the world.[1]

The prescriptions of the radical global centralists, like those of the advocates of a great power concert, have the merit that they take account of the need for some framework of co-operation among the major powers if goals of minimum world order are to be achieved. Moreover, unlike the model of a great power concert, the global centralist position recognises that a consensus confined to the great powers is insufficient, and seeks to accommodate the demands of the 'have-not' countries for radical change. They assert the desirability of a consensus that involves international society as a whole, and not merely its ruling or dominant elements, and the need to achieve a wider range of goals than those simply of peace and security.

A weakness of Falk's approach is that in his search for a wider consensus he does not take account of what the demands of the Third World states actually are, and does not consider how far they can be reconciled with the perceived interests of the other main groups of states. He instead bases his prescriptions on a conversion of the whole planet to a comprehensive array of goals that reflect his own detailed preferences, a conversion which is to be brought about simply by his own and his colleagues' powers of persuasion and exhortation.

We have already noted that the demand for global central direction at the present time comes almost exclusively from the Western countries, and that the countries of the Third World and of the Socialist Commonwealth are vehement defenders of state sovereignty (see Chapter 12). Underlying the position of the two weaker of the three main groups of states, and particularly that of the Third World countries, is the perception that a move towards greater centralisation of power now would be likely to result not in a redistribution of wealth, resources and power favourable to themselves, but in a consolidation of its present distribution. The radical globalists, like all advocates of a centralised authority, implicitly assume that it will embody their own values. What is perhaps more likely is that a centralised authority will reflect the values of the presently prevailing great powers, who alone could make it a reality.

In this connection it is worth noting the critique of the radical global centralists delivered by an Indian writer, Rajni Kothari, whose views we shall consider more closely below. Kothari writes that he and his Indian colleagues are 'averse to the hollow sounds of comfortable, angry men from the Northern Hemisphere, hopping from one continent to another in a bid to transform the whole world – the latest edition of the white man's burden'.[2] The radical one-worlders, like the conservative ones, he maintains, are 'myth-makers utilising modern mass media and communication and conference facilities for building elaborate defences around basic structures of political and intellectual domination'.[3]

While the distribution of wealth, resources and power in international society remains as unequal as it is at present, the prospects of movement towards a more centralised global political structure, based upon a process of consensus, appear slight. It may be argued that if such a movement is eventually to take place, there must first be brought about a redistribution of wealth, amenities of life and power in favour of the states and peoples of the Third World.

At all events it seems hardly likely that a centralised global structure can be created and imbued with the values of the Western radicals by resort to the salvationist exhortation favoured by Falk and his colleagues. They vow that they will avoid blueprints or 'static utopias', but it is blueprints that they present. They speak of a situation of unprecedented global emergency, but what they mean by this is simply that the reality of world politics does not conform to the goals of peace and justice which they prescribe for it, which is as true of every past period in world politics as of the present. They tell us that we must make a new beginning and design a new world order, but we are in the middle of a process, not at the beginning of one, and there can be no such thing as a 'fresh start'. There is a certain naiveté about their plans for 'consciousness-raising', as if this had never been tried before, and a certain presumption in their claim that they speak for 'spaceship earth'. There is also a fundamental pessimism that underlies the superficial optimism of their pronouncements that disaster will immediately befall us unless drastic transformations are effected, which they themselves must know to have no prospect of being carried out.

Regionalism: A Third World Model

Another approach to the reform of the states system is to seek a wider role for regional organisations which occupy the middle ground between states on the one hand, and global organisations on the other. On the one hand, it is argued, regional organisations are capable of fulfilling some at least of the functions envisaged for global organisations in relation to peace and security, economic justice, and environmental management. On the other hand, they are not open to some of the objections that can be levelled at global organisations, for example that they may lead to domination of the states system by the great powers, that they are subject to break-down because of the difficulty of achieving consensus for the states system as a whole, and that they do not allow for regional autonomy and diversity.

Joseph Nye, in his study of *Peace in Parts,* distinguishes five doctrines, all of them of recent origin, that assert a connection between the development of regional organisations and a more peaceful world order: that they work against the concentration of power in the hands of the two super powers, and thus against the special dangers of the so-called 'bipolar system' (an argument often used in connection with the European regionalist movement); that by bringing about the combination of small, weak states that are only nominally sovereign by themselves, but may become viable by joining together, they remove a temptation to foreign intervention and conflict (an argument advanced by Nkrumah in relation to African regionalism); that by creating institutions beyond the state which qualify or diminish its sovereignty, they are helping to reduce the classic dangers of the sovereign states system (the argument that was considered in Chapter 11 above, in relation to the emergence of a 'new mediaevalism'); that by tying states together in a tight web of economic, social and cultural relations, they inhibit resort to war among regional states (a regionalist version of the functionalist approach to world order, often advanced in relation to the European Economic Community); and that they are specially able to control conflicts among their member states, on the one hand because they serve to insulate the region from global conflicts, and on the other hand because they enjoy advantages over remote global organisations in understanding the causes of conflicts within their own region and the conditions under which they can be resolved (a claim often made, for example, on behalf of the Association of South East Asian Nations).[4]

Regionalism as an approach to world order is not always connected with the attempt to escape or modify the dangers thought to flow from domination by the great powers. On the contrary, a reorganisation of world politics on regional lines has sometimes been envisaged as a division of the world into great power spheres of influence or responsibility (see Chapter 9). However, in the post-1945 era, characterised as it has been by the ascendancy of the United States and the Soviet Union, whose conflict has been widely perceived as the chief danger to peace and security, and whose co-operation has been seen as the chief obstacle to just political and economic change, regionalist approaches have often been connected with attempts to limit or combat the influence of the super powers. It is no accident that the five 'regionalist peace doctrines' noted by Nye are doctrines that have emerged in this period.

We may take as an example Dr Rajni Kothari's *Footsteps Into the Future,* in which proposals for a reorganisation of world politics on regionalist lines are closely connected with advocacy of Third World resurgence against domination by the super powers. Kothari's principal theme is the need for autonomy – both of individual human beings and of states and nations. The realisation of autonomy he sees as being frustrated in the rich countries by over-development and an ethic of consumption, in the poor countries by under-development, organised exploitation and 'structural violence', and in both by 'an approach to human organisation that is making men a burden on the planet, work a superfluity and machine the most potent source of life'.[5]

Kothari, while proscribing policies to promote autonomy on a universal basis, places his main emphasis upon its attainment by the countries of the Third World. He is concerned that the poor and formerly colonial territories should consolidate their independence, and asserts that the world of autonomous nation-states should not merely be accepted as a reality but endorsed as a 'preferred reality'. The object is to make the autonomy of states more real than it is in the world of today, in which there is a division between super, intermediate and marginal states.

Kothari is opposed not only to world government but also to proposals for global centralisation of power that fall short of it. He thus dismisses the 'Kissinger model' of a great power concert or directorate, and, as we have seen, also rejects the position of the American radical proponents of globalism. He looks to the proliferation of nuclear technology, to the formation of a tight-knit Third World bloc, and to pressures exerted upon the Western powers, such as those exemplified by the 1973 Arab oil embargo, to help redistribute power or influence in favour of the Third World.

To provide a form of world order that will allow greater scope for autonomy to the Third World states and others at present living under the shadow of the great powers, Kothari proposes a system of twenty to twenty-five regional federations. These are chosen on the basis of geographical contiguity and complementarity of resources and economies, and, while they are not necessarily uniform in size and power, they would represent a system of more equal units than those which exist in the world at present. The great powers are cut down to size: the Russian Region includes in addition to the U.S.S.R., only Mongolia; China is assigned Tibet and Taiwan, both regarded by the Peking government as parts of China; the United States is given nothing – Canada is put in a separate region with Greenland, and Mexico is linked with Central America. India is given South Asia, and it is suggested that this might eventually link up with the South East Asian Region and a South Pacific Region that includes Australia, New Zealand and the Pacific island states. Other proposed regions include Northern Europe, East Central Europe, the E.E.C., the Arab World, East, West and South Africa, the Caribbean, Andean South America, the Plate River Region, Brazil.

As we have already noted, there is much force in Kothari's contention that a move towards centralised authority now would consolidate the existing political and economic order, with its attendant injustices. Even if we hold that movement towards a more centralised authority is ultimately desirable, this would presuppose a consensus among the main sections of the world community as to what kind of an authority it will be and what policies it will implement; and it is unlikely that any such consensus will develop until there has been a redistribution of power in favour of the Third World countries. Such a redistribution, as Kothari perceives, is likely to be brought about only by the efforts of the Third World countries themselves to mobilise their resources, combine with one another and challenge the prevailing authorities.

Even if we could assume (which, as argued above, we cannot) that a world authority created now would embody the values of the Western radicals, this would be unlikely to entice the Third World countries into co-operating with the system. The Third World is alienated from the Western states not simply because of the latters' lack of high-mindedness but because of their overwhelming power, and the concern of the Third World countries, as Kothari perceives, is to bring about a redistribution not merely of wealth, or resources, or amenities of living, but of power – including military power, of which they are still in most cases deprived.

Three objections may be stated in relation to Kothari's proposals. First, it is difficult to conceive that a structure of regional organisations can sustain world order unless it is held together in some global framework. These regional organisations or (as Kothari calls them) 'federations' would themselves be major powers, and the existence or otherwise of order in the world would depend largely, perhaps chiefly, on the relations among them. If we ask how relations among the regional powers are to serve the goal of order, we are led back to a consideration of the traditional devices for achieving order in the anarchical society, which were reviewed in Part 2 of this study.

Kothari does provide for a global level of world political organisation as well as a regional level. In particular, he favours making the Economic and Social Council the principal organ of the United Nations, the creation of a World Parliamentary Assembly of national legislatures, the strengthening of the specialised agencies, and even the placing of an armed force at the disposal of 'the world body' (he does not say what 'world body').[6] These are, of course, utopian proposals; what Kothari does not tell us is how a global framework of order can be created from the political forces in the world that actually exist. He dismisses what he calls the 'balance of power' approach of founding peace and security on great power co-operation, which he says is precarious and unstable and condemns the majority of the human population to a position of dependence. But his own projected world of regional federations would be a world of conflicting concentrations of power, and a global framework of co-operation would have to be found that took account of these realities if goals of minimum world order were to be sustained.

Second, Kothari's discussion of his proposed regional federations is in some respects unsatisfying. He does not explain what factors in world politics will help to bring his regional federations about. He says very little about the processes of integration within them; nor does he deal adequately with the difficulty that if a region is insulated from the influence of external powers, the smaller states within it are left at the mercy of the dominant regional state. This is why Pakistan, Nepal, Sri Lanka and Bangladesh would not wish to be assigned to a South Asian region in which they would be left alone with India. It is also why Papua/New Guinea, Fiji, New Zealand and the other small South Pacific states would not wish to be left alone with Australia in the regional federation in which Dr Kothari puts them.

In many of the regions which Dr Kothari discusses, the deepest fears of the smaller units are in fact of their larger neighbours, rather than of external great powers, and the influence of the latter is valued as a check on the dominance of the former. From this point of view, the desire of India, for example, to exclude the great powers from the Indian subcontinent and ocean is like the desire of the United States, through the Monroe Doctrine, to exclude the European powers from the Americas; it is one side of a coin, the other side of which is the desire to use India's natural predominance in the region to settle things in its own way. The difficulty might in principle be surmounted if it were possible to develop, within each of Dr Kothari's regions, a sense of community strong enough to ensure that among the inhabitants of the smaller states the affairs of the region would not be perceived in terms of state-to-state relations. But this is a matter to which Dr Kothari does not address himself.

Third, there is a certain ambivalence in Dr Kothari's attitudes as between, on the one hand, the attempt to prescribe footsteps into the future for mankind as a whole, and on the other hand the attempt to prescribe a course of policy for India and the Third World. His book is concerned formally with the future of all mankind, and uses the language of common human solutions to common human problems. But many of his prescriptions concern the future only of India and the other Third World countries, and are addressed to this more restricted audience. 'The need for regional consolidation', he writes, 'is real not so much for the world as a whole but for the two-thirds of it that is poor and divided. The other one-third is well organised and can at any time mobilise both economically and politically, despite power conflicts and historical antagonisms.'[7]

One of the difficulties in all prescriptions about future world order is to determine to whom they are being addressed. While these prescriptions are in most cases apparently directed towards all and sundry, there is usually the tacit assumption of a particular audience. Mankind as such is not a political agent or actor, and it is inevitable that prescriptions about its future be addressed to particular groups that are politically competent. From this point of view it is a strength of Dr Kothari's approach that he chooses as his principal audience a group of powers with certain concrete common interests and a capacity for action. It also illustrates, however, the difficulty of prescribing universal solutions to universal problems in an age of slight and possibly shrinking consensus.

Revolution: A Marxist Model

Another path to the reform of the states system is that of universal proletarian revolution, designed to remove the exploitation of man by man both within states and between them. It is true that Marx and Engels may be taken to have held that universal revolution would lead ultimately to the disappearance of the state, and hence of the states system, and thus to favour transcending the states system rather than reforming it (see Chapter 10). But the various contemporary Marxist and neo-Marxist prescriptions for revolution are essentially directed towards the revolt of oppressed classes, so as to achieve justice within states, and the revolt of oppressed nations, so as to achieve justice among them: demands for the abolition of the state itself, or of the nation, do not figure in these prescriptions, except as speculations about the remote future. It is impossible in this short section to come to grips with the whole Marxist system of thought of which these prescriptions are part. But it is nevertheless important, in a survey of contemporary proposals for the reform of the states system, to take account of them.

We may take as a leading example the variety of Marxist revolutionism that emanates from China. A central feature of it is that it asserts the priority of just change over order, at least in the sense of the preservation of the existing order.

> The present international situation [Chou En Lai stated in his report to the Tenth National Congress of the Communist Party of China] is one characterised by great disorder on the earth. 'The wind sweeping through the tower heralds a rising storm in the mountains.' This aptly depicts how the basic world contradictions as analysed by Lenin show themselves today. Relaxation is a temporary and superficial phenomenon, and great disorder will continue. Such great disorder is a good thing for the people, thus helping the international situation develop further in the direction favourable to the people, and unfavourable to imperialism, and modern revisionism, and all reaction.[8]

The priority of just change over the preservation of the existing order is the theme of the Chinese polemics of the 1960s directed against Khrushchev, Tito, Togliatti, Thorez and other 'revisionists' who were accused of failing to recognise the basic 'contradictions' in the world.[9] These were the contradictions between the socialist and imperialist camps; between the proletariat and the bourgeoisie in capitalist countries; between the various monopoly-capital cliques; and – the primary contradiction of the present phase – between the oppressed nationalities and imperialism. The 'Khrushchev revisionists', it was argued, sought to conceal these contradictions or to reconcile them, and shirked the path of revolution and class struggle; especially, it was argued, they denied that the contradiction between the imperialists and the oppressed nations of Asia, Africa and Latin America was the primary one.[10]

'The storm of the people's revolution in Asia, Africa and Latin America', proclaimed *Renmin Ribao* in 1963, 'requires every political force in the world to take a stand. This mighty revolutionary storm makes the imperialists and colonialists tremble and the revolutionary people of the world rejoice. The imperialists and colonialists say, "Terrible, terrible!" The revolutionary people say,

"Fine, fine!" The imperialists and colonialists say "It is rebellion, which is forbidden." The revolutionary people say, "It is revolution, which is the people's right and the inexorable current of history." '[11] The Soviet revisionists, it charged, while mouthing the slogans of revolution, in effect were siding with the imperialists. In saying that colonialism had entered its final phase, they ignored the fact that it had been replaced by neo-colonialism: 'the wolf has left by the front door, but the tiger has entered through the back door'.[12] In speaking of a 'new stage' of the national liberation movement, which had economic tasks as its core, they were denying the primacy of political struggle against imperialism, which becomes armed struggle when the imperialists resort to armed repression. In speaking of the role of their economic aid to newly independent countries, the revisionists failed to recognise that the national independence and social progress of liberated peoples are primarily due to the revolutionary struggles of their own peoples. In visualising co-operation with the American imperialists in giving aid, disarmament as a means to increasing assistance to new states and a role for the United Nations in the abolition of colonialism, they were implying that the imperialists would bestow freedom upon oppressed peoples without a struggle.

There could be peaceful coexistence between different social systems, the Chinese polemics maintained, but this does not mean that there can be peaceful coexistence between oppressed classes and nations and their oppressors. The revisionists maintained that 'atomic weapons do not respect class principles' and proclaimed the danger of war between 'the two military blocs' and the need to pursue disarmament. But war remained the continuation of politics by other means, and some wars were just: nuclear weapons did not undermine the Marxist-Leninist view of war, which was not to be confused with bourgeois pacifism or a sentimental view of war. War could not be eliminated, nor disarmament achieved while imperialism continued to exist. Nuclear war would be a calamity for all mankind, but this was no reason to be paralysed by fear of it, or to engage in 'capitulationism' towards the American imperialists, typified by Khrushchev's withdrawal of the Soviet missiles from Cuba in 1962, after having rashly placed them there ('one day adventurism, the next day capitulationism'). Nuclear weapons do not determine man's fate, and history leads to the destruction of nuclear weapons by mankind, not to the destruction of mankind by nuclear weapons.[13]

Proposals for proletarian revolution, as adumbrated by the Chinese Marxists and others, have the merit of recognising goals that are left out of account in some of the earlier models for reform within the states system that have been considered: the need for drastic change in the political structure of many countries, in order to achieve human justice in the economic and social fields; the need for drastic change in the political structure of relations among states, in order to achieve international or interstate economic and social justice. The paths of revolution and confrontation are not the only ones that promise means to effect structural change in the pattern of dominance and dependence between and within states that characterises the relations of some strong and rich to some poor and weak societies today, but it is beyond our present purpose to consider their respective merits.[14]

Marxist revolutionary prescriptions are in no way inherently hostile towards international order in the sense in which it was defined at the outset of this volume. In the name of just change a threat is delivered to the existing political and economic structure of the world, in the course of which order, in the sense of a pattern of activity that sustains elementary goals of social life, is disrupted. But this is followed by the establishment of a new political and economic structure in which order is restored; the object of revolution is to replace an order that sustains the old set of values with an order that sustains a new set of values, and it is to the old values that revolutionary prescriptions are inherently hostile, not to the quality of order itself.

Moreover, we have already argued that international order at the present time has to be built upon a strengthening of consensus within the society of states, and that this is unlikely to be achieved without a radical redistribution of resources and power in favour of the weak and poor states of the Third World which constitute a majority of states and of the world's population. The revolutionary model provides one possible route towards such a redistribution.

The Marxist revolutionary model, however, does not address itself to the issue which the present study examines – how order is maintained and strengthened among independent political communities – except by saying that order can be achieved through the abolition of capitalism and of the exploiting classes. The world in which the issue of international order arises, however, is one in which capitalist states exist, and in which, moreover, socialist states, in their relations with one another, quite evidently enter into conflict in the same way that states of other kinds have always done. Proletarian revolution, however desirable it may be, does not remove the system of states, in which independent political communities dispose of power and pursue objectives that come into conflict. The question how international order is maintained thus arises in relation to the world that might follow universal proletarian revolution, just as it arises in the world at present. Moreover, in the world at present, it arises as much in the relations of socialist states with one another, as in the relations of capitalist states with one another, and in the relations between capitalist and socialist states. To this question about order among states the revolutionary model does not provide any answer; indeed, it does not recognise the validity of the question. Whether or not the revolutionary model points a way to just change in international society, it leaves us unable to dispense with the range of ideas concerning the maintenance of order, with which the bulk of this volume has been concerned.

The Prospects for International Society

The present argument suggests the following tentative conclusions as to the conditions under which the states system might continue to provide a viable means of sustaining world order. First, the states system can remain viable only if the element in it of international society is preserved and strengthened. This depends, in the first instance, on maintaining and extending the consensus about common interests and values that provides the foundation of its common rules and institutions, at a time when consensus has shrunk.

This consensus must include a sense of common interests among the great powers, sufficient to enable them to collaborate in relation to goals of minimum world order, and especially the avoidance of nuclear war. However, a consensus, founded upon the great powers alone, that does not take into account the demands of those Asian, African and Latin American countries that are weak and poor (they are, of course, not weak or poor in all cases) who represent a majority of states and of the world's population, cannot be expected to endure.

It is hardly likely that these demands for just change can be met without a radical redistribution of the world's wealth, resources and other amenities of living; we should recognise also that behind the demand of the 'have-not' states for just change there lies also a demand for a radical redistribution of power, including military power. Steps towards greater global centralisation of power seem possible only after such measures of redistribution have taken place, and not before; and it may be right to see as one of the steps that can promote this redistribution a consolidation of regional organisations, as proposed by Dr Kothari.

Revolution may provide the only available means of securing just changes within some states, and may help to bring about the mobilisation of political resources of weak states, and the combinations among them, that will facilitate processes of international redistribution. But it does not in itself provide any means of escaping the classic issue of the maintenance of order among independent states.

Finally, the prospects for international society are bound up with the prospects of the cosmopolitan culture that at present underlies its working. It was noted in Chapter 1 that all historical international societies have had as one of their foundations a common culture. On the one hand, there has been some element of a common *intellectual* culture – such as a common language, a common philosophical or epistemological outlook, a common literary or artistic tradition – the presence of which served to facilitate communication between the member states of the society. On the other hand, there has been some element of common *values* - such as a common religion or a common moral code – the presence of which served to reinforce the sense of common interests that united the states in question by a sense of common obligation.

In considering the role of such common cultures in relation to international society, it is worth distinguishing between the diplomatic culture, of which mention was made in Chapter 7 – the common stock of ideas and values possessed by the official representatives of states – and the international political culture, by which we mean the intellectual and moral culture that determines the attitudes towards the states system of the societies that compose it. It is clear that the European international society of the eighteenth and nineteenth centuries was founded upon a diplomatic culture and an international political culture that do not now underpin the world international society of today.

We may say that in this world international society there is at least a diplomatic or elite culture, comprising the common intellectual culture of modernity: some common languages, principally English, a common scientific understanding of the world, certain common notions and techniques that derive from the universal espousal by governments in the modern world of economic development and their universal involvement in modern technology. However, this common intellectual culture exists only at the elite level; its roots are shallow in many societies, and the common diplomatic culture that does exist today is not powerfully reinforced by an international political culture favourable to the working of the states system. Moreover, it is doubtful whether, even at the diplomatic level, it embraces what was called a common moral culture or set of common values, as distinct from a common intellectual culture.

The future of international society is likely to be determined, among other things, by the preservation and extension of a cosmopolitan culture, embracing both common ideas and common values, and rooted in societies in general as well as in their elites, that can provide the world international society of today with the kind of underpinning enjoyed by the geographically smaller and culturally more homogeneous international societies of the past. To say this is not to imply that any cosmopolitan culture is likely to become dominant throughout the world, engulfing cultural particularisms, or that it is desirable that such a development should take place. We have also to recognise that the nascent cosmopolitan culture of today, like the international society which it helps to sustain, is weighted in favour of the dominant cultures of the West. Like the world international society, the cosmopolitan culture on which it depends may need to absorb non-Western elements to a much greater degree if it is to be genuinely universal and provide a foundation for a universal international society.

14

Conclusion

It was stated at the outset that the purpose of this inquiry was not to advance any 'solution' to the problem of maintaining order in world politics, or to canvass any set of policies as representing 'the way ahead'. It is evident, however, that the argument has taken a definite direction, and that certain recommendations appear to be implicit in it, or may be read into it. Here I shall state briefly what the direction of the argument has been, but also why it should not be read as a set of prescriptions or recommendations.

The argument is an implicit defence of the states system, and more particularly of that element in it that has been called international society. In Part 1 it was in terms of the idea of international society that the concept of order in world politics was given meaning, that order in world politics was shown to exist, and that an explanation was advanced as to how it was maintained. In Part 2 an account was given of how order is provided in the contemporary states system in terms of the continuing vitality of the traditional rules and institutions of this society of states. In Part 3 the argument was put forward that, despite the existence in principle of alternatives to the states system of various kinds, there was no clear evidence that the states system was in decline, or that it was dysfunctional in relation to basic human purposes, provided that the element of international society in it could be preserved and strengthened, in ways that were indicated. International society today is in decline, but such prospects as there may be for order in world politics lie in attempts to arrest this decline rather than to hasten it.

However, to derive from this an endorsement of the existing society of states, and its rules and institutions, would be to overlook certain other points that have also been stressed throughout the argument. In the first place, it has been contended that international society is only one element in world politics, that this element of society shares the stage of world politics with the elements of war or conflict, and the element of human community, and that the working of what have been called the rules and institutions of international society have to be seen in relation to these other two elements, as well as in relation to international society.

In the second place, it has been maintained that world order, or order within the great society of all mankind, is not only wider than international order or order among states, but also more fundamental and primordial than it, and morally prior to it. The system of states has constantly to be assessed in relation to the goal of world order. In Part 3 it was concluded that arguments to the effect that the states system was in decline, or was unable to serve goals of world order, were unconvincing. But such a conclusion stands in need of continual re-assessment.

In the third place, it has been contended that order in world politics conflicts with goals of justice – international, human and cosmopolitan – and that while there is a sense in which order is prior to justice, it does not follow from this that goals of order are to be given priority over goals of justice in any particular case. It was argued that a study of order in world politics, such as the present one, needs to be complemented by a study of justice. To make recommendations on the basis of an examination of human goals as incomplete as that provided in the present study would be unwarranted.

The search for conclusions that can be presented as 'solutions' or 'practical advice' is a corrupting element in the contemporary study of world politics, which properly understood is an intellectual activity and not a practical one. Such conclusions are advanced less because there is any solid basis for them than because there is a demand for them which it is profitable to satisfy. The fact is that while there is a great desire to know what the future of world politics will bring, and also to know how we should behave in it, we have to grope about in the dark with respect to the one as much as with respect to the other. It is better to recognise that we are in darkness than to pretend that we can see the light.

Notes and References

Chapter One

1. Augustine, *The City of God,* bk xix, ch. xii (Everyman's Library, 1950) p. 249.
2. There are many sources for this analysis, but see especially H. L. A. Hart's account of 'the simple truisms' that constitute 'the core of good sense in the doctrine of Natural Law': *The Concept of Law* (Oxford: Clarendon Press, 1961) p. 194.
3. For an attempt to view international relations as a special case of the relations of powers, see Arthur Lee Burns, *Of Powers and their Politics: A Critique of Theoretical Approaches* (Englewood Cliffs, N.J.: Prentice-Hall, 1968).
4. Raymond Aron, *Peace and War: A Theory of International Relations* (London: Weidenfeld & Nicolson, 1966) p. 94.
5. See Martin Wight, *Systems of States* (Leicester University Press and London School of Economics, 1977) ch. 1.
6. Ibid.
7. See especially *System and Process in International Politics* (New York: Wiley, 1957).
8. Kaplan defines a system of action as 'a set of variables so related in contradistinction to its environment, that describable behavioural regularities characterise the internal relationships of the variables to each other, and the external relationships of the set of individual variables to combinations of external variables': ibid. p. 4.
9. I owe this point to Martin Wight, *Systems of States.*
10. See A. H. L. Heeren, *A Manual of the History of the Political System of Europe and its Colonies,* Göttingen, 1809 (Oxford: Talboys, 1834) vol. I. p. v.
11. See note 8.
12. Heeren, *Manual,* pp. vii-viii.

Chapter Two

1. This threefold division derives from Martin Wight. The best published account of it is his 'Western Values in International Relations', in *Diplomatic Investigations,* ed. Herbert Butterfield and Martin Wight

310   *Notes and References*

(London: Allen & Unwin, 1967). The division is further discussed in my 'Martin Wight and The Theory of International Relations. The Second Martin Wight Memorial Lecture', *British Journal of International Studies*, vol. II, no. 2 (1976).

2. In Kant's own doctrine there is of course ambivalence as between the universalism of *The Idea of Universal History from a Cosmopolitical Point Of View* (1784) and the position taken up in *Perpetual Peace* (1795), in which Kant accepts the substitute goal of a league of 'republican' states.

3. I have myself used the term 'Grotian' in two senses: (i) as here, to describe the broad doctrine that there is a society of states; (ii) to describe the solidarist form of this doctrine, which united Grotius himself and the twentieth-century neo-Grotians, in opposition to the pluralist conception of international society entertained by Vattel and later positivist writers. See 'The Grotian Conception of International Society', in *Diplomatic Investigations*.

4. Otto Gierke, *Natural Law and the Theory of Society 1500 to 1800*, trans. Ernest Barker (Boston: Beacon Press, 1957) p. 85.

5. See 'Third Letter on the Proposals for Peace with the Regicide Directory of France', in *The Works of the Right Honourable Edmund Burke*, ed. John C. Nimmo (London: Bohn's British Classics, 1887).

6. E. de Vattel, *The Law of Nations* (1758) Introduction, translated by Carnegie Institute (1916) p. 3.

7. Martin Wight, 'International Legitimacy', *International Relations*, vol. IV, no. 1 (May 1972).

8. James Lorimer, *The Institutes of the Law of Nations* (Edinburgh, 1883) vol. I, pp. 101–3.

9. See Igor de Rachewiltz, 'Some Remarks on the Ideological Foundations of Chingis Khan's Empire', *Papers on Far Eastern History*, 7 (March 1973).

10. See, for example, Francisco de Victoria, 'De Indis et de Jure Belli Relectiones', trans. J. P. Bate, in *The Classics of International Law*, ed. E. Nys (Washington: Carnegie Institute, 1917).

11. Grotius, *De Jure Belli ac Pacis*, trans. Francis W. Kelsey (Oxford: Clarendon Press, 1925) II, xxii, 2.

12. Ibid.

13. Vattel, *Law of Nations*, III, iii, 34.

14. See *The European Anarchy* (London: Allen & Unwin, 1916) and *The International Anarchy* (London: Allen & Unwin, 1926).

15. See my 'Society and Anarchy in International Relations', in *Diplomatic Investigations*. The present section incorporates some material from this essay.

16. Thomas Hobbes, *Leviathan* (Everyman's Library, 1953) ch. 13, p.65.

17. Ibid. p. 66.

18. Ibid. p. 64.

19. Ibid. p. 65.

20. Spinoza, *Tractatus Politicus*, III, ii, in *The Political Works of Spinoza*, ed. A. G. Wernham (Oxford: Clarendon Press, 1958) p. 293.

21. Carl von Clausewitz, *On War*, trans. Jolles (Modern Library Edition, 1943) pt I, ch. I, p. 8.
22. Ibid. pp. 7–8.
23. Hobbes, *Leviathan*, p. 63.

Chapter Three

1. This concept of the 'protection' of the rules may seem to carry the sinister implication of justifying conduct that is contrary to the rules, or of placing persons 'above' them, but I have not been able to think of a better term.
2. See, for example, M. Fortes and E. E. Evans-Pritchard, *African Political Systems* (Oxford University Press, 1940); John Middleton and David Tait (eds), *Tribes Without Rulers, Studies in African Segmentary Systems* (London: Routledge & Kegan Paul, 1958); and I. Southall, 'Stateless Societies', in *Encyclopaedia of the Social Sciences,* ed. David L. Sills (New York: Free Press, 1968). I am also indebted to Roger D. Masters's penetrating article 'World Politics as a Primitive Political System', *World Politics,* vol. XVI, no. 4 (July 1964).
3. Masters, 'World Politics as a Primitive Political System', p. 607.
4. See Schapera, *Government and Politics in Tribal Societies* (New York: Watts, 1956) ch. 1. For Maine's view see *Ancient Law* (London: John Murray, 1930) p. 144.
5. Fortes and Evans-Pritchard, *African Political Systems*, p. 10.
6. Ibid, p. 18.

Chapter Four

1. Ali Mazrui, *Towards a Pax Africana* (London: Weidenfeld & Nicolson, 1967).
2. The distinctions between general and particular justice, formal and substantive, arithmetical and proportionate, commutative and distributive, are all to be found in Aristotle. For contemporary analyses see Morris Ginsberg, *On Justice in Society* (London: Heinemann, 1965); and John Rawls, *A Theory of Justice* (Oxford University Press, 1972).
3. *Laws*, bk VI.
4. See Telford Taylor, *Nuremberg and Vietnam, an American Tragedy* (New York: Random House, 1970).
5. Kenneth Boulding, 'The Concept of World Interest', in *Economics and the Idea of Mankind,* ed. Bert F. Hoselitz (Columbia University Press, 1965) p. 55.
6. Julius Stone, 'Approaches to the Notion of International Justice', in *The Future of the International Legal Order: Trends and Patterns,* ed.

C. Black and Richard A. Falk, vol. I (Princeton University Press, 1969).

7. Mazrui, *Towards a Pax Africana,* p. 137.

Chapter Five

1. 'Une disposition des choses au moyen de laquelle aucune puissance ne se trouve en état de prédominer absolument et de faire la loi aux autres': de Vattel, *Droit des Gens,* bk III, ch. ii, section 47, text in J. B. Scott, *The Classics of International Law, Le Droit des Gens* (Washington: Carnegie Institute, 1916) p. 40.

2. In Morton Kaplan's terms the only historical 'bipolar' systems have been 'loose' not 'tight'. See *System and Process in International Politics,* ch. 2.

3. See, for example, Quincy Wright, *A Study of War* (University of Chicago Press, 1964) abridged, p. 122.

4. Burke, 'Third Letter on the Proposals for Peace with the Regicide Directory of France', p. 441.

5. Ibid.; Friedrich von Gentz, *Fragments on the Balance of Power in Europe* (London, 1806); and Heeren, *A Manual of the History of the Political System of Europe and its Colonies.*

6. See J.-J. Rousseau, *A Project of Perpetual Peace* (London: Danderson, 1927); and Arnold Toynbee, *A Study of History* (Oxford University Press, 1935–59) vol. III, pp. 301–2.

7. See David Hume, 'Of the Balance of Power', in *Essays Moral, Political and Literary,* vol. I (London: Longmans, Green & Co., 1898).

8. Sir Herbert Butterfield argues persuasively that contrary to Hume's famous argument that it derived from the ancient world, the doctrine that a balance of power should be maintained throughout the international system as a whole 'seems to come from the modern world's reflection on its own experience'. See 'The Balance of Power', in *Diplomatic Investigations,* p. 133.

9. L. Oppenheim, *International Law,* 1st edn (London: Longmans, 1905) vol. I, p. 73.

10. For valuable discussions of the multiple meanings of the term, see Wight, 'The Balance of Power' in *Diplomatic Investigations;* and Inis L. Claude, *Power and International Relations* (New York: Random House, 1962).

11. See J. H. von Justi, *Die Chimare des Gleichgewichts in Europa* (Altona, 1758); and Richard Cobden, 'Russia', in *Political Writings* (London: Ridgeway, 1867 and London: Cassell, 1886).

12. See I. Kant, *Perpetual Peace,* trans. H. O'Brien (Liberal Arts Press, 1957).

13. See Lord Acton, *Lectures on Modern History,* ed. J. N. Figgis and R. V. Laurence (London: Macmillan, 1910).

14. *Oeuvres choisies de Fénelon*, tome IV; quoted in Charles Dupuis, *Le principe d'équilibre et le concert européen* (Paris: Perrin & Cie, 1909) pp. 26–7.
15. For a survey of some of these concepts, see Morton H. Halperin, *Limited War in the Nuclear Age* (New York: Wiley, 1963).
16. See Kaplan, *System and Process in International Politics*, pp. 50–2.
17. I have set this out in *The Control of the Arms Race* (London: Weidenfeld & Nicolson, 1961) ch. 2; and in 'Arms Control: A Stocktaking and Prospectus', in *Problems of Modern Strategy*, ed. Alastair Buchan (London: Chatto & Windus, 1970).
18. André Beaufre, *Dissuasion et stratégie* (Paris: Armand Colin, 1964).
19. See Robert S. McNamara, *The Essence of Security* (New York: Harper & Row, 1968).
20. See *The Control of the Arms Race*, ch. 5.
21. Ibid. ch. 9.

Chapter Six

1. See Myres S. McDougal and Associates, *Studies in World Public Order* (Yale University Press, 1960) esp. ch. 1. See also Rosalyn Higgins, 'Policy Considerations and the International Judicial Process', *International and Comparative Law Quarterly*, vol. 17 (1968).
2. Hobbes, *Leviathan* (London: Blackwell, 1946) ch. 13, p. 83.
3. John Austin, *The Province of Jurisprudence Determined* (originally published in 1832, and London: Weidenfeld & Nicolson, 1954) lecture VI.
4. Hans Kelsen, *The General Theory of the Law and State*, trans. A. Wedberg (Harvard University Press, 1946).
5. ibid. ch. VI.
6. I have elaborated this argument in 'The Grotian Conception of International Society', in *Diplomatic Investigations*.
7. See Hart, *The Concept of Law*, p. 77.
8. Ibid. p. 79.
9. Ibid. p. 90.
10. Ibid. p. 92.
11. Ibid. p. 90.
12. Ibid. p. 231.
13. For a discussion of this threefold division, see Georg Schwarzenberger, *The Frontiers of International Law* (London: Stevens & Son, 1962) ch. 1.
14. Oppenheim, *International Law*, vol. I, ch. 1.
15. See, for example, Myres S. McDougal, Harold D. Lasswell and W. Michael Reisman, 'The World Constitutive Process of Authoritative Decision', in *The Future of the International Legal Order*, ed. Richard A. Falk and Cyril E. Black (Princeton University Press, 1969) vol. 1. See also C. Wilfred Jenks, 'Multinational Entities in the Law of

314   *Notes and References*

Nations', in *Transnational Law in a Changing Society, Essays in Honour of Philip C. Jessup,* ed. Wolfgang Friedmann, Louis Henkin and Oliver Lissitzyn (Columbia University Press, 1972).

16. See Philip C. Jessup, *Transnational Law* (Yale University Press, 1956).
17. See C. Wilfred Jenks, *The Common Law of Mankind* (London: Stevens & Son, 1958); and Percy E. Corbett, *The Growth of World Law* (Princeton University Press, 1971).
18. B. V. A. Röling, *International Law in an Expanded World* (Amsterdam: Djambatan, 1960) p. 83.
19. Wolfgang Friedmann, *The Changing Structure of International Law* (London: Stevens & Son, 1964).
20. See J. L. Brierly, *The Basis of Obligation in International Law* (Oxford: Clarendon Press, 1958); and Hersch Lauterpacht, *International Law and Human Rights* (London: Stevens & Son, 1950).
21. Richard A. Falk, *The Status of Law in International Society* (Princeton University Press, 1970) p. 177.
22. Ibid. ch. 5.
23. See E. McWhinney, *International Law and World Revolution* (Leyden: Sijthoff, 1967) ch. 4.
24. Rosalyn Higgins, *The Development of International Law Through the Political Organs of the United Nations* (Oxford University Press, 1963) p. 5.
25. See C. Wilfred Jenks, *Law, Freedom and Welfare* (London: Stevens & Son, 1963) ch. 5.
26. Ibid. p. 83.
27. See Higgins, 'Policy Considerations and the International Judicial Process'.
28. See Richard A. Falk, 'McDougal and Feliciano's Law and Minimum World Public Order', *Natural Law Forum,* vol. 8 (1963) p. 172.
29. Martin Wight, 'Why Is There No International Theory?', in *Diplomatic Investigations,* p. 29.
30. Ian Brownlie, *International Law and the Use of Force by States* (Oxford: Clarendon Press, 1963) p. 424.
31. See, for example, ibid. pp. 432ff.
32. For some cogent criticisms of the doctrine of consent, see Brierly, *The Basis of Obligation in International Law,* ch. 1.
33. Higgins, 'Policy Considerations and the International Judicial Process', p. 62.
34. For a further discussion of this point see my 'International Law and International Order', *International Organisation,* vol. 26, no. 3 (Summer 1972).

Chapter Seven

1. Harold Nicolson, *Diplomacy* (Oxford University Press, 1950) p. 15.
2. Sir Ernest Satow, *A Guide to Diplomatic Practice,* 4th edn (London: Longmans, Green & Co., 1957) p. 1.

3. See Philippe Cahier and Luke T. Lee, 'Vienna Conventions on Diplomatic and Consular Relations', *International Conciliation*, no. 571 (January 1969).
4. Michael Hardy, *Modern Diplomatic Law* (Manchester University Press, 1968).
5. Ragnar Numelin, *The Beginnings of Diplomacy. A Sociological Study of Inter-tribal and International Relations* (Oxford University Press, 1950) p. 124.
6. Sir Geoffrey Butler and Simon Maccoby, *The Development of International Law* (London: Longmans, Green & Co., 1928) p. 74.
7. Ibid. p. 80.
8. See François de Callières, *On the Manner of Negotiating with Princes,* trans. A. F. Whyte (University of Notre Dame Press, 1963).
9. Ibid. p. 11.
10. Ibid p. 9.
11. Ibid. p. 47.
12. See Alfred Vagts, *The Military Attaché* (Princeton University Press, 1967).
13. Johan Galtung and Mari Ruge, 'Patterns of Diplomacy', *Journal of Peace Research*, no. 2 (1962) p. 127.
14. See Nicolson, *Diplomacy;* and *The Evolution of Diplomatic Method* (London: Constable, 1954).
15. See especially Eugene R. Black's plea for a corps of 'development diplomats' in *The Diplomacy of Economic Development* (Harvard University Press, 1960).
16. R. B. Mowat, *Diplomacy and Peace* (London: Williams & Norgate, 1935).

Chapter Eight

1. B. V. A. Röling, *International Law in an Expanded World* (Amsterdam: Djambatan, 1960) p. 19.
2. Raymond Aron, *On War: Atomic Weapons and Global Diplomacy* (London: Secker & Warburg, 1958) ch. VI.

Chapter Nine

1. See, for example, George Liska, *Imperial America. The International Politics of Primacy,* Studies in International Affairs, no. 2 (Washington: Centre of Foreign Policy Research, Johns Hopkins University, School of Advanced International Studies, 1967).
2. See speech by Mr Eisaku Sato in the United Nations General Assembly (October 1970), *The Japan Times* (22 October 1970); and speech in the Diet (November 1970), *The Japan Times* (26 November 1970).

3. Ranke wrote: 'If one could establish as a definition of a great power that it must be able to maintain itself against all others even when they are united, then Frederick had raised Prussia to that position.' See *The Great Powers*, translation in T. H. von Laue, *Ranke, The Formative Years* (Princeton University Press, 1950) p. 203.

4. This is the theme of Sir Herbert Butterfield's essay on 'The Great Powers', in *Diplomatic Investigations*.

5. W. T. R. Fox, *The Super Powers: The United States, Britain and the Soviet Union – Their Responsibility for Peace* (New York: Harcourt Brace, 1944).

6. But see Oran Young, *The Politics of Force: Bargaining During International Crises* (Princeton University Press, 1968); and Coral Bell, *The Conventions of Crisis: A Study in Diplomatic Management* (Oxford University Press, 1971).

7. See Carsten Holbraad, *Super Powers and International Conflict* (London: Macmillan, 1979) ch. 5.

8. See Georg Schwarzenberger, 'Hegemonial Intervention', *Yearbook of World Affairs* (London: Stevens & Son, 1959).

9. On the 'Brezhnev Doctrine', see Theodor Schweisfurth, 'Moscow Doctrine as a Norm of International Law', *Aussen Politik*, vol. 22, 1 (1971).

10. Lord Curzon, *Frontiers* (Oxford: Clarendon Press, 1907) p. 42.

11. M. F. Lindley, *The Acquisition and Government of Backward Territory in International Law* (London: Longmans, 1926).

12. Quoted in ibid. p. 208.

13. Walter Lippmann, *U.S. War Aims* (Boston: Little, Brown & Co., 1944).

14. Curzon, *Frontiers*, p. 43.

15. These terms are analysed at length by Carsten Holbraad in 'Condominium and Concert', in *The Super Powers and World Order*, ed. Holbraad (Canberra: Australian National University Press, 1971).

16. See John Strachey, *On the Prevention of War* (London: Macmillan, 1962).

Chapter Ten

1. See the 'Revised Soviet Draft Treaty on General and Complete Disarmament under Strict International Control' of 24 September 1962, and the United States' 'Outline of Basic Provision of a Treaty on General and Complete Disarmament in a Peaceful World' of 18 April 1962. Both are printed as appendices to Sir Michael Wright, *Disarm and Verify* (London: Chatto & Windus, 1964).

2. The argument of the next few paragraphs is set out in greater detail in *The Control of the Arms Race*, ch. 2.

3. Litvinov first put forward the proposal at a meeting of the preparatory commission of the League of Nations Disarmament Conference on the occasion of the first appearance of Soviet delegates at Geneva in 1927, and elaborated it most fully at the World Disarmament Conference in February 1932. See League of Nations, 'Conference for the Reduction and Limitation of Armaments', *Verbatim Records of Plenary Meetings*, vol. I, p. 82.
4. However, the speed, cost and destructiveness of war in a 'disarmed world' would not be determined by the size or sophistication of arms alone but also by moral and social factors.
5. I have discussed this doctrine in 'The Grotian Conception of International Society', in *Diplomatic Investigations*.
6. See Kaplan, *System and Process in International Politics*, pp. 50–2; and Arthur Lee Burns, 'From Balance to Deterrence', *World Politics*, IX, 4 July 1957).
7. Ibid.
8. Kant, *Perpetual Peace*, pp. 19–20.
9. *Hegel's Philosophy of Right*, trans. T. M. Knox (Oxford: Clarendon Press, 1942) pt III.
10. Raymond Aron, *Peace and War, A Theory of International Relations* (London: Weidenfeld & Nicolson, 1962) pp. 99–104.
11. See 'Rousseau on War and Peace', in Stanley Hoffmann, *The State of War. Essays in the Theory and Practice of International Politics* (London: Pall Mall Press, 1965).
12. This is quoted by Richard Cobden at the beginning of 'England, Ireland and America': see *The Political Writings of Richard Cobden* (London: Cassel, 1886) p. 3.
13. Ibid. p. 216.
14. John Stuart Mill, 'A Few Words on Non-Intervention', in *Dissertations and Discussions*, vol. III (London: Longmans, Green, & Co. 1867).
15. See, especially, Cobden, 'England, Ireland and America' and 'Russia, 1836', in *Political Writings*.
16. Strachey, *On the Prevention of War*.

Chapter Eleven

1. On this point see S. Prakash Sinha, *New Nations and the Law of Nations* (Leyden: Sijthoff, 1967).
2. See Joseph Nye, *Peace in Parts: Integration and Conflict in Regional Organisations* (Boston: Little, Brown & Co., 1971).
3. See, for example, Lord Gladwyn, 'World Order and the Nation-State: A Regional Approach', in *Conditions of World Order*, ed. Stanley Hoffmann (New York: Simon & Shuster, 1970).
4. See *Keesing's Contemporary Archives* (February 12–18, 1973) p. 25, 725.

5. See International Committee of the Red Cross, *Draft Additional Protocols to the Geneva Conventions of August 12, 1949* (Geneva, 1973).
6. I have discussed these examples, and the wider question of private international violence, in 'Civil Violence and International Order', *Adelphi Papers*, no. 83 (1971).
7. See Samuel P. Huntingdon, 'Transnational Organisations in World Politics', *World Politics*, vol. xxv, no. 3 (April 1973).
8. Ibid. p. 336.
9. See George Ball, 'The Promise of the Multinational Corporation', *Fortune*, vol. 75, no. 6 (1 June 1967); and J.-J. Servan-Schreiber, *Le Défi Américain* (Paris, 1968).
10. Robert Gilpin, 'The Politics of Transnational Economic Relations', in *Transnational Relations and World Politics*, ed. Joseph Nye and Robert Keohane (Harvard University Press, 1972).
11. Huntingdon, 'Transnational Organisations in World Politics', p. 363.
12. Z. Brzezinski, *Between Two Ages* (New York: Viking Press, 1970) p. 3.
13. Ibid. p. 19.
14. Karl W. Deutsch and Alexander Eckstein, 'National Industrialisation and the Declining Share of the International Economic Sector 1890–1959', *World Politics*, vol. xiii (January 1961).
15. See Geoffrey Blainey, *The Tyranny of Distance: How Distance shaped Australia's History* (Melbourne: Sun Books, 1966).
16. This is stated most clearly in Richard A. Falk, 'A New Paradigm for International Legal Studies', *Yale Law Journal*, vol. 84 (1975). Professor Falk's views are discussed also in Chapters 6, 12 and 13.
17. Nye and Keohane, *Transnational Relations and World Politics*.
18. These views are not on the whole taken by Nye and Keohane, who make so many concessions to their potential critics that their thesis becomes a very mild one. They do, however, hold the second of the five views I reject, namely that transnational interactions are now clearly more important in world politics than in earlier eras. See *Transnational Relations and World Politics*, Introduction.
19. Aron, *Peace and War*, p. 105.
20. For a persuasive statement of this view, see Osvaldo Sunkel 'Development, Underdevelopment, Dependence, Marginality and Spatial Imbalances – Towards a Global Approach', a paper presented to the Conferencia del Pacifico, Vina del Mar, Chile (1970).

Chapter Twelve

1. See Cyril E. Black and Richard A. Falk (eds), *The Future of the International Legal Order*, vol. i (1969); and Richard A. Falk, *This Endangered Planet: Prospects and Proposals for Human Survival* (New York: Random House, 1971).

2. See Karl W. Deutsch *et al., Political Community in the North Atlantic Area* (Princeton University Press, 1957).
3. I have developed these points in 'Society and Anarchy in International Relations', in *Diplomatic Investigations.*
4. J. N. Bhagwati writes that 'one looks almost in vain in literature and sociological and political writing before the Second World War for any systematic, coherent and sustained discussion of the "gap"': see *Economics and World Order From the 1970s to the 1990s* (London: Macmillan, 1972) p. 6.
5. On this point, see ibid. pp. 5–10.
6. *This Endangered Planet*, p. 98.
7. The idea of 'the tragedy of the Commons' is developed by Garett Hardin in *Science* (13 December 1968). It refers to the destruction of the common pastures in England through the overgrazing of herds.
8. Linda P. Shields and Marvin C. Ott, 'The Environmental Crisis: International and Supranational Approaches', *International Relations*, vol. IV, no. 6 (November 1974).

Chapter Thirteen

1. Falk, *This Endangered Planet*, ch. VII.
2. Rajni Kothari, *Footsteps Into the Future: Diagnosis of the Present World and a Design for an Alternative* (New Delhi: Orient Longman, 1974) p. 10.
3. Ibid. p. 7.
4. Nye, *Peace in Parts*, ch. I.
5. Kothari, *Footsteps Into the Future*, p. xx.
6. Ibid. p. 141.
7. Ibid. p. 156.
8. 'Report to the Tenth National Congress of the Communist Party of China, 24 August 1973', *Asia Research Bulletin*, vol. 3, no. 4 (September 1973) p. 2116.
9. On the Chinese polemics see the collection of Chinese statements in *Whence the Differences* (New Era, no date); G. F. Hudson, R. Lowenthal and R. MacFarquhar (eds), 'The Sino-Soviet Dispute', *China Quarterly* (1961); and W. E. Griffith, *The Sino-Soviet Rift* (London: Allen & Unwin, 1964).
10. See 'The Khrushchev Revisionists' Fear of Contradictions', *Red Flag* (31 July 1965) pp. 34–41.
11. *Apologists of Neo Colonialism*. Comment on the Open Letter of the Central Committee of the C.P.S.U. by the Editorial Departments of *Renmin Ribao* and *Red Flag* (Peking: Foreign Languages Press) pp. 1–2.
12. Ibid. p. 4.
13. On these points, see especially *Two Different Lines on the Questions of War and Peace* (Peking: Foreign Languages Press, 1963); and *On*

Khrushchev's Phoney Communism and Its Historical Lessons for the World (Peking: Foreign Languages Press, 1964).

14. Alternative strategies for structural change are reviewed in Johan Galtung, 'A Structural Theory of Imperialism', *Journal of Peace Research*, no. 2 (1971) especially pp. 106–9.

Index

UNIVERSITY OF WOLVERHAMPTON
LEARNING & INFORMATION SERVICES